HOW THE RED SOX EXPLAIN NEW ENGLAND

HOW THE RED SOX EXPLAIN NEW ENGLAND

Jon Chattman
and Allie Tarantino

TRIUMPH
B O O K S

Library of Congress Cataloging-in-Publication Data

How the Red Sox explain New England / Jon Chattman and Allie Tarantino.
    p. cm.
  ISBN 978-1-60078-802-4
 1. Boston Red Sox (Baseball team)—History. 2. Baseball—New England—History. 3. New England—Social life and customs.
I. Tarantino, Allie.
  GV875.B62H69 2013
  796.357'640974461—dc23
                                    2012044219

This book is available in quantity at special discounts for your group or organization. For further information, contact:

Triumph Books LLC
814 North Franklin Street
Chicago, Illinois 60610
(312) 939-3330
www.triumphbooks.com

Printed in U.S.A.
ISBN: 978-1-60078-802-4
Design by Patricia Frey
Photos courtesy of AP Images unless otherwise indicated

*Jon Chattman dedicates this book to
his parents, Gary and Patti; his wife, Alison;
and his son, Noah.*

*Allie Tarantino dedicates this book to
his parents, Ralph and Diane; his wife, Shira;
and his children, Cyrus and Juniper.*

Contents

Foreword

Baseball is such a familiar game. It's played almost every day, and most people have played it at one time in their lives. There's a connection there. In New England people just get caught up in it. And I mean all of New England. The best way I can put it is—it's a way of life. Wherever you go as a player in Boston, the fans recognize you, they want to be with you and want to be a part of it all.

There will be people in Maine eating lobster on the back porch on a sunny afternoon in late August, and they'll be listening to the Red Sox. It's an event there, and it's all encompassing. It's just 24/7. As a player, you can never get away from it. I would go fishing to decompress mentally. Players need that. On the West Coast, there are a billion other things to do. It's not as fervent. People are not as rabid about their team as New Englanders. You'd go to the park, and you'd see the people coming in, and it was apparent to me pretty quickly that people knew what they were talking about. If a player on another team had a great game, they applauded. Now, they didn't want him to win, but they respected his performance. You could tell they were knowledgeable. The fans came early, and they stayed late. I used to love that. You don't notice those things as much until you go someplace else, and you miss that electricity.

Part of it is the allure of Fenway Park and the people who played there. I felt it. I was in the same outfield where Ted Williams and Mickey Mantle played. Great players were there before me, and it was really cool. The fans know that stuff. The atmosphere there is like no other. When the team is doing well, it's great. And when they're not, the fans will let you know it, and that's okay, because we're professionals. They don't want you to lose, and neither do we. In Boston you do really learn about yourself when you're not doing well or when your team is not doing well. But you have to stand up and answer the questions. When you go to the park, you better be ready mentally.

I'm kind of the shy and introverted type. When I signed with Boston, I heard about the people and the media. I was just told to "Listen to the questions they ask you, and answer them. Don't volunteer anything else." That was great advice, and I wasn't a quotable guy. We had plenty of guys on the team who loved to talk and all those kinds of things. It gets a lot easier as time goes on, and I had some preparation. My background was for big-stage things, and I had a pretty good pedigree. I'm really a West Coast guy with roots in the Midwest. I was born in Chicago, but when I was two years old, my family moved us out West. We were a blue-collar family with a middle-class upbringing. I walked to school each day, even though the bus went right by our house. I was shy growing up except when it came to athletics. I wasn't a forceful guy when I played. I just played the game and adapted to all the other things that came with it as I went along.

So I wasn't some naive kid. I had played ball in college and played international baseball for three years, representing the United States each time. The international ball was as much media as you could get at that time. So I had a pretty solid base athletically and media-wise. Because of my background in college, I was a high draft pick. I didn't sign right away in June 1973. I played another year internationally for the U.S. All-Stars against Japan. The Red Sox said to finish that out, and my pro career started in mid-July of that year. I started in Double A in Bristol, Connecticut, where ESPN is now located. I was there only a month and a half, when I was called up to the Triple A World Series, which we won. I played four months in Pawtucket, Rhode Island, before I was called up and got a taste of the majors in September 1974. Since I did pretty well down there, I wasn't in the minors for a long time. I've always been pretty good at seizing the moment, especially when it's young guys playing against older guys who sort of discount you. That's the worst.

The Giants were my favorite team growing up, and here I was, with Orlando Cepeda and Juan Marichal as my teammates, sitting and talking with them on the bench. I felt totally comfortable on the field—a little awkward off the field. What helped the next year was that we had a core group of young players. We were all going through the same thing. Jimmy Rice and I were there. Dwight Evans was there at that point, and Pudge (Carlton Fisk) was only 26 or 27. We were all young and we all hung out. The focus wasn't just on me, so there really was no pressure. And we were pretty bad up until that point, so nobody expected anything of me or the team. We didn't know what we had, and nobody expected rookies to do anything. There was never any mention of an MVP or Rookie of the Year. We were just trying to win for the first time since 1967. It was fun, and Jimmy and I got into the middle of the lineup quickly. I feel badly for Miguel Cabrera, who's been playing for a while, and now it's all about the Triple Crown, and Mike Trout and his rookie year. The media is just all over the place now. I don't know if I would've handled it as well in today's game. It's hard to say.

In 1975 we weren't getting national attention as a team—not until mid-June when I drove in 10 runs and hit three homers. All of the sudden, people were like, "Who is this guy?" The people on the West Coast knew, but we weren't on TV, so nobody else did. We had a few nationally televised *Game of the Weeks,* and I made some good plays. I helped put *This Week in Baseball* on the map. The team was playing really well, I was playing really well, and questions started being asked. "Can the Red Sox do it? Can they pass the Yankees?" And, no one mentioned curses back then…it was probably because no team had gotten close.

But at least we were in the fight. After the 1978 playoff loss to the Yankees, that might've started the seed for The Curse. And it was in its full-blown glory in 1986. But we didn't have to worry about that kind of thing. Our group of guys in the '70s helped put the Red Sox on the map nationally, and that's when this kind of thing evolved. But it was never about me. It was about the team. If I was playing now, I probably would've gotten endorsements mid-season that year. I would have an agent fielding offers for this and that, but I didn't even have an agent back then!

When I left the Red Sox, it wasn't under the best of circumstances. Unfortunately, it happened to a number of players under the old regime. When you're traded away, you want to do well against your old team. The fans were pissed off they got rid of us, but at the same time, you become the enemy right away. I'm pretty good at leaving things behind that are out of my control. You have to put the blinders on, the ear plugs in, and just go on. That's why some guys who come from small markets fail in New York or Boston. They can't handle the pressure and the press. Instead of three guys in the locker room after a game, it's 50, and they're asking, "How come your sinker isn't sinking?" Some guys handle it; some can't. I always kind of looked forward to facing the Red Sox. But in the 1986 playoffs, I pulled for them. When you play in the American League, you pull for the league. I hate to see teams lose when I think they should win, and 1986 was hard.

I've always followed the Sox, and when this new ownership took over in 2002, they initiated a Red Sox Hall of Fame, and I've been part of the club since that year. I go back several times a year. I've always been a fan of baseball and I always watch the teams I played for. I pull for them. A Trojan, I pull for USC, too. Those loyalties never end. And the same is true with the fans of New England. They just voted me on the All-Fenway Team to celebrate the 100th anniversary of Fenway Park. I was one of the starters, and that's pretty meaningful to me. One hundred years, and I'm in the starting nine? It means my play was really appreciated. When you're older, it's nice to hear from people who say, "I remember that catch you made at Yankee Stadium." Sometimes they remember better than I do. It's very gratifying. Those kinds of events, like that celebration, are not only fun for the fans, but they also are fun for me. I get to see some of my old teammates and also talk baseball with guys I didn't play with. But seeing teammates of mine is great fun. It's as if time stands still. We may look older, but we don't think older. We fall back instantly.

—Fred Lynn
Boston Red Sox (1974–1980)

Introduction

I grew up in Needham, Massachusetts, roughly 20 minutes from Fenway Park and Boston Garden and 35 minutes from Foxboro. It, though, took just 15 minutes if your dad drove to the Pats game and left the house at 12:48 for a 1:03 kickoff, which also included parking in a self-created spot behind some yellow tape. For me, it was all but impossible not to be a fan of the Patriots, Bruins, Celtics, and Red Sox. During my lifetime, all four have experienced mountaintop highs and some horrific lows. Much like a family and the seasons of New England, there is an ebb and a flow and an unpredictability, which is why being a passionate sports fan offers so much to one's development of coping mechanisms. The low points—ball through Bill Buckner's legs, the David Tyree catch, Magic's hook shot—have a value as great, if not greater than, a Bobby Orr end-to-end rush or a Larry Bird no-look pass to the Chief for a dunk. Losing happens, winning happens, and if you are lucky enough to enjoy both, then you, too, are ahead of the game.

As a little boy in New England, I did not so much adopt the four teams, as the four teams adopted me. Their homes were my homes, especially Boston Garden and Fenway Park. Some New Englanders profess that as children they were attracted to the Cowboys because of the star on the helmet or—God forbid—the

Yankees, because they loved New York City. Not acceptable. With that said, and in my current role as host of a nationally televised sports program, ESPN's *Baseball Tonight*, I think it's appropriate to admit that I don't believe anyone in my position—even those who preach neutrality and objectivity—are deep down not fans of a team or teams from the city they grew up in or lived nearby.

From his three-point shooting contests to his wars with the Sixers, Lakers, and Pistons, Larry Bird defined my world in the 1980s. There was the final day of May 1984, when my best friend, John Dinneen, and I detoured from our landscaping duties to deliver a 12-pack of Budweiser to the Legend's house—a good-luck gesture for that night's Game 2. Dina answered the door and said Larry was sleeping; though, there was a tall guy with long, hairy legs sitting at the kitchen table. She graciously accepted our liquid offering. The Celtics won in overtime that night and took the series in seven. Bird was named series MVP and regular-season MVP, as well. Life couldn't get any better, or so I thought. But soon the new century came knocking, and my relationship with Fenway Park blossomed.

The year 1999 was magical. Six years into my ESPN experience, the Major League Baseball All-Star Game came to Fenway Park. Steroids was the bubble gum of choice for certain superstars that year, of course, and the Home Run Derby was one for the ages. A ballpark built in the early 1900s hosting players built by synthetics? It was a toxic combination of size and strength, overpowering a building with a Green Monster that had stood for almost a century. How many monsters were actually there that night? Having grown up in the shadows of Fenway Park, the '99 All-Star Game was the eye-opening moment for me, as I truly came time to understand the significance of Fenway.

As host of *Baseball Tonight* since 1995, I have developed a relationship with commissioner Bud Selig, speaking frequently with him. Sometimes the conversations are pleasant—other times not so much. But when it comes to conversing about the history of baseball, I could see his face light up through the telephone. He embraces the history of baseball the way one embraces a child who had just found out his best friend of five years was moving away. He cares for it, empathizes with it, and glorifies it. The ceremony on the field before the '99 All-Star Game—Bud's baby—was the biggest hug one could give to a child, and it came wrapped in the arms of the sweetest and most comfortable caretaker on the baseball planet: Fenway.

Ted Williams, suffering from strokes and a bad hip, was driven onto the field that was already occupied with the living legends of the game, including Willie Mays, Hank Aaron, and Stan Musial. The current players were drawn to the golf cart like bees to honey. They swarmed around him, many with tears in their eyes, as a weakened Williams came to life, talking baseball and hitting on the same field he played on 60 years earlier. I was standing no more than 20 feet away and could feel the intensity of the moment. On this same dirt and grass, the present and past were colliding and connecting in a way so unique it would take years to understand how special it was.

After Williams threw out the first pitch, Pedro Martinez took the mound and put on a power pitching display for the ages. He struck out four of the six batters he faced, including Hall of Famer Barry Larkin and home run kings Mark McGwire and Sammy Sosa. I don't believe Pedro was ever the same again and I know Fenway Park roared to decibels it had not reached in 80 years—but not quite to the levels it would in 2004 and 2007.

By 2004 and especially in light of another nightmarish American League Championship Series loss in 2003, we Red Sox fans generally understood that World Series titles were reserved for the Yankees. They won them often, and the Red Sox had not since 1918. But everything changed with new ownership and a brash young general manager named Theo Epstein. Like me, Epstein had grown up within a handful of miles of Fenway Park and understood how the history of the team had affected the present as well as the future. The owners led by John Henry recognized Fenway for what it was—a once-in-a-lifetime edifice made even more significant by the events that bind generations. Combine the brains in the front office with the Idiots (a self-proclaimed nickname of the 2004 team), and the ingredients for an earth-shattering event were in place. Voilá—a World Series championship after 86 years, featuring an epic comeback in the ALCS against the Yankees.

In neither 2004 nor 2007 did the Red Sox clinch the World Series on their home field. To deny the impact upon Fenway Park—the Green Monster, the manually operated scoreboard, the wood seats, the uneven concourse cement, the greenest grass you ever saw—is the ultimate conspiracy. It would've transformed memories of the millions who had sat in the building. None of the factors that led up to a championship would have had been in place had it not been for the building on Yawkey Way. Now the conversation had changed.

The Red Sox were world champions, and finally friendly Fenway Park had become home to a champion. Fenway did not need it, but it is richly deserved. The stadium lives, breathes, and shines, not because of the people who have played on its field, but because of the connection it has to the millions who have shared a bond with it. Fenway Park is the single-most recognizable and comfortable house ever built.

—Karl Ravech,
host of ESPN's *Baseball Tonight*

Preface

The Red Sox are a religion. Every year we reenact the agony and the temptation in the garden. Baseball's child play? Hell, up here in Boston, it's a passion play.

—George V. Higgins, *Time*

Across the tapestry of New England, myriad people and topography emerge whose scope are full of beauty, integrity, and wonder. Yet, there is one tie that serves to bind the region together—the national pastime of baseball. Okay, it's not baseball per se. New England is defined by the love of one particular team, and it certainly isn't the New York Yankees. As fast as you can say "Pawtucket," it's obviously the Boston Red Sox.

Unlike other regions of the United States stretched across hundreds and hundreds of miles, New England's state-to-state proximity is like six siblings who are each born a year apart and decide to spend their lives in an old college town. Although the six New England states certainly are different, you get the gist of the analogy. Connecticut, Rhode Island, Massachusetts, Maine, New Hampshire, and Vermont are each diverse with their own respective identities. But other than Fairfield County, Connecticut—a New York Yankees territory within a real Yankees territory—New England is the heart that pumps Red Sox Nation.

That region is symbolized by a classic scene in the 1998 movie, *Good Will Hunting*. While trying to pick up a girl at a bar, Ben Affleck's character is confronted by a ponytailed Ivy Leaguer who takes it upon himself to outsmart his "Southie" adversary by name-dropping moments he's read about in history. Will Hunting, played by Matt Damon, steps in and blasts the know-it-all for plagiarizing passages and playing them off as his own to impress a girl. The scene ends with the infamous line, "Do you like apples? Well, I got her number. How do you like 'dem apples?" What the scene doesn't illustrate, however, is that no matter what class, creed, or pretty much anything else, there is one common train of thought in New England. Whether it's a bar in Beantown, an oyster farm in Maine, or an eatery in Rhode Island, New Englanders live for the Red Sox. It's pretty fair to say without the Red Sox, outsiders might generalize New England solely as Kennedy country, a region where rich, clean-cut royalty spend and get away with everything. But as long as they've existed, the Boston Red Sox remind us all that New England isn't just for Connecticut suits and vacation-compound mainstays in Hyannis Port. It's also the home of working-class heroes who often don't shave and are sometimes rugged, down-to-earth "idiots."

Baseball is followed in other regions, states, and cities. But Chicagoans can choose to root for the Cubs or the White Sox. New Yorkers can follow the front-running Yankees or root for their red-headed stepchildren, the New York Mets. Californians have a plethora of teams to cheer. For New Englanders, however, there's only one show. In this region, it's a common religion, where perhaps an Ivy Leaguer with a bad ponytail might find himself matching wits in a bar with Will Hunting one night but high-fiving him the very next day at Fenway Park. From Plymouth Rock to the Industrial Revolution to Thoreau and Dickinson, New England is known for a lot of things. But if you ask any New Englander what defines them, it'll come down to the boys in navy and red.

The Red Sox explain New England, and New England explains who the Red Sox are. You love the Red Sox when they are good, bad, and 2012 ugly. The term "die-hards" gets overused in sports today, but you will not find a fan base more worthy of using that term than Red Sox fans. Whether it's flooding the Huntington Avenue Grounds after the Sox defeated the Pittsburgh Pirates in the very first World Series in 1903 or flooding the plane when the Sox came back to town after their World Series win against the Colorado Rockies in 2007, the fans live, breathe, die, eat, sleep, drink, cry, and any other verb you can use, with this team.

You'll read a collection of essays here that illustrate this passion. From a tour guide reliving his childhood by taking visitors on a tour of Fenway to comedians whose humor were shaped by the team who abused them growing up, this notion that the Red Sox are an extension of everyone who calls New England home will hit you upside the head like a Luis Tiant fastball.

When the Sox win, the fans win. When the team loses, they lose. When the team trades away the fans' favorite player, they take it personally. When a manager calls out a devoted player, the fans will call out the manager. Whether you still live in New England, moved away years ago, were born there, raised there, called it home for a few days, knew a man from Nantucket, or got wicked plastered at a Yawkey Way bar, the Red Sox are home for New England and explain all you need to know about one of the most historic regions in America. Never underestimate the power of baseball...and the power of a fan base.

1

America's Park: Fenway

Coming to Fenway Park as a visiting player was awesome, but there was nothing like being at Fenway Park playing for the Red Sox! The passion you feel from the Boston faithful in such a storied landmark as Fenway was second to none. I'm forever grateful for getting to experience playing for the Boston Red Sox. You could feel the history in that park every single night.

—Sean Casey, 2008 Red Sox first baseman/designated hitter

On April 6, 1992, the Baltimore Orioles hosted the Cleveland Indians in their brand-new ballpark, Orioles Park at Camden Yards. Camden was a new, supersized stadium but with a retro feel. The move from Memorial Stadium to the shiny happier place along the Inner Harbor in Baltimore made other owners follow suit. Among the ballparks that took after Camden's model were Coors Field in Colorado, Busch Stadium in St. Louis, and most recently Citi Field in New York and arguably New Yankee Stadium—home of the Yankees. Yes, despite the lure, the magic, and the memories, the Bronx Bombers opted to tear down their history in place of a new, bloated stadium that includes a Hard Rock Café—and probably a Tiffany's. Longtime Yankees fans felt a connection to the other stadium more than this imitation, an inflated one that lacks any history. Perhaps that changed when the Sox's rival bought their World Series in 2009—the first year in their new digs—but some old-school fans still balk at the new park. And that brings us to the Red Sox. They have called their park home—and will continue to do so—since their first major league game on April 20, 1912. "When you walk up the ramp, see the field and the Green Monster with the city in the background, there is nothing that compares to it," said Randy Adams, general manager of McGreevy's 3rd Base Saloon. "You walk in, you smell the sausages, you hear the Boston accents saying 'selling tickets,' and you see it's always packed. It will make the hair stand up on your arms. I still get chills."

Even Yankees fans would probably agree that the park located at 4 Yawkey Way represents all that is good and holy about baseball and its rich history. It's a classic that has been altered. (There have been additions and renovations. Seats atop the Green *Monstah* are new school.) In 2012 the park celebrated its 100th anniversary by being added to the National Register of Historic Places. "Everybody who's ever been to Fenway," said Larry Callahan, chief judicial marshall in Hartford and Cromwell, Connecticut, "when they walk through the tunnel, the green of the place just startles you. I've always gotten that feeling. It's a great old park. It's a national monument."

Every major league city should have a park like Fenway, but let's be honest: we're glad they don't. It's fitting that a little more than a decade into the 21st century that the oldest American League ballpark resides in America's first frontier, New England. While several states (California, New York, Pennsylvania, Illinois, Texas, Florida, Missouri, and Ohio) have more than one franchise located within their borders, the entire region of New England sinks its collective teeth into their Boston Red Sox.

Most New Englanders remember the movement in the 1990s to replace Fenway Park in Boston. Many major league teams had succumbed to what Rick Reilly described as "bulldozing real vintage ballparks like Tiger Stadium and Fenway Park to put up fake vintage ballparks." The sentiment to keep Fenway Park vital was shared by many, as online ventures to save the stadium endlessly popped up. It led Bob Costas to declare on a *Game of the Week* in

The Green Monster outfield wall adds uniqueness to Fenway Park and is part of what makes it a special baseball stadium. (Getty Images)

1999, "When we lose Fenway, we lose the sense that somebody sat here and watched Ted Williams hit." As fortune would have it, new owners would come and not only keep Fenway, but also pave the way for a Red Sox renaissance similar to when the stadium opened 100 years ago. Fenway Park has inspired all comers to wax poetic at the 100th anniversary in April 2012. "When you walk and come to Fenway, it's just like it was 30 years ago," Major League Baseball commissioner Bud Selig said. "The beauty and stability here is why the park means so much to many generations."

Two of Selig's predecessors spoke fondly of Fenway, including Bowie Kuhn, who oversaw the game from 1969–1984. "As commissioner, you're supposed to be objective," Kuhn said. "It wasn't much of a secret, though, that I loved Fenway Park, especially how it made you a participant." The late A. Bartlett Giamatti served briefly as commissioner before his untimely death in 1989, but he was a lifelong Boston Red Sox fan. "When I was seven years old, my father took me to Fenway Park for the first time," he said. "As I grew up, I knew that, as a building, it was on the level of Mount Olympus, the pyramid at Giza, the nation's capitol, the czar's Winter Palace, and the Louvre—except, of course, that it was better than all those inconsequential places." You'll be hard-pressed to find any baseball fan or player (okay, maybe those of the Chicago Cubs) who disagree with those sentiments.

During his three years with the Red Sox, pitcher Bronson Arroyo lived in the Back Bay of Boston and used to walk to Fenway. Arroyo, who played on the 2004 championship squad, moved on to the Reds in 2006. He has enjoyed success in Cincinnati, posting double-digit victory totals five times and twice reaching the postseason, but part of him yearns for those walks to Fenway and the atmosphere of the historic park. "I definitely miss the excitement of Fenway," Arroyo said. "There's such a long history—generations after generations have been going to this place…Baseball is closer to football and soccer fans there. They act almost like they're playing 17-game seasons instead of 162. It's a life-or-death feeling every time. As a player, you feel that. It's part of what drives you."

The Fenway atmosphere not only drives the players, but it also provides lifelong memories for the Red Sox fans. The beauty of sports is that you remember exactly where you were when a noteworthy or historic event happened. Each generation has its own top pivotal moments that become mythologized and rhapsodized beyond a lifetime. These events have even more sizzle when you watched them inside the ballpark where they actually transpired.

Long before Matthew P. Mayo became a published author and editor who has written fiction, nonfiction, and has contributed to countless anthologies, he was a Fenway and Sox fan. Loving the home team was just something that he gravitated to before he wrote his first manuscript. He'd often visit Fenway while living in Rhode Island, but when his family moved him to Vermont's

Northeast Kingdom, a piece of him stayed there. "I loved it there, on a riverside farm way out in the country. I fished every day and played pickup ballgames with other farm kids. But I missed my old friends, my Red Sox-loving grandma, and my occasional forays to Fenway," Mayo said. "I went to Montreal a few times to see the Expos play, and while the dome was impressive when you first walked in, even as a kid I knew it didn't hold a candle to Fenway's historic grace."

A few years after he moved to Vermont, Mayo received Sox tickets from his parents. "My mom; my best friend, Johnny; and his mom all went to Boston," he said, noting the BoSox played the Cleveland Indians on that day. "The game started out great, and, as I recall, it just kept getting better—one of the Indians swung, let go of his bat, and it helicoptered at Dennis Eckersley's legs. Eck jumped, and it missed him. But he was not pleased, his teammates were not pleased, Fenway fans were not pleased."

It didn't end there. The same thing happened an inning or two later. "I seem to remember Eck stripping off his glove and hurtling toward home plate before his feet landed back on the mound. Dugouts emptied. There was a bit of a brawl on the field, and two kids [and their moms] from northern Vermont, sitting along the third-base line, thought the entire affair was so very cool."

Yes, the game was cool, but the day got better afterward. "We waited by the players' parking area and saw a Caddy, I think it was, parked outside the gate with *Rice 14* on the license plate. Alas, it was a decoy. Jim Rice blew through those gates in a different car, right past everyone. But Dennis Eckersley stopped, climbed out of his van, and signed autographs and posed for photos, smiling the whole time." It was quite a day for Eck and quite a birthday weekend for Mayo. The next day, Mayo and his family were checking out of their hotel, when they saw Indians player Ron Pruitt hanging around the lobby. While he was too shy to go up to him, nothing could stop Mayo's mom. "She came through for us. It turned out Mr. Pruitt was very kind, not at all how we'd pictured those bat-chucking Cleveland players…Oddly enough, I would, many years later, marry a Cleveland girl who harbors a lifelong love of her own home team, the Indians. To date, she has not thrown a bat my way. However, I've kept Eck's technique in mind, should the situation arise."

Mayo's Red Sox adoration remains a fixture of his life. "I write books for a living, all sorts, Westerns among them. Yep, cowboys, and six-guns, and cattle drives, and range wars. But I do it from my home in Maine, wearing my old Red Sox cap and, in season, I listen to games radioed in from Fenway. And I'm always planning my next drive down the coast to Boston to catch another game…

"A visit is a singular experience: Emerge out of any Fenway passage and see the bold red, white, and green of the perfectly tended field before you, then spot the squat might of the Green Monster, see the billboards and the lights, hear the vendors yelling, 'Ice CREAM! Get your ice CREAM here!' (No matter where you sit, those guys can land a treat snack smack-dab in your lap)…the smells of hot dogs, beer, and pretzels, watching all those other fans looking for their seats, hear the rising hubbub of voices….

"Then come the warm-ups, the organ impossibly loud, the scoreboard, the players' uniforms as they take the field, the announcer's voice, the national anthem, the thunder and roar of the crowd, then…play ball! And that never gets old."

Yes, even today Mayo's heart is at Fenway and with the team he used to follow religiously when he lived in Rhode Island and when he moved to Ben & Jerry's country. Mayo was at a convention out West a few years back, and another author whose work he had long admired, looked at him and said, "Them's fightin' words."

"What are?" Mayo said, genuinely worried. "What had I done to offend this titan of writin'?"

"That hat," he said, cracking a grin and nodding again…at his trusty Red Sox cap.

"Oh?" Mayo said, squaring off. "Then bring it on.

"You can toy with my writing, mock my diminishing hairdo, even laugh at my dog, but do not mock this man's home team. Because while you might take the boy out of Fenway, you can't take the Fenway out of the boy."

Reliving the Dream

Like Mayo and so many others, Vincenzo DiGirolamo isn't simply a Red Sox fan. He lives and breathes for the team. You might even say he was born into it. Raised in Medford, just 10 minutes outside of Boston, the now 27-year-old, recalls being taken to Fenway Park with his brother countless times by his avid Sox fan dad and immersing himself in all things navy and red. DiGirolamo's father came to America from Sicily when he was just seven years old and instantly fell in love with the game of baseball—specifically the Red Sox. As a matter of fact, his dad went to games at Fenway before he knew much English and before he understood any of the rules of baseball. "He used to think it was an out when the left fielder caught the ball off the wall," DiGirolamo said. "Needless to say, he quickly learned that wasn't the case and developed an understanding of the game."

Because of his father's undying love for the game, Vince said he can't remember a time in his life that he A) wasn't a baseball fan and B) wasn't a Red Sox fan. "He got me started with baseball and the Red Sox at a very young age. And for that, amongst many other things, I'll always be grateful to him," he said.

As Vince's big brother, Bernardo, recalled, "My dad's a chef and has been working in restaurants and kitchens his whole life. And every season, I would look forward to seeing, where he would tape up his Red Sox schedule in the kitchens or restaurant office. Seeing that small, unfolded schedule taped to the wall meant Opening Day was coming up. A new beginning. Another chance. He would mark off every game with a *W* or an *L*, and soon I was doing the same thing with my own schedule in my room. I would meticulously mark *W*s and *L*s, like I was the official wins and losses keeper for the team. When there were a few *W*s in a row, I was happier; things in Boston were happier. On the flip side, when the Sox would get knocked out of the playoffs or not make the playoffs at all, there was the 'there's always next year' feeling that Sox fans got very familiar with throughout the years before 2004."

Over the past 22 years, DiGirolamo has immersed himself in Sox lore: the Curt Shilling sock highs and the Bobby V. lows. "It's a roller coaster ride I will never get off," he said. DiGirolamo's earliest memory of this wild ride dates back to when he was five years old and learned everything about the players. "My father would throw out a name, and I would know the roster number," he said. He doesn't know why he enjoyed memorizing the names and numbers, but it was important to him. Red Sox tickets may be hard to come by now—especially since they won World Championships in 2004 and 2007, but DiGirolamo recalls a time when tickets were a lot easier to get. As a result, he said, he and his family went to countless games together. Although he can't pinpoint the first game he went to, he said it's probably around the time he started the game of "throw out a name" with his dad.

His favorite name—or player—was Jody Reed. He wasn't a star player, but the infielder hit well in Beantown, and he loved him for that. Reed made his major league debut with the Sox in September 1987 and stayed with Boston through 1992. His best year was in 1990, when he smashed 173 hits and led the American League with 45 doubles. DiGirolamo was drawn to Reed because he played his little league positions of middle infield and third base. That Reed's jersey had his favorite number, the No. 3, on the back also helped. He was also of the right stature. "He wasn't the biggest guy, and neither was I," DiGirolamo said. "He was smaller and scrappy, and I could relate to that. And today that's translated into being a huge fan of Dustin Pedroia, because he's built and plays the same way." Pedroia is about 5'8", while Reed was listed as 5'9".

DiGirolamo and his older brother were huge card collectors back in the day, and to this day, his uncle gives him a hard time about some of the terrible card trades he made just so he could acquire Jody Reed cards. Needless to say, by 1993, when Reed was selected by the Colorado Rockies in the expansion draft, DiGirolamo was crushed. "I was at my grandparents' house when I heard this. I immediately started crying and locked myself in the bathroom. I was devastated. I remember my grandmother yelling in half-Italian, half-English for me to come out and saying how everything would be okay. Granted, yes, it turned out it was not the end of the world. But it took me a while to realize that," he said. Reed finished his career after 11 years, playing for the Sox, Los Angeles Dodgers, Milwaukee Brewers, San Diego Padres, and Detroit Tigers.

DiGirolamo took solace post-Reed by knowing he'd be having a birthday party at Fenway with or without his favorite middle infielder. "My birthday is in October, and my brother's is in November, so that's not exactly baseball season," he said. "But that didn't stop my parents. I remember several times being at a game, and then all of the sudden getting an overwhelming smell of smoke. Before I could even say anything, my parents put a small cake or cupcake in front of us and sang 'Happy Birthday.' It didn't stop there. The whole section would even join in on the singing. To us this was the coolest thing ever. We felt as though Fenway Park was singing 'Happy Birthday' to us."

These stories resonate even more, because DiGirolamo now actually works at Fenway Park. A communications and marketing professional by day, the man, who is arguably Jody Reed's biggest fan, moonlights as a tour guide for the old park today. Memories such as the Reed expansion draft drama and so much more flow out of him every time he steps out of Yawkey Way and into the Boston landmark park.

DiGirolamo took the job three years ago after seeing an ad posted on the website. He went to a job fair in the State Street Pavilion at Fenway and waited for hours with hundreds of other people who wanted to work at Fenway—be it as a tour guide or hot dog vendor. When he was finally called in, the human resources person there asked him what he was there for. DiGirolamo didn't know. He told her he worked in marketing, and she suggested giving tours. "After a few weeks of observing and a brief audition, I became a Fenway Park tour guide," he said.

From the very first day on the job, DiGirolamo relived all the memories he had as a kid: his father taking him to the games, his parents taking him there for birthday celebrations, hearing stories of past Sox heroics like Carlton Fisk's "waving" home run in extra innings during the 1975 World Series against the Cincinnati Reds to heartbreakers like the Bill Buckner fielding gaffe of 1986, his uncle busting his chops, and, of course, Jody Reed. But many of Vince's memories are of the redemptive the 2004 and 2007 seasons.

Each time he leads a tour group, he's reminded of Dave Roberts' stolen base in 2004—the biggest steal in Red Sox history. In the bottom of the ninth inning, down by a run, Kevin Millar drew a walk from immortal Yankee closer Mariano Rivera. Roberts pinch ran for him, and stole second base. Bill Mueller hit a single, and Roberts scored the tying run. The Sox would go on to win that game, head to the World Series, and win it all for the first time since 1918. "I know I don't have to set the scene, but I will," he said. "The Red Sox are down three games to none, to the bad guys—the Yankees. The previous three games I had watched all at different locations. The setting for Game 4 was at my parents' house, with my mother, father, and brother. If the Red Sox were going to get swept, I was going to be surrounded by my loving family and we would all share in the pain together.

"Going into this game, I wasn't feeling great about it. No team had ever come back from a 3–0 deficit to win a series. And after the way we lost Game 3, most of Red Sox Nation was expecting the worst. But it wasn't over yet. I remember a phone conversation I had with my father the day before, in which I asked him what he thought about their chances. His response, 'You know something—it's not over! I think this team can do it. I don't care what everybody says, I think they still have a good shot.' This phone call rejuvenated me. I remember getting excited after hearing my father say that, and I was completely sold. 'This isn't over!' I thought to myself. And with the team the Red Sox had that year, I knew they had something left in them. We all know how that game, and series, ended up playing out. But that steal set everything in motion. I will always get chills when I see that play."

The mantra of "This isn't over" has been repeated by DiGirolamo on his tour, but mostly he and the other guides stick to a set plan. For about an hour, they provide the groups with information about Fenway Park and the Boston Red Sox, cramming more than 100 years of history into a 60-minute tour, while answering any questions anyone may have.

The tours take patrons to three or four locations throughout the park, including the grandstands, Green Monster seats, the press box (when the team's away), and the right-field roof deck. He'll detail stories—like Ted Williams' 502-foot home run into the right-field bleachers on June 9, 1946 (hence the infamous "red" seat where it landed) and also incidents he witnessed firsthand—be it Derek Lowe's no-hitter against the Tampa Bay Rays (then called the Devil Rays and also very terrible) on April 27, 2002 or Jon Lester's no-no against the Kansas City Royals on May 19, 2008. "Tours can sometimes be as small as two people or as large as 150 people," he said. And they feature "all kinds of characters." There are young fans who probably would think a ball ricocheting off the left-field wall was an out as well, and old fans who remember back to the days of Pesky. There are die-hard Red Sox fans and casual fans. There are those who never set foot in a baseball stadium before and tourists from foreign countries who are learning the game just like DiGirolamo's dad did.

"As a tour guide, I am blessed with having a wealth of baseball information stored in my brain, and not just relating to the Red Sox. Oftentimes during a tour, I will throw out a trivia question to the group. What's the third-oldest active ballpark in the major leagues? Whose No. 42 is retired on the right-field façade, and why is it blue? What is the meaning of the dashes and dots hidden on the Green Monster? These are a few examples of the questions I throw out there," he said. "Sometimes I'll have a few people on my tours who know the answers. Other times it will be crickets. Playing trivia is fun for me, because when I give my tour the answers, I can see that they are learning something. It's rewarding to me, when I can see that my patrons are not only having fun, but they're also learning something new."

On the flip side, DiGirolamo said there are times when people on his tour try to challenge his baseball knowledge. "There are instances on tours when a patron may know, or may think they know, more than you. This comes up when a patron poses a trivia question my way or has a previous understanding of something that I talk about. If I had one dollar for every time somebody tried telling me the red seat marks the landing spot of Teddy [Williams'] last ever home run, I'd have a lot of dollars," he joked.

"I've always been a student of the game of baseball, so I'm always excited to learn something new. I don't know everything." Most tour groups, though, are appreciative of his tour guiding skills. DiGirolamo said he's been approached countless times by those who thank him for his insight. He said he's even been able to recruit some new fans to the Sox, and somehow managed to make Yankee fans on the tour from New York appreciate their rival's ballpark. "Some are just *waaaaiting* to hear the mention of 1918," he said, but overall they grow to appreciate the deep roots of America's most beloved ballpark. "While we all pledge our allegiances to different teams, above all, we are baseball fans. And that is why they're there. Fenway Park is the oldest park in all of Major League Baseball. Fans across the country, and the world, want to be able to say that they visited Fenway Park," he said.

DiGirolamo most enjoys instructing Red Sox fans that have never been to Fenway Park before—whether it's six-year-old girls or 70-year-old men. "I love sharing this moment with them. I feel as though I'm reliving my first Fenway experience through them. The look of awe and excitement on their faces is what I do this job for. I have fun giving tours either way, but it's the tours like this one that are my favorite," he said.

And for DiGirolamo, the son of a hardworking restaurateur who came here from Sicily and instantly fell in love with the blue-collar Red Sox, working at Fenway and sharing stories of the Sox past and reliving his own has brought him closer to his childhood and his dad. "I remember during my first year, a patron came up to me and said, 'This must get old to you, huh?' My response: 'Absolutely not.' Patrons always ask me to take their pictures during the tour, and I oftentimes want to ask them to take mine, too. I'm just as excited to be there as they are. I'm inside Fenway Park. I'm talking about the park I basically grew up in and the team I've followed religiously for as long as I can remember. So no, being a tour guide will never get old to me," he said.

"Generally, I'll never forget the feeling of going to a game when I was a little kid," he said. "Back then, everything is bigger than you. But at Fenway, everything is larger than life. I remember walking through the concourse and up the tunnels to get to our seats. That moment, when I could see the Green Monster and the field, I was in complete awe. I was this little kid who could barely see over the backs of the seats, but I was taking in everything I could. I was a kid in a candy store, except I was in Fenway Park."

Rites of Passage

Dave Zapponi was born and raised in Massachusetts and attended UMass. "[I am] Massachusetts through and through, so trips to Fenway have been aplenty," he said. Sitting in section 25, box 60, row M, seat 1, he watched the Sox play pivotal games against the Yankees en route to their second title in four seasons. According to Zapponi, "Yankees general manager Brian Cashman walked up the aisle just after a controversial call at first. I nudged my buddy and pointed him out. [Cashman] overheard us and proceeded to jokingly argue the call with us. We all had a good laugh about that from those seats." A few seasons earlier from those same seats, he saw Donald Trump, who had just made it big time again with *The Apprentice*, throw out the first pitch. "Boo birds were out, of course," Zapponi said. "He walked off the field, and to my surprise, walked unescorted right behind my seats, wearing his trademark trench coat, suit, and tie with that old smug look on his face. Well, you know the 'overrated' chant in sports? I then looked at him and chanted 'overleveraged.' It was enough to get a smirk and a nod from him as he passed by those awesome seats at Fenway Park."

Bethany Paupeck grew up in Wrentham, Massachusetts. As a child, her family always went to see the Pawtucket Red Sox, New England Patriots, and Boston Bruins. However, she only saw the Red Sox in action in Fort Myers, Florida, for spring training, and that was during her freshman year in high school. So it was very odd that her first Red Sox game in Fenway came when she was 23 years old. "I went to college at Georgia Southern University and moved to Jackson, Wyoming, after graduation," she said. "I made several friends in Wyoming who worked in Cape Cod during the summer. They were dying to go to a Red Sox game, so I asked my father to get us four tickets. He managed to score us four box-seat tickets…It was a cold day in April 2003. I figure the temperature was in the mid-50s. Walking into our box and seeing the sight of Fenway from the inside, seeing the field and the Green Monster was amazing. We were the only four people sitting outside in the seats that were attached to our box out of any of the boxes in the whole park. This is because we had just come from a Wyoming winter, and we actually thought it was warm out. I even had sandals on. The other people in our box kept on telling us that we were crazy."

Because the vast network of crazy BoSox fans extends outside New England and even beyond the 50 United States, it's called Red Sox Nation for a reason. Take Scott Robertson, who is an Edmonton, Alberta, native. The Canadian has been a Red Sox fan more than 20 years. This has never been a popular choice back home for Robertson, as the 1992 and 1993 World Champion Toronto Blue Jays (and for a while the Montreal Expos) were Canada's baseball teams. However, despite growing up in a city where Wayne Gretzky made his name, Robertson stuck with his beloved team in hopes of one day walking into Fenway Park and getting a chance to see the Pesky Pole and the Green Monster.

On July 1, 2004, the Red Sox trailed their rival New York Yankees by 8.5 games. At the same time, they were two games behind the wild-card-leading Oakland Athletics. By the end of that month, they still trailed the Yanks by 8.5 but only trailed by one in the wild-card race behind the Texas Rangers. Scott's friend, Heidi, presented him with the ultimate gift: an opportunity to see the Sox play at home in the playoffs. "I had no idea how she was going to pull this off, but I was excited nonetheless," he said. "Now all we needed was for the Red Sox to make the playoffs."

Forty-two wins in your final 60 games will most likely punch your playoff ticket, and that's exactly what the '04 Sox pulled off, finishing the season only three games behind the Yankees for the division and winning the wild-card race by seven games. With the playoff spot clinched, Heidi secured seats (bleacher C, section 41, row 14, seats 16 and 17) in right field on eBay.

Upon arriving in Red Sox gear, Scott and Heidi booked a tour of Fenway Park, the first item on any Sox fan's checklist. Elderly tour guide speaking with a strong Boston accent. *Check.* The smell of many years worth of blood, sweat, and tears filling the Fenway air. *Check.* Sitting atop the Green Monster, staring at the famous Citgo sign, and walking the warning track. *Check, check,* and *check.* "We sat atop the Green Monster and walked the warning track, which became a picture that sat on our mantel for many years," Robertson said. "The scene was set for a series-clinching victory and the memory of a lifetime." But as Red Sox fans know it's never that easy.

After having won Games 1 and 2 at Angels Stadium in Anaheim, California, behind Curt Schilling and Pedro Martinez, the five-game series shifted to Fenway. Game 3 starters were Bronson Arroyo for the Sox and Kelvim Escobar for the Anaheim Angels. As this was the first home playoff game since shortcomings of the 2003 season, Robertson described the scene as a mix of personal joy and Red Sox Nation anxiety. "We took a cab and got there in plenty of time to experience Yawkey Way and climb down behind the dugout and watch batting practice," he said. "You could feel the buzz in the air. Kind of a nervous buzz. We bought our beers, hot dogs, and peanuts, and, of course, a souvenir baseball that sits on a shelf in my home office."

With 35,547 in attendance, Robertson was one of those who liked the Sox's chances after knocking Escobar out early. "By the end of the fifth inning, we were up [five runs] and cruising. Arroyo and his patterned braids were pitching well. We spent much of the first half, high fiving everyone: 6–1! This is it," he said. "Then boom! Reality hit." The seventh inning started innocently enough with Doug Mientkiewicz replacing Kevin Millar at first for defensive purposes. Arroyo, however, faced his last batter upon walking Jeff DaVanon. Mike Myers proceeded to walk the only batter he faced, Jose Molina. With first and second occupied, Mike Timlin momentarily calmed things down by inducing a pop-up from Curtis Pride. The always-pesky David Eckstein loaded the bases with a single to right, followed by a much-needed strikeout of Chone Figgins. Timlin walked Darrin Erstad and brought 2004 MVP Vladimir Guerrero to the plate. Off an 0–1 count, he jacked a grand slam. Good-bye 6–1 lead. "That grand slam in the seventh made me sink," Robertson said. "The score was now tied. This couldn't be. How much Heidi had spent on these tickets would never erase the memory, but a win would make it so special."

As everyone in the Nation knows, this story does have a happy ending. Four hours and 10 minutes after the first pitch, Robertson described the scene. "It was do-or-die time," he said. "Two outs, bottom of the 10th, me—a Canadian from a small town outside of Edmonton, Alberta, Canada—watching Big Papi walk up and stroke a walk-off home run…I was in shock. Time stopped. Pandemonium! We hugged and celebrated with so many fans, stayed in Fenway as the players came out, and walked the warning track celebrating their victory with us. We didn't want to leave or the experience to end. In my memory it never has!

The memory is alive. My basement has a 2004 signed Curt Schilling World Series jersey; my mantel a collector's baseball; the wall behind my desk at work, a blown up 3x4 picture I took of the field with the Sox coloring the grass around the mound; my house a scrapbook filled with pictures; and now a brick from the walls of Fenway with the words: 'Go Sox Go! A Memory Forever.'"

Lights! Camera! Fenway!

The 2005 comedy *Fever Pitch* starring Jimmy Fallon and Drew Barrymore was a modest success when it opened nationally, but it significantly epitomized many in Red Sox Nation. The film, directed by New Englanders Bobby and Peter Farrelly (of *There's Something About Mary* fame), is about a woman competing with the Red Sox for her boyfriend Ben's affection. It focused a huge microscope on die-hard Boston Red Sox fans who literally put their lives on hold for the Sox. The movie was supposed to focus on how Ben's character gives and gives to a team that historically lets him down. Before 2004, as we all sadly remember, the Sox had not won a World Series Championship since 1918. But the film, which had been made during the miracle season of 2004, needed reshoots once the Sox swept the St. Louis Cardinals. *Pitch* ends with what Boston Red Sox fans had needed for 86 years: a very happy ending.

Jessamy Finet was born and raised in Boston, and lives, breathes, and dies for her Red Sox. A female equivalent of Ben, she has gotten even more fervent. "I have always been a fan," she said, "just not as obnoxious or over the top as I've become." With her brother and father, sports "was a family affair." She went to Boston Latin Academy, which is within steps of Fenway, and attended most Opening Day games.

But Finet has a more direct tie to *Pitch*. After she and her roommate were interviewed for the documentary, *Still We Believe*, it led to a role in the Farrelly Brothers film. "We couldn't believe it. A casting company called us and literally said that their call was not a joke, but the Farrelly Brothers had requested that we both audition for a part in their movie…We were excited and nervous as hell, but how freakin' cool was that?"

Finet said she "screwed up" her lines during the audition but got the role anyway. For two to three weeks, Finet was a working actress, trying to memorize her lines and loving every minute of 15-hour filming days at Fenway. "I had a trailer on Lansdowne Street and had almost free range to the park, including a little time in the clubhouse, which was interesting. All in all it was a once-in-a-lifetime experience."

Her exploits in 1999 demonstrated that she deserved a place in that movie. It was in that year that her best friend and current roommate started taking road trips. "Our first major trip was to Cleveland for Game 5," she said. "Once you witness something like that it gets very addictive." Finet and her friends had gone to Game 4 of the series the night before in Boston, and after bawling her eyes out after an amazing victory, she and her pals spontaneously decided to travel to Cleveland for Game 5. They kept talking about it throughout the night as they celebrated with spirits, and it became a running gag all night long. They even tried to recruit some fans at the bar to come with them. "No one took us seriously," Finet said. "Needless to say we woke up very early the next morning. We probably got two hours of sleep, and we said to one another, 'We're still on, right?' And we were off."

Without even looking up directions, Finet and her friends jumped into the car and headed to Cleveland to see the conclusion of this magical year. They continue to take road trips, but 2004, of course, was a magical year for her and all of Red Sox Nation. Not only did the Sox shake the Babe Ruth curse, she literally gained from the whole experience, launching her role as Teresa in *Pitch*.

Filming at Fenway Park has become a trend of late since that Jimmy Fallon movie. Films like *A Civil Action*, *Good Will Hunting*, and *Blown Away* showcase America's most beloved ballpark, but after *Fever Pitch* and the Sox-winning ways in 2007 and beyond, more and more films are shooting there—from *The Town* to *Ted*. And there's a reason. "It's a cathedral," beloved Red Sox pitcher Tim Wakefield said. "Why wouldn't you want to make a film in the most famous park in the world?" Finet, who knows a thing or two about acting in a Fenway film, agrees. "From the Citgo sign to Yawkey Way, there aren't many parks you can compare the awesomeness to," Finet said. "You can't beat our city nor our park between the history, nostalgia, and quaintness."

Fenimonial: There's No Place Like Home

Close your eyes, tap your heels together three times, and think to yourself, there's no place like home, there's no place like home.

—*The Wizard of Oz*

Glinda, the Good Witch of the North, must have been a baseball fan.

Like everyone else who has ever been in the place, when asked to describe Fenway Park, I think first of the Wall. In recent decades it has acquired a new handle, the Green Monster, but for those of a certain age, it was in the beginning, is now, and ever shall be simply the Wall.

Yet when I am seated in the park, whether it is empty or full, there's no place like home, home plate, that is. That is where my eye is invariably drawn. It's where the action is. It is where I have seen Teddy Ballgame, Yaz, Pudge, and Big Papi take their stances and it is the very spot where, before them, Jimmie Foxx, Babe Ruth, and Tris Speaker stood. It is where countless others have stood, helpless, while a Pedro Martinez fastball blazed by or a Tim Wakefield knuckler danced tantalizingly past into the catcher's mitt. It is where catchers have stood for a hundred years, fearlessly bracing themselves as they prepared to block the plate, catch the ball, and apply a tag while absorbing the crash of a runner hurtling down the third-base line.

In 1960 Ted Williams' final blast nestled into the bleachers beyond the Red Sox bullpen, and in 1975 Fisk's clout that won the Greatest Game Ever clanged off the foul pole in left, but they both were launched from home plate. It is there where the battle of the pitcher and the hitter is decided. It is where everything in baseball begins and ends. And it has been happening at home plate in Fenway Park longer than anyplace else.

Standing at the plate back in the '40s, Johnny Pesky would occasionally rub his needle nose. Dom DiMaggio, leading off first base, would read the signal, and the special play they had cooked up would be on. DiMaggio would take off on the next pitch, forcing the shortstop to cover second. Pesky would artfully bunt the pitch down the third-base line, and the third baseman would have to charge in for the ball, whereupon DiMaggio would keep going around second and cruise into an unguarded third base, a two-base advance on a ball hit only about 30 feet. The play worked well. In fact, it worked too well. It got written up in the newspapers. One day against the Yankees, Pesky rubbed his nose and DiMaggio took off. He rounded second and steamed into third, only to find catcher Bill Dickey waiting there with the ball. As he applied the tag, Dickey looked down at DiMaggio, grinned, and said, "I read the papers, too."

It was at Fenway's home plate that I witnessed what must be the greatest insult of an umpire in the game's history. Carl Yastrzemski was batting, and Red Flaherty was umpiring behind the plate. Flaherty was having, in Yaz's estimation, a bad day, a really bad day. When he got rung up on strikes, on what Yaz considered a particularly egregious call, he took matters into his own hands—literally. Rather than get involved in a shouting match he knew he couldn't win, the usually undemonstrative Yastrzemski dropped his bat, crouched down, and with both hands made a pile of dirt that completely covered home plate. Then he stood up and stalked off, leaving the umpire standing there sputtering. Yaz got thrown out of the game, as he knew he would, but he was already well on his way back to the dugout by the time Flaherty pulled the trigger.

As a kid growing up on the sandlots of Quincy, Massachusetts, home plate was not a particularly friendly place for me. I couldn't hit the ball out of the infield. That is not, though I wish that it were, hyperbole. It got so bad that, when I came up to hit, the kids playing in the outfield would lie down in the grass. I never did give them a reason to regret it.

What must those kids have been thinking on a July evening in 2002 when I stepped up to home plate in hallowed Fenway Park holding in my hand—not a baseball bat—but a microphone? The occasion was the closest thing to a funeral that Ted Williams ever had, a tribute the Red Sox put on a few weeks after he died. It drew old teammates—military buddies such as John Glenn—and 25,000 other fans and mourners.

Several months before that event, I had driven from Boston with DiMaggio and Pesky to Williams' home in Florida to visit him for three days. We all knew how gravely ill he was. To justify my presence in the company of the great heroes of my boyhood, I did a quick rewrite of a grand old baseball ballad I'd been reciting ever since my college days, Ernest Lawrence Thayer's immortal "Casey at the Bat." I reworked it so that it was about the great post-World War II Red Sox teams, when DiMaggio batted leadoff, Pensky hit second, and Williams third. The new version became "Teddy at the Bat." I recited it for the first time before an audience of three, DiMaggio, Pesky, and Williams, in The Splendid Splinter's living room. They were the luminaries for whom the rewrite had been done, and I assumed that would be the end of it. But when word of our trip got back to Boston, I began to get asked to repeat the recitation at venues such as BoSox Club events. Then, when Williams died, the Red Sox great impresario, Dr. Charles Steinberg, invited me to do "Teddy at the Bat" at the Fenway Park tribute.

So there I was, the kid who couldn't hit the ball out of the infield, standing at home plate in what was even then the most sanctified baseball shrine in existence. All eyes were upon me. But there was a problem. Until a completely new sound system was installed in the park a few years ago, one's amplified voice did not go out over the loudspeakers until several seconds after the words had been spoken. To say, it was disconcerting to a speaker, is an understatement of gargantuan proportions. To attempt to recite from memory a poem of more than five minutes in duration, in the face of the distraction of one's own voice repeating what had just been said, in front of 25,000 people live, for crying out loud, is like playing Russian roulette. I felt like one of the Flying Wallendas, the daredevil high-wire walkers who always worked without a net. It turned out they couldn't fly after all, and when they fell, they fell hard.

I made it through. I'm not quite sure how, but I made it through. In the ensuing years, I have been asked to recite other poems at home plate on occasion, but with the new sound system and no delayed feedback, it is, relatively speaking, a piece of cake.

Still, though I had stood at home plate in Fenway, I hadn't done so with a baseball bat in my hands. But my moment was to come.

Each year the Red Sox generously make the park available for a day to the Genesis Fund, which is dedicated to the care and treatment of children with birth defects and brain injuries. It's a wonderful cause, and the event that ensues is equally wonderful. It's called Yaz Day at Fenway. Carl Yastrzemski has been a committed supporter of the Genesis Fund for many years and he does much more than give his name to the event. He signs autographs, mingles with the participants, and even gives instructions. The participants get to bat at home plate, run the bases, field balls hit off the Wall, and pitch against the speed gun. I have been on the fund's board of directors for years and I show up do the announcing.

One year there was a little lull in the action. I saw my opportunity and I took it. I grabbed a bat and strode manfully to the plate. Taking my stance in the left-hand batter's box, I waved the bat menacingly. I can't say that I intimidated the pitcher, since I was hitting against a machine. It was programmed to deliver the ball at a pace just fast enough to keep it from being a leisurely lob, perhaps 55 miles per hour. It made Wakefield look like Nolan Ryan. This was my chance to show those kids from my sandlot days—those of them who were still alive, anyhow—just what I could do.

The balls came drifting in from the machine and I, consistent as ever, was hitting my usual quota of weak dribblers and pathetic pop-ups. I did foul one back into the seats, and that was pretty cool. But my window of opportunity was closing. There was only time for one more swing. I dug in—determined that I would not be denied.

In came a heater, about 56 miles per hour. I turned on it and caught it right on the sweet spot of the bat. As I followed through, the ball majestically soared toward right field.

Way back. WAY BACK! It's outta here!

Not out of the park, out of the infield. It landed in the grass behind first base, about 10 inches beyond the skin of the infield. Admittedly, if a first baseman had been on duty, he'd have caught it while standing in the infield. But it landed in the grass, and damn it, that's the outfield.

It might not seem like much to anyone else, but I'm the guy, who as a kid couldn't hit a ball as far as the outfield, and yet, when I was in my 60s, I did just that. That tells me one thing. As the years go by, I must be getting stronger and stronger. At the rate I'm progressing, I might hit one out by the Pesky Pole when I'm in my late 90s.

Fenway Park has the Wall, it has the Pesky Pole, it has the triangle in right center, and, as Glinda said to Dorothy all those years ago, there's no place like home.

—Dick Flavin, *Red Sox Magazine*

2

Backyard Fenway

It comes back to why the ballparks matter to us—because exactly comparable people played a comparable game in this ballpark for generation after generation.

—George Will

America's houses of worship may not take your breath away like those in Europe, but our green cathedrals are our historic ballparks. Fenway Park, after all, has served as the heart of New England for one century and counting. It has served as a home to not only the Red Sox, but also to the Braves (of Atlanta, Boston, and Milwaukee), the Boston Bruins, Patriots, and several college teams. Visiting that sanctuary is incomparable and inspiring. Fans of baseball, the Sox, or any team come away with the same notion—they've just seen a game at a venue like no other. The seats, with sightlines that may have made sense 100 years ago, are a reminder that generations have come to the stadium to celebrate the national pastime.

The old adage "Always replicated, never duplicated" never seemed truer than in the 1990s, when it became vogue for major league teams to build new, retro-stadiums. Major league franchises are not the only ones to try and replicate Fenway's grandeur. Many fans, whether it be in a dorm room, basement, or Little League field, have done their best to bring a little bit of Fenway nostalgia to their homes or neighborhoods. Being New Englanders, some have done so not for vanity, but charity. Little Fenway in Vermont and Mini-Fenway in Maine have roots in giving back. Their noble existences have been a benefit to their communities, both in the thrills they have provided, and in creating a better way of living for those they have helped.

Little Fenway is an amazing structure, an accurate miniaturized version of Fenway Park. While Fenway Park hosts the national pastime, Little Fenway hosts the sport many of us grew up playing: wiffle ball. Some of the most thrilling parts of playing as a kid are aiming at the strike-zone box painted on the wall, which is in place of an umpire, or hitting one past the thorn bush, which marks home run territory. The game can be played anywhere: the beach, blacktop, a campsite, or a busy intersection. Possibly the only thing missing from everyone's collective wiffle ball experience is playing the game on a legitimate playing surface. Well, New Englanders have not had that problem since July 4, 2001, thanks to Pat O'Connor's Little Fenway in Essex, Vermont. Located 210 miles from the real Fenway Park, his 23 percent-scale replica of Boston's hallowed field provides adults a chance to create new wiffle ball memories while giving back to those in need. "Everyone is a kid," O'Connor said, "when they are out there playing."

Growing up in a military family, O'Connor moved around a lot, and as a little kid he found himself a California Angels fan. He moved to New England in 1981, after getting out of the coast guard and landing a job with IBM in Vermont. At that point Pat started to make the pilgrimage to Fenway Park as often as possible. For each summer expedition, the O'Connors kept returning to Boston to get their Fenway fix and see the aquarium and museums. By 1992 they moved eight miles with their three kids from Jericho, Vermont, to Essex to their current house, which rests on 11 acres of land. The idea for the field developed in 1993. "I planned a baseball trip with my two brothers to see all 28 teams in the space of 17 days," O'Connor said. "We met in Pittsburgh and ended in Pittsburgh and rented a van with unlimited miles. The tour got rained out in New York and almost got rained out in Boston." That Fenway game

Youngsters play a wiffle ball game at Essex, Vermont's Little Fenway, which is an exact 23rd percent-scale replica of Fenway Park.

Pat O'Connor changes the Little Fenway scoreboard by hand—just as it's done in the real version on Yawkey Way.

started at 10:30 PM. The storm followed them on the trip, but they saw the New York Yankees on another day and kept schedule.

Good Morning America had the brothers on television, because at that time those types of extensive baseball road treks were very unique. "In comparing all the ballparks, it was clear to me that Fenway was my favorite park we visited," O'Connor said. "Little Fenway started to percolate in my mind. Wouldn't it be nice to do something here in the yard? But then you get caught up in everything else. In late '90s after many more trips to Fenway, I thought why don't we bring a little bit of Fenway Park to Vermont." Because of the work required, he figured he should scale it for wiffle ball. So he drew it up on a napkin and took it in to work to his friend who thought it was a great idea. "Next thing we know we're digging holes," O'Connor said.

A great deal of research and precision was required to capture the feel of the ballpark on a wiffle ball scale. Extremely meticulous, O'Connor coerced a groundskeeper at Fenway into getting him a vial of dirt from third base. He recalled the cross-eyed glance he received, but that didn't stop him from further pursuits. "I was feeling kind of bullish, so I went over to the first-base side by the tarp," O'Connor said. "I found another groundskeeper and asked if he would give me a scoop of the track dirt." Afterward, he went to a couple of different quarries in Vermont to match up the granular and color. And then a friend of O'Connor's went to the real Fenway and scraped a piece of paint off the Red Sox dugout. "Back then they wouldn't give out the shade of green they used to the public," O'Connor explained. "About five years ago, they directed me to a place to get the color, but when I was first exploring this, they wouldn't give out that formula."

Most of the people who visit Little Fenway are hard-core Red Sox fans who want to take a crack at the Green Monster. During the fall of 2000, Bernie Carbo, pinch-hitting hero of the 1975 World Series, became the first Red Sox player to visit Little Fenway. The Green Monster was up, but the sod was not yet in place. Carbo signed the wall where he hit his home run, while sharing some of his favorite Fenway Park stories. Former Red Sox starting pitcher Bill Monbouquette has visited a number of times, and Vermont resident Bill "Spaceman" Lee comes all the time. Other major leaguers to appear at Little Fenway include pitchers Jim Neidlinger and Vermont's own Len Whitehouse.

Pat tries to organize a schedule to play on Little Fenway, in between scheduled visits by the many people who come by to see it and Little Wrigley, which was added in 2007. The focus of the fields is on the charity events, but they have been used by many organizations and schools, including the cub scouts, a senior center, and the University of Vermont hockey team. The latter used it for team-building exercises. The action on the field is secondary to the good work being done. "When there is an event taking place, people mostly comment about the magic and the electricity of the place," O'Connor said. "They haven't been to a place where there is this much fun. [They remark], 'It's so cool, it's so different, it's so unique.' They can't believe how people could just come together and have such a blast. If people are coming and they just see the field when no one is on it, they get a real kick out of the Citgo sign, the scoreboard, and the Monster itself. A lot of people comment, it's smaller than they thought."

Measuring 100 feet to center and 70 feet to 75 feet down the lines with plenty of room for bleachers in right field, nine players can comfortably field the ball. "It's very hard to get a triple. That's one of the things I love about the design of this field," O'Connor said. "We experimented a lot with distances, even though the distance from home to the wall is 23 percent of Fenway. All the way across, the distances to the bases are 41½ feet, which works out really nice. If you hit a ground ball to third, and if he fields it cleanly and throws it across, you generally get the guy by a step or two."

Equipped to seat 1,000 people, Little Fenway includes the Ted Williams seat, 35 seats in right, and eight to 10 seats in center field. The wind determines whether it is a hitter's park or pitcher's park. Yet it is more of a hitter's park than Little Wrigley, where wind blows in more.

The event that creates the most magic is the annual Travis Roy Foundation Wiffle Ball Tournament. Twenty-four teams competed in the 11th annual tournament, raising $430,000 for the Travis Roy Foundation in 2012. Despite a bit of rain, which caused the need to bring out the tarp, everyone had a blast at the festive event that takes a year of planning. Each year at least 20 teams of nine players return to display their wiffle ball skills, raise funds, and bring awareness to spinal cord injuries. There is even a waiting list, which welcomes new blood to the ranks every year. Amazingly, four teams have come all 11 years, including one from Staten Island, New York. Most of the teams are from Vermont, Massachusetts, and Maine, but some have traveled from as far as Indiana to take part in the fund-raising tournament. "Out of the field, about 10 to 12 are local teams," O'Connor said. "With 24 teams you get a range of talent, but the top-end teams are very good wiffle ball players. Some of the teams have stayed together, so as players from the teams have moved and scattered across the country, they've flown in from all parts of the U.S. They plan their summers around it, which is a tribute to them."

While Little Fenway is used predominantly for wiffle ball, that signature event benefits a former hockey player. Travis Roy was a freshman Boston University hockey player for the defending champions, who won the 1995 Frozen Four. Roy was paralyzed 11 seconds into his first shift. His No. 24 is the only retired hockey number at a university with great hockey tradition. "He was probably destined for the NHL, playing as a freshman on the team that had just won the national championship," O'Connor said. "When he was in the hospital, he realized he was blessed with NCAA coverage and all the fan support. There were a lot of people in his condition that didn't have that support. So in 1997 he formed the Travis Roy Foundation to help spinal cord injured survivors. The tournament has become their big event." From 2010 to 2012, the tournament has raised $1.2 million, which goes toward motorized wheel chairs, home ramps, adaptive equipment, research, and financial help for spinal-cord-injured survivors. Among many other aspects of this tournament, the lights, music, and generators are all donated.

The tournament has an umpire chief, rules committee, a schedule maker, and instant replay. All game balls and bats are issued for the tournament, meaning nobody can bring their own. While no metal cleats are allowed, fielders can peg base runners. However, if you hit the base runner in the head, it counts as a miss. A radar gun, controlled by the umpires, is available to enforce a speed limit on pitchers, if necessary. Although there has yet to be a no-hitter, there once was a triple play.

O'Connor detailed one of his favorite memories, which shows the intense zeal of the sport mirrors baseball. "We brought technology into the Travis Roy Tournament. All the games are broadcast on the Internet. Multiple cameras are set up, and we even have a television at the concession stands, so you can go get food and watch the game. The memory to me that sticks out—a guy made a fantastic catch right by the Pesky Pole. The umpire called it a home run, because he said it tipped the Pesky Pole before he caught it. We have a rule that if you donate $50 to the Travis Roy Foundation, you can appeal the play. We went into the tent and looked at the instant replay. We zoomed in on the ball going by the Pesky Pole to determine that it didn't change direction. We declared that it was the first time instant replay had been used to determine the outcome of a wiffle ball game."

The first ever Little Fenway Winter Classic was played the Saturday of Super Bowl XLVI weekend. O'Connor contacted his friends at Wiffle Ball, Inc. He asked the grandson of the inventor of wiffle ball, Dave Mullany, "How do they keep balls from cracking every time they are hit in cold temperatures?" The Connecticut company didn't have a model, and nobody had ever pressed them to figure out the solution to playing wiffle ball in freezing temperatures. "It was cool to have that discussion and speak about different ways we could keep those balls warm," O'Connor said. "We got heated coolers that umpires kept next to them, balls spray-painted red for Fenway and blue for Wrigley. We have to come up with a new rule for next year when a ball is hit and cracks in two, and the fielder only catches half."

O'Connor keeps a busy schedule. In addition to running Little Fenway's annual events; he is also the owner and team president of the New Bedford Bay Sox of the New England Collegiate Baseball League. Red Sox veteran Rick Miller earned 2012 NECBL Manager of the Year honors while leading the Bay Sox to a 25–17 record and second place.

Ready to spend even more time in baseball, O'Connor has a really nice spot for a third park right next to Little Wrigley, and it won't be Little Yankee Stadium. "We are probably going to do Little Field of Dreams," he said.

Like every New Englander, O'Connor has a favorite experience at the *big* Fenway Park. His occurred after winning first place at Red Sox Fantasy Camp in 2007. While playing at Fort Myers, Florida, for manager Bill Lee, O'Connor was catching, and one of his good friends was pitching. That battery induced a ground-out, winning the fantasy camp tournament and thus the right for O'Connor and his teammates to be introduced at Fenway.

Enjoying the chance to take that legendary field and decked out in Red Sox uniforms, O'Connor played catch with his teammates on Fenway's third-base line. Some young fans mistook him for a major league Red Sox player. As O'Connor was leaving the field, he took his brand new ball and flicked it to a young Sox fan. "The kid's eyeballs were huge," O'Connor said. "It was really cool to be on that side of the experience. There's always something on a trip to Fenway that makes me remember that particular game."

Mini-Fenway

"Many baseball fans would not look favorably on a fan that changes sides, especially the ones who are just following the winners—your typical fair-weather fans. Even worse, a cardinal sin would be if you change sides to your hated rival," Ken Walsh said.

With those words it's easy to want to label Walsh a "pink hat," a term which has come to describe a Red Sox fan that jumped on the bandwagon as a result of the 2004 and 2007 World Championships. After hearing the heartwarming side of his story, however, you might change your opinion.

Walsh is a self-described baseball lifer. "I truly love the game of baseball," he said. "It's been in my blood since I was a little kid playing sandlot baseball with my brothers and friends in my backyard. Like many kids I dreamed of playing baseball at the major league level. I made it to the college level and played for 10 years in adult leagues, Stan Musial [baseball league] and tri-state leagues. Baseball was always a key part of my life."

In 1992 Walsh came to Maine to run the Waterville-area Boys & Girls Club, leaving New Rochelle, New York, which is just 20 minutes from the Bronx, where he was assistant executive of New Rochelle's club for seven years. He arrived in Maine as an avid Yankees fan, who got to celebrate years of Bronx Bombers dominance and the rebirth of excellence through the 1990s.

He quickly realized that the state of Maine is very much part of Red Sox Nation. Walsh's reaction to the situation was that of a stereotypical New Yorker; he had to stir things up by displaying his love for the Yankees in every way possible. From bumper stickers on his car, photos of the Yankees greats in his office, and, of course, a Yankees flag hanging outside his house, Walsh gloated for years, as the Yankees were on their '90s upswing, and the Red Sox struggled. All of that changed in the summer of 1998.

Earlier in 1993 Walsh met Harold Alfond, a member of the Maine Baseball Hall of Fame and a recipient of the Ted Williams Distinguished American Award. The Maine resident and philanthropist assisted Walsh during the development of the Boys & Girls Club in Waterville. Alfond, the creator of the Dexter Shoe Company and an owner of the Boston Red Sox beginning in 1978, gave millions of dollars away to support the efforts of youth development. Through Alfond's support, the largest Boys & Girls Club in the nation was built in little old Waterville (population 15,000). He also helped bring together a unique partnership with the YMCA, creating the only merged YMCA and Boys & Girls Club in the nation. Walsh explains the partnership, "like pulling together the Yanks and the Red Sox to one franchise."

Walsh and Mr. Alfond had baseball in common. "Harold in his 80s still enjoyed the game immensely, flying to many ball games as he had his own owner's box right next to the President/CEO John Harrington's box," Walsh said. "Harold, over his lifetime, went to many World Series games and had Ted Williams, Yaz, and other Red Sox greats as his friends. He took a liking to me and always joked about me being the lone Yankee fan in Waterville. Baseball connected both of us as well as helping kids."

Walsh's conversion to the good side happened gradually. "Over a five-year period, Harold always invited me down to Fenway to see a ballgame. I laughed and said I could not bring myself to enter the park of the Yankees' biggest rival, unless they were playing the Yankees," Walsh said. "I received a phone call on August 14, 1998 from Mr. Alfond, and he said, 'Meet me at the Waterville airport at 5 PM. We're going to a game tonight.' I arrived at the airport, and a Red Sox jet waiting for me, Harold, and a few other Boys & Girls Club/YMCA board members, flew to Fenway for my first game at this historic park. The next part was pretty breathtaking to me. Harold led us to ground level of the field through the press box and onto the Fenway Park ballfield while the Sox were taking batting practice before their game against the Minnesota Twins. I was out of my mind, being right on the field with professional ballplayers right next to me. Harold brought me into the Red Sox dugout to meet Pedro Martinez. Pedro was as professional and outgoing as he was on the mound...I went over to the batting cage and stood next to Hall of Famer Jim Rice and listened to the advice he was giving to players like Nomar Garciaparra, Jason Varitek, John Valentin, and Mo Vaughn. I ended up getting autographs from each. Manager Jimy Williams came over to say hello and talked it up with Harold. I stepped away and spotted Hall of Famer Paul Molitor. Paul was in his last year as a major leaguer. We talked for a moment, and I asked him how much longer he was going to play. He said that, most likely, he was going to end his career this year. I told him he has been a major asset to the game. He autographed my ball, and we all headed to the owner's box for the game."

Access like this was not something Walsh took for granted. He said, "Being at Fenway for the first time was like going to baseball heaven. This old rustic park gave you the sense of family immediately. From the Green Monster wall, to the big Coke bottle in left field, to the seating arrangements—all of it created the character of this unique park. Perhaps Harold knew what he was doing, spinning his web that caught a Yankee fan off guard. Whatever the case, it helped bring me over from the Dark Side."

The Red Sox beat the Twins that evening 13–12, and Walsh began questioning his commitment to the Yanks. "Within months my Yankee flag went down, and I began to watch more Red Sox games. The core Yankee fan in me began to erode away, as the Red Sox Nation grew stronger. However, I still do get ribbed by my buddies in Maine, telling me that my roots will never disappear.

"Since that August 14th night, I've seen many Red Sox games—more than I can count. I saw the great October 16, 1999, Pedro vs. [Roger] Clemens playoff match, where the Sox knocked Clemens off the mound in little over two innings, winning the game 13–1. I can remember the thunderous crowd chanting, 'Roger, Roger,' as I sat in the owner's box with Harold. I remember watching my first World Series game in 2004 right at field level and again in 2007. Recently, my wife and I sat on the Green Monster wall for the first time, enjoying a great game."

The 2004 season was magical in many ways for Walsh; he married his wife, Suzanne, who is a die-hard Red Sox fan. Like many other members of Red Sox Nation, who were also married in '04, they welcomed their first child, Sean, as the Sox hauled in another World Series title in 2007. "Over his crib was a wall-size mural of Fenway Park," Walsh said.

Shortly afterward, the friendship with Alfond resulted in the only licensed mini-Red Sox stadium. Walsh recounts, "Harold Alfond called me shortly after the birth of Sean and asked me to meet him in the Boys & Girls Club/YMCA parking lot. He was there with his driver. He rolled down the window and threw me a baseball. He said, 'I want your son to get the first baseball from me.' On the baseball it was inscribed: 'To Sean, Best Wishes, Harold Alfond.' After months of fund-raising and working with Major League Baseball, Cal Ripken Sr. Foundation, and the Red Sox, Mini-Fenway was built. I brought Harold Alfond, who was suffering with cancer at 93 years old, to the newly built field. He got out of his car driven by his oldest son. He was amazed at the exact identity of Fenway; he was overwhelmed to the point a tear came from his eye. I said, 'Harold, this field is dedicated to you, it will be called the Harold Alfond Fenway Park.' In late September Cal Ripken Jr. came to Maine to dedicate the field and honor Harold. It was a tremendous afternoon and a day many of us will always remember."

On November 16, 2007, Alfond passed away. Before he passed, he had Mini-Fenway Park dedicated to him, and the Red Sox won the World Series. "Now the Harold Alfond Fenway Park hosts many regional and local tournaments as well as the Junior Red Sox Baseball Camp," Walsh said. "The Major League Baseball Association delivers ballplayers each summer to give our kids exceptional instruction at our historic Mini-Fenway. The Red Sox Nation lives well at the Walsh house, and we all wear proudly our blue and red shirts and hats wherever we go, including Yankee Stadium."

3

Misery Is Comedy

Laughter and tears are both responses to frustration and exhaustion. I myself prefer to laugh, since there is less cleaning up to do afterward.

—Kurt Vonnegut

For way too many years, the Boston Red Sox were on the wrong end of a punch line. How many "1918" chants did we need to hear? How many Bucky Dent references have been made? How many Bill Buckner lines were doled out during the winter of our discontent, following the 1986 Fall Classic? For comedians from Boston, however, laughing through the pain got them through all the tragedies of our boys in navy and red. But, once the Sox started their winning ways in 2004 and 2007, in many cases, the jokes about the "joke of a team" faded. It's hard to crack a joke about a team that's winning—well, unless you buy the World Series, like the Yankees historically have done. In any event, four comedians know heartache all too well about their team, and it has fueled the belly laughs that they've caused those outside of New England. It's easier to laugh off 1975 or Aaron Boone than deal with the crushing reality of what happened to your team. The Sox have shaped these comedians' humor and provided them with countless jokes to tell for fellow long-suffering fans and those beyond the wall of the Green Monster.

A dejected Bill Buckner reacts to making an error in Game 6 of the World Series. That play is a source of misery—and material—for Boston-area comedians.

It's too bad Brian Kiley came from a good home. Had he endured a crappy childhood, the comedian is convinced his act would be a lot funnier. "There's something about pain that causes comedy," he said. Lucky for Kiley, an Emmy Award-winning writer who has been with Conan O'Brien since they called 30 Rockefeller Plaza home, he's a Boston Red Sox fan. Yes, the Massachusetts native said rooting for the boys in red and navy has enabled him to make a living in the funny business and helped shaped his self-deprecating style of humor. "There's something about losing and failure that lends itself to comedy," he said. "I used to do this joke back when the Red Sox and Patriots were terrible. I don't remember exactly how it went, but it was something like, 'I had to go to a funeral, and I was looking to wear my most depressing clothes. So

I went there with a Red Sox shirt and a Pats hat.' It used to be a killer joke for me back when the Pats were terrible, and the Sox were breaking hearts."

Up until the Red Sox won it all in 2004, Kiley was used to having his heart broken by his favorite team. He grew up in Newton, Massachusetts, and regularly went to games at Fenway Park and would arrive very early. "I'd get to the park at 9 AM on Saturday morning and would sit outside the parking lot to get autographs from all the Sox players and the opposing teams. I was 12 or 13 and got tons of autographs—Nolan Ryan, Rod Carew—some pretty big names," he said. On one occasion Kiley interviewed the "Needle" himself, Johnny Pesky, in that parking lot for his high school journalism class.

For Kiley, rooting for the Sox was a given from the second he burst out of his mother's womb. "It's that thing, where your dad would take you to games, and his dad took him to games," he said. Even after Kiley's father retired to Florida, he felt compelled to come back to Fenway. "When my son was seven years old, my dad came home. He felt he should take him to a Red Sox game," Kiley said. "It's just part of being a grandfather in New England. It's very much a generational thing."

Yes, going to Fenway Park and cheering on the Sox is a time-honored tradition for Bostonians and New Englanders. Going to the ballpark and rooting for the Sox is just in your DNA. Trips to Fenway can be as common as churchgoers going to mass each Sunday. And Kiley stresses it's not just a guy thing. "You can go to Maine on a Sunday afternoon, and you can see an old lady listening to the Red Sox game while she's making cookies. My great aunt lived to 97, and I remember the last few years she'd just repeat her stories over and over. She'd tell us how she saw Babe Ruth at Fenway and how the fans cheered him when he hit a home run and booed him when he struck out. She'd tell that story three or four times a visit. It became a running joke within our family. Any time someone would break a glass or knock something over, we'd say, 'And then they booed him!'"

Being a Red Sox fan plays a roll in your everyday life, and it doesn't just stay in New England. In 2009 Kiley and his family moved to Los Angeles when Conan O'Brien replaced Jay Leno as host of *The Tonight Show* after a decade-plus run as host of *Late Night*. After Leno returned to *The Tonight Show* (boo!) and O'Brien moved on, creating *Conan* for TBS, he remained in L.A. As a Red Sox fan residing in La-La-Land, Kiley—still a writer for *Conan*—said he's noticed a lot of Sox bumper stickers, hats, and attire on the West Coast. "It's this weird fraternity," he said. "There's a certain romantic feel to the Sox. People love Fenway, and there's something romantic about the sad, long curse the Red Sox went through. People have pulled for them in a way because they're the anti-Yankees. People embraced that."

September 2011 was a perfect example of that. On the final day of the season with the Red Sox and Tampa Bay Rays tied in the race for the American League wild-card, Sox closer Jonathan Papelbon blew a 3–2 lead against the Baltimore Orioles, and the Sox lost 4–3. Minutes later, the Rays won their game against the New York Yankees because of Evan Longoria's game-ending home run. The Sox had been up by as many as nine games in the final month of the season but epically collapsed. "Something happened that September—something behind the scenes that people don't know about," Kiley said. "They needed to play .333 ball to make the play-offs and couldn't do it."

In the middle of that Sox collapse, Kiley's father passed away. Naturally he fielded many condolences from staffers at his Warner Bros. lot offices in the days and weeks that followed. "People would say 'I'm sorry,' and I'd just say 'Thanks.' But it turned out they weren't even talking about my dad. They didn't even know about my dad. They were talking about the Red Sox." Kiley didn't realize that until a few obvious instances. "They'd say, 'I'm sorry, but there's always next year.' And I'd be like, 'What? No there isn't. He died.' Or they'd say, 'The pitching fell apart.' Looking back it's kind of funny."

As Kiley pointed out, pain breeds humor when you're a Sox fan. He's not sure he'd have had as successful a career had he rooted for a different team. Had he cheered on the Yankees and was born in the Bronx, it's clear—at the very least—his comedic style would be vastly different. "There's nothing funny about winning all the time," he said.

Rooting for an underdog or a lovable loser team that seems to have arguably had more moments like the Papelbon blown save than the heroics of 2004 or 2007 victories has allowed Kiley to keep the same outlook. Case in point: The 2012 Red Sox campaign was terrible. With the team constantly trying to avoid the basement of the AL East, Kiley said he can't help but continue to watch just how bad they can be. "My normal day starts by watching the game I DVR'd the night before the next morning," he said "I'll be on the stationary bike for 25 minutes and fast-forwarding through the game. It's my routine, and it doesn't matter how bad they are. I'll keep watching. It's like a car accident or something," Kiley said. However, he noted that the Yankees losing to the Detroit Tigers in the 2012 ALCS and missing the World Series provided some salvation.

Coming up with illogical logic has been the norm for Kiley and countless Sox fans. When Aaron Boone ended the 2003 American League Championship Series with a walk-off Game 7 home run off Tim Wakefield, Kiley said he took solace in knowing it wasn't the worst defeat ever. In his history book, the two most painful losses were failing to win the 1986 World Series against the New York Mets, despite being within a strike away more than once, and the 1978 season, which on all accounts ended infinitely times worse than the Papelbon screwup. As Red Sox Nation knows all too well, the Sox blew a 14-game lead in the division, ended the season tied with the Bronx Bombers atop the AL East, and lost a one-game playoff, when Mike Torrez served up a home run to Bucky "Fucking" Dent of all people. "There's always just this 'expecting doom' feeling," Kiley said. "When we lost in 2003, I took consolation, knowing it was only the third-worst loss they ever had. It was not the most heartbreaking. It was kind of like the guy who gets hit by a bus, but he tells himself, 'It wasn't as bad as the time I got hit by a train or the time an airplane fell on me.'"

Being a Red Sox fan makes it a whole lot easier to make people laugh and to laugh at yourself. When Kiley was at the funeral of his friend's father a few years back, he actually noticed something funny. "We were at the cemetery, and a plot nearby had these floral arrangements, and in the middle of the flowers was a baseball cap centered in it," he said. "It was a Yankee-hater hat. I just thought to myself, 'Wow, for all of eternity, he can hate the Yankees.'

"I'm not sure hatred is the idea of the afterlife. I remember thinking, 'Is this really the message you want to send?' It's one thing to have a Red Sox hat on, but a Yankee-hater hat? It just made me laugh."

Like Kiley, comedian Paul Nardizzi surely would agree that a Yankee-hater hat is a bit too much to take with you to the grave. Born and raised in Dedham, roughly 20 minutes away from Fenway Park, the acclaimed New England comic and Boston Comedy Festival winner said he's far more of a lackadaisical fan these days anyway. Since the team started spending like their rival New York Yankees, he's said he has become somewhat dissatisfied. "At some point I realized in the recent years, rooting for them is the same as rooting for the Yankees. They are just a money machine," he said.

But way back when, you couldn't find a bigger fan than Nardizzi, who grew up on the team thanks to his parents and his maternal grandmother. Nardizzi was a hard core fan and went to many games throughout his childhood. When he was about seven years old, he was at Fenway with his brother and father, and they sat in front of a fan who would, for some reason, say "Oooooooweeeeeee!" "He'd say it over and over. It was funny to a seven-year-old," Nardizzi said. A young Nardizzi constantly looked back at the fan in the hopes he'd make that sound again. He did something much better—and stranger. "[In] about the fifth inning, he takes a pear and he eats some of it. Who brings pears to a ballgame? It's real ripe and juicy, and then he chucks the rest of it. And I swear I will never forget the sight of that thing hitting this bald guy in the back of the head several rows down." The impact of the pear being flung made its juices go all over the man's head. "I was in hysterics, the 'Oooooooweeeeeee' guy was my hero," he said. Naturally, Nardizzi'a father didn't think much of it. "Of course my father explained this is not how you act, and so on. I wanted to bring the guy home with us."

Nardizzi had another fond Fenway experience, when he and his friends "helped" change the outcome of a game—at least he likes to think so. "I sat above the bullpen one game in the 1986 season, Buckner's year. The Sox were in a pennant race, and this guy for the [California] Angels was warming up," Nardizzi said. "My buddies and I were drinking and giving it to the guy real good, and he was getting pissed. Then, he went out there, and the Sox lit him up and won in late innings." Perhaps that trash-talking took the pitcher off his game. "It was such a key win. People were dancing on cars when we left and partying in the streets," he said, before quipping, "no cars were tipped over. We save that for the playoffs and World Series."

As everybody in Red Sox Nation knows all too well, New York Mets speedster Mookie Wilson hit a slow dribbler right through Buckner's legs during Game 6 of the World Series. Terrible losses like that may have shaped Nardizzi's humor. "I never thought about it in those terms, [but] it certainly could have. Having a team every year that finds some way to lose, you learn to laugh at it," Nardizzi said. "You bond with other fans and that type of thing."

On the stand-up circuit, there's even a fraternity of Boston comics who bond over Sox losses and victories. "Comics tend to huddle in the back, and the ones who follow sports discuss it a lot. A lot of sarcasm and ripping of local athletes goes on…so when the Sox lose, it's talked about, and, of course, as comics, we have all the answers," he said. "Some comics know their stuff. Then there is the guy or two who hangs on the fringe and offers a comment or two just to fit in but should know to keep his pie hole shut!"

Making fun of his favorite team had always been a slam dunk for Mike Donovan. Then the Boston Red Sox won the World Series in 2004, their first title since 1918. "Just like BC and AD, there is a before 2004 and after 2004," the stand-up comedian explained. "Before 2004 I had a few jokes about the futility of being a Red Sox

Comedian Mike Donovan used to joke about the Red Sox's tragic playoff history, which includes annoying Aaron Boone and his 11ᵗʰ inning home run to win the 2003 ALCS.

fan." Donovan, who was born and raised in South Boston, recalls a bunch of them. One joke in particular worked wonders with his audiences in the 1980s. "I have a Red Sox watch on. It works fine in April. Every October the battery dies," he said. Yep, in that Alf and Cyndi Lauper decade, self-deprecating Sox wisecracks worked on many, though, as he looks back now, they might have struck out with some. "I'd say sometimes it worked and made the show better, but sometimes it was maybe a little too inside for much of the crowd—a little inconsiderate," he said.

That was all pre-2004. That was before the Sox defeated the rival New York Yankees in four straight games after dropping the first three during the ALCS. That was before Keith Foulke closed out Game 4 of a four-game sweep against the St. Louis Cardinals, and it was certainly well before Pedro Martinez ever entertained Nelson de la Rosa in the clubhouse. Before that salvation took place, Donovan was born at Boston City Hospital on January 26, 1955 and raised in South Boston. Like many Red Sox fans, he was born into it. His father and grandfather cheered for the Sox, and Donovan probably frequented Fenway Park more times than Frodo roamed around the Shire. Naturally, the comedian, who started performing in the mid-1970s and headlined shows by the end of that groovy decade, has countless memories of the team and of Fenway.

A key highlight came in the fall of 1990, when the devoted fan was the only one to capture a clear video shot of outfielder Tom Brunansky making a sensational catch to clinch the division on the final day of the season. "For two days no one in New England was 100 percent sure that Brunansky maintained complete control of the ball when he hit the ground," Donovan said. But Donovan knew and had proof. "I showed up at Channel 4 with a homemade Panasonic video and became a tiny part of Red Sox history," he said proudly.

Red Sox history also has provided inspiration for his act. Onstage he's done impressions of Ken Harrelson, Jim Rice, Joe Castiglione, and Sox public address announcer Sherm Feller. A few months after Feller passed away, an audience member came up to Donovan after a show and told him a wonderful story. "He worked with Feller and said that when Sherm heard there was a local comedian who impersonated him, he showed up and watched his show and secretly made a tape recording of the set. He loved it, but he never told the comedian, which was me," Donovan said. "He used to force visitors to listen to the crowd laughing while I mocked him in my act. He kept the tape in the front drawer of his desk at all times. When the guy cleaned out Feller's desk, he remembers taking that tape out and remembering the good times when Sherm Feller made people listen to my act. And I never met him."

One of Donovan's enduring Red Sox memories is a painful, yet historic game. It was October 22, 1975—Game 7 of the World Series between the Cincinnati Reds and the Red Sox. The game followed one of the biggest wins in franchise history, when Carlton Fisk hit a game-winning home run in the 12th inning to tie the series at three games. Fisk waved his arms, signaling the ball to go in fair territory, and that gesture is etched in our hearts and souls.

"I had just enough money for a standing-room ticket to Game 7," Donovan said. "I had to wait all night outside Fenway to get it. I walked to the game from my house and walked home…about 2.7 miles."

Bill "Spaceman" Lee was on the mound that night, and kept The Big Red Machine to two runs over the first six innings. Eventually the Reds went ahead in the ninth on an RBI duck-fart single by Joe Morgan. The Sox were sent down in order by Will McEnaney to end the inning and the Series in the ninth. Needless to say, it was a long walk home for Donovan. "It was very quiet, when Cincy won," Donovan said. "You could hear the slaps on the backs from the Reds through the park as they celebrated."

During a much more joyous Red Sox time, Donovan was onstage in Las Vegas in 2004 while the lifelong fan's team won their first World Series since 1918. He said he felt more sad than happy about the historic event. "It really took a lot away from it for me. It's a sad memory that I missed it," he said. "The other comic was from Boston, and he stuck his head out from behind the curtain and gave me the thumbs up that they had won it all over Cardinals. I was already well into the act and had already done a lot of sports material, so I shared it all with them about how I was from Boston, and at least I was sharing it with 'a nice crowd like you.'

"It was packed at the Tropicana, and it was a really nice crowd, like a 9.1 on a 1 to 10. The crowd actually gave me a nice cheer, and then I went back to the act. But it is actually a sad memory. All that work and then to miss the moment."

The 2004 win has shaped Donovan's humor as of late. Since that year, he said, he rarely talks specifically about the Sox onstage. "I do talk and joke baseball in general," he said. So gone are the jokes about the Sox watch, though he said he had gotten miffed that two different people asked him to retire it when they had won. "[They] said sort of angrily, 'Now you can stop basing your act around making fun of them.' Basing your act? One joke in a 45-minute set?"

Now even when he's given an opportunity to hit a meatball out of the park, he won't take it. The 2012 Red Sox lost 93 games, finished in last place, and featured all kinds of internal dissension. On a September night, he appeared on Boston's CBS affiliate, WBZ, for four hours, and the host read a story about how the team had just lost their seventh straight. Donovan held back. "I was going to joke that the new promo for NESN [New England Sports Network] says, 'Watch the Sox lose! Tonight at eight!' But I've had my fun with them, so I didn't hit 'em when they're down. I held my tongue, and I know the host would have laughed."

———

The Red Sox were a significant part of Mike McCarthy's act before 2004, but it's certainly changed since Kevin Millar and his merry band of Idiots took the gold in that magical season. "Something certainly changed in my makeup after we won," the 25-year stand-up veteran explained. Up until that point, he said his humor was more pessimistic and superstitious when addressing the Sox. Why wouldn't it be?

Born and raised in Medford, Massachusetts, and the youngest of eight kids, he grew up idolizing the Sox, even though they constantly let him down. Case in point: When the Sox lost the 1986 World Series, his parents threw him out of the house for "smashing stuff." His explanation for the act? "I'm Irish."

As an adult, McCarthy couldn't help but feel dejected and angry each time the Sox came close. "It runs deep," he said of his fandom, noting he's never wavered, even though the Sox relationship was one-sidedly abusive. Despite the key losses and frustrations prior to 2004, he's loved his team no matter what. His dog is named Tessie, and his daughter would have been named Carlton (as in Fisk), had she been a boy.

And he has his Sox superstitions. McCarthy said he had been "carting around" his father's Bushmills whiskey for years. It had one shot left in it, and since his father passed away, the comic was waiting for an appropriate moment to finish off that bottle. In 2004 he took a swig and did a lot more. "I ran around the block naked in 2004 after taking a sip," he said. "[My dad] passed before he could see them win, but they beat the Skankees in Game 7 on his birthday."

Life for McCarthy and every Sox fan has gotten a whole lot more celebratory since 2004, even if the team has failed to make the postseason the last few seasons. But McCarthy explains it's all irrelevant, since the Sox ended their World Series drought in 2004 and won again in 2007. "Before 2004 I was more pessimistic onstage, but since then I focus on the positives," he said. "If they lost Game 7, I would be institutionalized. I believed they'd come back because I had no choice…Now it's all house money."

It has changed his style of humor, too. "I try to make fun of myself more than anything else," he said. "I kid you not. It changed me as a person. I had given them so much."

4

Wakefield of Dreams

Tim Wakefield has represented the best of the Boston Red Sox...In the long, proud history of this franchise, few men have brought greater honor to the uniform.

—former Red Sox general manager Theo Epstein to RedSox.com

How do the Red Sox explain New England, and vice versa?
New England is the Red Sox fan base. I don't know of any other baseball team that has a fan base that encompasses six states. It's amazing. The passion that pours from our fans from this region compares to no one else in the country.

Why do you think this region cares so much about the team? Paint a picture of the fan base.
It has a lot to do with the history of the team as well as the commitment from the team to the fans. The belief in the Red Sox has been passed from generation to generation and has spread throughout the entire country as well. Even as we traveled around the country to play, we ran into Red Sox Nation wherever we went.

What's your most memorable moment at Fenway Park?
I have two. The first is winning the '04 World Series and bringing it back to Boston to share with the millions of fans from all different

Starting pitcher Tim Wakefield, who played for the Red Sox for 17 years, throws during Game 1 of the 2004 World Series against the St. Louis Cardinals. (Getty Images)

generations, and to see the pleasure in their faces brought us a ton of joy. The second was when I won my 200th game, and coming back onto the field to celebrate with the 38,000 fans that stayed in their seats, waiting for me to come out and allow me to thank them for their support over my 17-year career.

What is your favorite New England hang out spot?
Obviously, I'm a little biased toward something I'm invested in; my favorite restaurant is Turner's Yard in Pembroke [Massachusetts]. But before that I was a regular, and still am, at The Capital Grille. As far as the other amenities that Boston has to offer, how can you go wrong with any choice you make? Boston is the greatest place to shop, eat, and raise a family. What more can you want?

What is your favorite aspect of Fenway Park?
My favorite aspect of Fenway is the history. So many great players have played there before me, as well as after. There is no greater place to play than Fenway Park. When you look into the stands, you see faces. Not a crowd. It has a feel of a neighborhood rather than a sporting event.

Do you think you would have had such a successful post-Pirates career had you not been playing in Boston?
Probably not. Playing in Boston brought out the best in me as well as everyone else that donned the Red Sox uniform. The fans demanded it, and you wanted to please them as much as possible. That's what made it great to play there.

5

For the Love of the Game

by Jess Lander

Where it began, I can't begin to knowin'. But then I know it's growing strong. Was in the spring, and spring became the summer. Who'd have believed you'd come along.

—Neil Diamond, "Sweet Caroline"

People seek to marry someone who shares not just mutual interests, but a deeper level of connection, often in the form of shared religious beliefs. Some unique couples, though, pray to the Boston Red Sox. And while many couples traditionally tie the knot in a church or religious setting, for Sox fans, their church, temple, and sanctuary is Fenway Park, where church bells chime, and brides saunter down the aisle to the tune of "Sweet Caroline."

And marriage requires a level of commitment with which Sox fans are already very familiar: a lifelong undertaking through the so good, not so good, and heartbreaking Bill Buckner-like moments. For even in the worst of times—after getting swept by the New York Yankees—the love is absolute, because vows were taken, and faith is forever unwavering. Not to mention, misery loves company.

For most, relationship deal-breakers might be smoking, unemployment, or a criminal record. But for Red Sox fans there's just one unbreakable rule: Thou shalt not date Yankees fans.

———

"Ladies and gentleman, boys and girls, welcome to Fenway Park, America's most beloved ballpark." Carol Merletti has uttered that sentence 32 times standing before 32 almost-married couples—and sometimes—before a crowd of Red Sox fans that ended up getting more than a baseball game with their ticket purchase. Donning her Sox cap, Merletti has to be both loud and quick, running through her justice of the peace spiel in the small window of the seventh-inning stretch. Two "I dos" and a kiss to seal the deal, and then at the sound of *Take Me Out to the Ball Game's* final "One, two, three strikes," it's time to sit back down before people start throwing Fenway Franks.

Merletti's first Fenway wedding was just weeks shy of the second championship, in September of 2007, during the Red Sox regular-season finale. It happened atop the Green Monster for the joining of two Red Sox fans from New York who wore personalized Mr. and Mrs. jerseys. "It was incredible. The crowd takes part in it. They're really sweet to the couples. They cheer them on," Merletti said. After waiting four years for the chance to officiate on Yawkey Way, Merletti realized a personal dream after marrying those Sox fans.

The 52-year-old Malden, Massachussets-lifer, Merletti, muted the Sox game for a recent interview but was definitely not about to turn it off. It didn't matter that Boston, dead last in the American League East, had already blown any chance of making the playoffs. What mattered was that they were down 2–0 to the Yankees in the bottom of the seventh and still had a chance to spoil it for the boys in pinstripes. Spoiler alert: the Red Sox lost.

She grew up with 11 siblings, who all had to take turns going to the games. "It's in my blood because my parents were Red Sox fans," Merletti said. When she got older, her mother became her routine date to Fenway, and so when her mother fell ill, Merletti embarked on a quest to fulfill her mother's dream of meeting Red Sox Hall of Famer Jim Rice. That quest had been in place since August 7, 1982, when Rice heroically rushed into the stands to help a bleeding child who got hit in the head with a line drive. After exhausting efforts, Merletti pulled through on her promise. The first jersey that Rice ever signed with *HOF* preceding his signature was for Merletti's mother and is now displayed in Merletti's Sox-shrined home office. Her mother passed away in 2011, but they both have mother-daughter 100th anniversary bricks at Fenway. Now whenever Merletti officiates a wedding or attends a game at Fenway, her game date is there with her.

Merletti officiates formal weddings in a majestically empty Fenway Park in addition to in-game weddings. Each wedding is unique. Each couple has their own story, their own touches, but each and every one symbolizes the union of a pair of die-hard Red Sox fans that leave with Merletti's custom-made Red Sox-themed marriage certificate. No cold feet here—every superstitious Red Sox fan knows that would be grounds for a curse.

On September 9, 2009 (09/09/09), Merletti circumnavigated the park to marry three couples during one game. She married a couple on the bittersweet day of 2012 when the blockbuster mega-trade sent John Beckett, Carl Crawford, and Adrian Gonzalez to the Los Angeles Dodgers, amidst the worst season in Sox history. She married a couple that lucked out by meeting Dustin Pedroia during batting practice. Merletti's seen it all, marrying couples not just from New England, but from Las Vegas, Tennessee, Pennsylvania, and Australia.

Merletti has wed a total of 733 couples to date. Each, though, is unique. She once turned down a request to dress up as Elvis for a ceremony. "If people want to consider my Red Sox weddings a Vegas-type wedding, that's all right by me, because I'm a fan, and it's right up my alley and I love it," Merletti said. "I love my Red Sox weddings. It ties in with me being a fan. I get to be down-to-earth. I get to be me."

Don Montgomery was in New Orleans for a business conference on October 8, 2003 when he parked himself at his hotel lobby's bar to watch his Red Sox play the Yankees in Game 1 of the American League Championship Series. When the Red Sox won 5–2, he stayed to celebrate with a couple of fellow New Englanders from Medford, Massachusetts, who were sitting at the end of the bar.

The Yankees eventually took the series in a gut-wrenching Game 7, when Aaron Boone hit a series-winning home run off of Tim Wakefield in the 11th inning. Most Red Sox fans remember that series as the last of the Red Sox heartbreakers before The Curse was finally broken the following year. But Don only focuses on that first game. If the Red Sox hadn't won it, he probably would never have met his wife. "The three of us were celebrating, and the only reason I stayed was because they had won," he said. "If they had lost, I would have been in bed. Denise arrived at the hotel late that night from Phoenix."

Although Montgomery's wife, Denise, is a San Francisco Giants fan first, the couple's mutual love for the game of baseball brought them together, as they embarked on a long-distance relationship after meeting in the hotel that night. And it wasn't long before Denise fell under the spell of Red Sox Nation. "It was almost an instant connection for us," she said. "At the time I was living in Arizona, so it was a way for us to stay connected while we were dating long distance. I adopted the Red Sox as my AL team and started following them from afar. When I was watching them, I kind of felt like I was with him, because it's what brought us together."

A year later she moved out to Philadelphia, where Montgomery lived, over Labor Day weekend, just weeks before the world changed for Sox fans. She still traveled a lot for work but would continue to watch the Red Sox on the road during playoffs. "I remember calling him from the lobby bar and saying, 'Your team is goddamn killing me! I don't know how you do this!'" she said.

Montgomery responded, "Try doing this for 37 years."

When Denise's parents were visiting, they got a taste of what it's like to watch a Sox game with him. With the Yankees just one win away from the World Series, it was Game 4 of the ALCS that turned the tide. But Montgomery never got to see Dave Roberts steal second base. He didn't see him score off of Bill Mueller's single, which blew Yankees pitcher Mariano Rivera's save and sent the game into extra innings. He also didn't get to see David Ortiz's two-run, walk-off homer in the 12th that kept the Sox alive. Instead, Montgomery had turned the TV off the second that Mueller walked up to the plate and with the Sox three outs away from the all-too-familiar saying, "There's always next year." "I actually said, 'Well, Mariano Rivera is on the mound. It's lights out. It's all over," he said. "My mother-in-law was like, 'I can't believe this. They could still win. I thought you were a fan!' But I'd watched this too many times. I actually said, 'It's hockey season now.'"

At 1 AM and in a deep sleep of familiar Sox misery, he got a call from an ecstatic Denise, who was yelling into the phone, 'Did you see that? Did you see that?' He hadn't, but with Denise back from traveling, the two watched the World Series together at a bar in Philly.

When they decided to get married, the pair was in search of a unique day. Self-proclaimed procrastinators, they tried to pull together a Leap Day wedding in 2008, but it didn't work out. In September of 2009 they were both heading to Boston for work, so they looked into getting Sox tickets. Denise happened to notice that one of those games was on September 9, numerically written as 09/09/09, just the kind of unique date they had been searching for. "I asked him, 'Want to get married at Fenway?' and he said, 'Yes,'" she said.

Denise had about three weeks to pull her wedding together, a task that would send most brides over the edge. She found Merletti to be their justice of the peace, the first of three Fenway Park weddings Merletti was slotted to preside over that day. Denise booked a photographer, and then the couple made T-shirts that read *09/09/09*. They bought tickets for the first row in the center-field bleachers, and that was that. "We had no idea where we were going to do it. We just said, 'Let's meet. Let's go to our seats and we'll figure it out,'" Denise said.

The small wedding party met up during batting practice before the game, and then an usher appropriately named Murph—this is Boston, after all—saved the day. He walkie-talkied a few security guys, who became the couple's witnesses, and they were ushered down to get married right on the field. Following the ceremony an Orioles player (whose identity they still don't know) passed the newlyweds a ball to keep as a memento. "After we got married, our whole section was cheering for us anytime one of us got up for a beer. One other man, who caught a ball, gave it to us. The people were just fantastic. It was such a great experience," Denise said. "It all came full circle. We wouldn't have met had they not won that day." Added the groom: "We had 35,000 guests at our wedding, and our wedding song is 'Sweet Caroline.' People say to me, 'Wow, you're the luckiest guy getting her to agree to that,' and I was like, 'It was her idea!'"

The couple both come from baseball backgrounds. "I became a Red Sox fan in 1967 with the unbelievable pennant race and in particular, the play of Carl Yastrzemski and Jim Lonborg," Montgomery, a Westborough, Massachusetts, native said. "I was six years old at the time, which is not a bad age to start getting into baseball, so my passion for the Red Sox goes back that far."

But his family's roots in baseball go back much farther. He had one grandfather, Joe Donald, who umpired Little League baseball for 40 years. Donald was a Yankees fan but also "the greatest man I ever knew in my life," said Don, who remembers that his grandfather passed away in 1986, on the day that the Red Sox moved past the Yankees in first place to stay. Don's other grandfather was a catcher at the University of Pennsylvania, and his father played catcher at Brown, even getting a tryout with the St. Louis Cardinals during the 1950s. His mother was the Little League president, and both of his brothers played catcher, too.

Don played baseball his whole life, finally retiring during a softball game when he was 45. But he hasn't forgotten the good years and isn't shy about them either. "I played for the 1976 Westborough team that won the Milford Babe Ruth Invitational, which, for all intents and purposes, in the 1970s was a state championship. I was the starting shortstop. I also was a cocaptain of the 1979 Westborough Senior Babe Ruth team, playing shortstop, third base, and the occasional center field, because I was the fastest guy in the league," he said.

Don remembers every key, painful moment of the Red Sox championship drought. He remembers being at football practice in 1978 during the playoff game against the Yankees, when Yastrzemski hit a home run in the second inning, and his coaches sent the team home to watch the game. Don came home to an empty house and was sitting by himself when Bucky Dent hit a three-run homer in the seventh inning to give the Yankees the lead and eventual win. "The game probably ended at about 5:30 in the evening, and the sun was starting to go down," he said. "I just sat there and let the room get dark."

He also can't forget the horrifying moment of 1986 when Bill Buckner let the ball roll through his legs in Game 6 of the World Series, allowing the Mets to win the game that would have given the Sox a championship at long last. "I was at Casey's Sports Pub in Worcester. The place was a madhouse until the ball went through his legs, and then it was just deathly silent. I remember the bartenders had a row of champagne glasses on the bar, and they were popping them open in the 10th inning, when the Red Sox were leading, and then they just had all these open bottles they couldn't use," Don said. "It's kind of like the Kennedy assassination. You remember exactly where you were, and I remember exactly where I was for all of them."

None of those moments, though, pushed Don away to another team. "I've never even considered rooting for another team even living in other cities. I don't know what keeps us this way. It's just a lifelong thing. I can chart certain things in my life versus what the Sox were doing at any given time," he said.

Sometimes those life events directly involved the Red Sox. "My first time at Fenway was July 20, 1969. During the game, they stopped the game to announce that Apollo 11 landed on the moon.

There was a moment of silence for the astronauts, and there was a guy with a tuba in the first-base upper-deck seats who stood up and played 'God Bless America,'" he said. "That game was against the Orioles, and the day I got married at Fenway was also against the Orioles. Paul Byrd was the starting pitcher. He had a short time in Boston, but we'll never forget it." The Red Sox won on both days.

Don expressed the significance that Fenway played in his life in his vows to Denise on his wedding day. They read:

> Now here we are, standing in a place that has been very special to me for 40 years; a place where I have seen and experienced my own childlike excitement hundreds of times; a place where I have stood as a little boy, as a teenager, as a young man finding his way, and as a brash 30-something who had thought he'd found his way—but boy, was so wrong. You didn't even know those Dons. Yet, you are the one who suggested we should be married here, in this place that is so special to me. You've given me this, and you're sharing it with me, just as you have given me so much joy in these past five years.

And now that day, too is a day in Red Sox history that Don will always remember.

———

The first time that die-hard Red Sox fans, Rebekah and Robert Refino, set foot in Fenway Park was on their wedding day. They were joined together on September 3, 2011, in left field underneath the Green Monster in front of their Yankees-loving families, while Boston's batting practice went on in the background. "My sister was determined to wear a Jeter jersey," Rebekah said. "And I just was not going to have it." Rebekah is the lone wolf in her family when it comes to her baseball allegiance and she settled on red bridesmaids dresses.

Having grown up in New Mexico, Rebekah's only guidance on professional sports teams came from her family, supporters of the pinstripes. But she chose to go rogue, adopting the Red Sox at the age of eight, following a trip to Boston. "My family was like, 'What are you doing, this is a Yankees family.' But I stuck to my guns. I'm a very outspoken fan and opinionated about my teams. Every year, I got to know the team better; I learned their birthdays, their colleges, their backgrounds; I studied up on them," she said. "We actually moved to Maryland, and my dad took me to my first Sox game at Camden Yards, when I was about 14. I remember it was the first time I saw Youkilis get up to bat and I heard the crowd do the 'Yoooouk!'—and that was pretty amazing to me."

Despite growing up in New England territory in Newport, Rhode Island, Robert still had to work hard to separate himself from his family's Yankees influence. His grandfather even tried taking him to Yankees games to bring him over to the dark side, but his father—the one Sox fan in the family—won the war. "He didn't like the way the Yankees put themselves on in general anyway, so he decided he wasn't going to be a Yankees fan. He really exposed me to the Red Sox. We'd always sit down and watch games together, always went to Paw[tucket] Sox games when we got a chance; Dave & Buster's, if they had a showing of it; or down to the movie theater, where they used to have showings," Robert said.

And so it was that the pair was born out of a shared love for the Red Sox. They met online through a mutual friend and fan, and it was that common interest…uh…obsession, that first got the conversation started and then kept it going. Without the Red Sox they admit that they might not be together today. "That was always one of the first things I would look for in a girl. She had to be a Red Sox fan or else it wouldn't work, and if she were a Yankees fan, it was doubly not going to work," Robert said. "It was one of our key talking points when we first started talking, and if it wasn't for being fans of the team or for our mutual friend, we wouldn't even probably have met."

The only problem was that Rebekah was in New Mexico and Robert in Newport. They started talking in August of 2010 and didn't officially meet in person until December, when Robert drove all the way across the country for her birthday. They got engaged by the water in Newport on Valentine's Day. And while wedding planning is a struggle for many couples, these two knew exactly what they wanted. "I've always wanted to get married at Fenway. He and I thought it would be perfect, because that's how we met. It was our first real conversation, and we both love the Sox. It was kind of a fairy tale for us," Rebekah said. Regarding her unique "fairy tale" wedding, she said, "It was a lot to take in. It was overwhelming, because I was at first getting married and then seeing the Red Sox, who I love too. It's unexplainable; to walk into the old tunnels… it's really cool." And even the Sox-Yankees drama was kept to a minimum.

Amazingly, the couple still hasn't attended an actual Red Sox game at Fenway Park. But they plan to make their first experience— on Opening Day—a family affair. It will be just weeks after the first baby Refino is due to be born. Although they don't yet know if their first Sox fan will be a boy or a girl, they've already got the middle name picked out: Yastrzemski. Ted Williams, Johnny Pesky, Curt Schilling, and Jason Varitek were also in the running. "The Red Sox have founded our whole relationship, so we really want to carry that on to our children," Rebekah said. "We want them to not just love the Red Sox, but baseball as a game, and I think that's really important."

Rebekah originally wanted to name the baby after her favorite player, Josh Beckett. But Robert knew. "I told her that 'we can't do people that are on the team now.' She wanted Beckett and I said, 'No, he might get traded.'" And he was right. Just weeks later, Beckett was sent to L.A. Besides, their choice seemed appropriate, being that the couple announced to family and friends that they were expecting on August 22, Carl Yastrzemski's birthday.

Little Refino has quite a name to live up to. He has Hall of Fame and Triple-Crown shoes to fill, but the couple is certainly not going to let their children sway away from family devotion the way they did from the Yankees. "My family thinks we're crazy for putting such a big name on a little baby," Rebekah said, "but it's what we want, and we want to root that baby in Boston."

———

In the era of online dating, there's a site for everyone. There's the traditional Match, eHarmony, and OkCupid. Then there's ChristianMingle and JDate for those seeking counterparts who share their religious beliefs. There are even sites for single parents, casual encounters, and committed relationships. But one New Englander realized a need for a dating site that catered to a different, specific, and very important goal: finding a Red Sox fan.

Timothy Lampa, who grew up in Quincy, Massachusetts, created and then launched MatchingSox.com in 2005. The site's slogan is "Turning Red Sox Singles into Doubles," and it features a pool of eligible men and women to browse and essentially draft. Most profile photos even feature Fenway Park in the background. Lampa's original motive behind the idea was simply to help Sox fans find fellow fans to go to games with. That, and the girl at Stand 12 who he'd fallen for when he worked at Fenway, selling hot dogs and sodas in college. "The popularity of the team and the new ownership had made it next to impossible to get tickets to Fenway Park. As a die-hard fan of the team and of the park, I was always looking for a way into the games," Lampa said. "During the playoff run to the World Series, I had noticed on Craigslist that some people were looking for companions to the game. I thought that if people had these extra tickets, then maybe there was a better or safer way to get them the company they desired."

MatchingSox.com has one big success: the wedding of Dawn Graham and Patrick Lowery. "My father always told me I was not allowed to marry a Yankees fan, so it was very slim pickings where I lived. Connecticut is half and half, but where I live, I'm closer to New York City, so in this general area, there are many more Yankees fans than Red Sox," she said. "I think something like that in common for me was super important. I know it sounds silly, but my household lives and breathes the Red Sox, and I think anyone else would probably think I was insane, because my family is just crazy." Her first date with Lowery would show that craziness.

The two met on the site in 2006 under the handles SoxGirl71 and NJRed. They were engaged three months later and married on September 30, 2007, a year after their first date, which took place at Fenway just as Lampa had envisioned. The date wasn't your traditional first date, however, as Graham invited Lowery to drive up from his home in New Jersey to attend a game. She had good seats behind the dugout that he couldn't pass up, but there was a catch. Also attending the game was Graham's best friend and mother. "It was a very, very strange situation," Dawn said. "Everyone teased him, saying, 'You must really like the Red Sox if you met a girl and her mother on your first date just to go to a game.'" But the date went well despite that awkwardness. Mom, friend, and most importantly, Dawn, approved. And the two didn't let the Red Sox loss that night deter them from a second date.

It was a good thing, too, because the couple could only have been good luck for the Red Sox, who clinched the division—Boston's first division title since 1995—two nights before their Sox-themed wedding. A three-up, three-down Papelbon special in the ninth secured the Sox's 5–2 victory against the Twins, and all of Red Sox Nation rooted for the Orioles to finish the job for them against the Yankees. With three runs off Mariano Rivera in the ninth, Baltimore came back from a 9–6 deficit and went on to top the Yanks in the 10th inning. Shortly after Graham and Lowery's honeymoon, the Red Sox won the World Series.

Graham was raised a Red Sox fan by her father, who took her to the first of her many games at Fenway, when she was just three months old and had no idea what baseball was. Lowery, on the other hand, found his own way to the Red Sox. "Patrick was from New Jersey, and all of his friends were either Yankees or Mets fans, and he lived in an area where the Red Sox were unheard of. He started following them and liking them when he was seven," Graham said. "He was always the odd man out growing up but never changed his mind about it." His team of choice can be linked to Dwight "Dewey" Evans, whose swing Patrick tried to imitate in Little League.

Both had previously dated non-baseball fans. "To be quite honest, the previous people that I dated really weren't into baseball, or even sports fans at all, for that matter. They would go to games with me and stuff like that but certainly were not into baseball like I was into baseball," Graham said. And it was the same story for Lowery. "He said he never dreamed that he would even meet a woman that was into sports or baseball as much as I am," Graham said. "There are women, yes, who are, but I guess most of the woman he dated or went out with were not truly fans of sports. When he saw the site, he was like, 'I can't think of anything better than to meet someone that actually likes the Red Sox.'"

This was a problem that Lampa had also hoped to solve. He knew that dating outside of the Fenway Faithful could be hard on a relationship. "Red Sox fans are a unique breed, a little crazier than a normal baseball fan. I think that if someone is dating a die-hard Red Sox fan, they might not fully understand how intense it can be," Lampa said. "The Farrelly Brothers movie *Fever Pitch* demonstrated it perfectly. If you can combine the passion for the Red Sox into a common interest, then dating can become easier. You wouldn't want the person you're dating to makes plans when the Red Sox are in the playoffs. You want them to be with you, rooting for the chance to watch the team advance."

And it was that very theory that brought Lowery and Graham together. He discovered the site on a bumper sticker outside of Fenway Park, while she caught it during her morning routine of watching NESN (New England Sport Network's) old show *Sports Desk* when Hazel Mae was doing a story on it. Neither thought they would ever meet their future wife or husband on the site but figured at the very least they'd find someone with whom to watch Red Sox games. For both, their first chaperoned date at Fenway was their first MatchingSox.com meet-up.

The Lowerys did get married in an actual church, opposed to Fenway Park—the official church of Red Sox Nation, but there was no absence of the team that brought them together in the first place.

For the ceremony Lowery had painted the bottom of his shoes with white nail polish to read *Go Red Sox* after they clinched the division two nights before. When he kneeled down at the altar the next day, it was visible for everyone, especially the couple's Yankees fan attendees, to see. The just-married pair left the church to "Sweet Caroline" and at the reception had a Red Sox cake topper and Red Sox toasting glasses. Graham had no objections to her groom donning his Sox cap for some of the photos.

Although the Red Sox haven't won another championship since, SoxGirl71 and NJRed are going strong. They make annual trips to spring training, sometimes with Lampa and the girl from Stand 12, who eventually became his girlfriend. The Lowerys live with their two dogs, Manny and Carbo, who are named after Sox players, Manny Ramirez and Bernie Carbo. But for the sake of Red Sox Nation, it might be time for the pair to renew their vows.

———

It's typical for brides to call all of the wedding planning shots, dragging around the grooms to fulfill all of their wedding dreams, however expensive, sparkly, or pink they might be. Such was the case in the Clough wedding, but there was nothing pink about it. The newbie Red Sox fan did, though, have to bring her husband-to-be Robert around to the idea of getting married at Fenway Park. He drew the line at his groomsmen donning jerseys for the occasion.

Robert grew up in New Hampshire and, like the typical New Englander, wasn't given much of a choice when it came down to choosing a baseball team. You were either a Red Sox fan or you were a Red Sox fan, and you definitely weren't a Yankees fan. As many would say, his father raised him right, taking him out to Fenway when he was young enough to stand on the street (before the Green Monster was built) to catch the balls that flew over during batting practice. His father once ran after a ball so hard that he ran into a parking meter, bending it over. Years later, Robert also saw Clay Buchholz throw a no-hitter.

His father only had one requirement for his son's future wife: "Before we were dating, [Robert] said to me that his dad told him that he didn't care what kind of girl he dated or married, as long as she isn't a Yankees fan," said Sarah, who actually had a sound argument for such a hypothetical unholy union. "With all the fighting, they'd have to make up a lot."

But much like her wedding, Sarah's Red Sox story is nontraditional. She grew up in a small town in Oklahoma and didn't start watching baseball, let alone any professional sports, until she was out of high school. Yet she remembers the exact date that everything changed. On April 21, 2007, at a California bar with friends (including Robert, long before they became an item), her interest was piqued by a baseball game on TV. That game just so happened to be Red Sox vs. Yankees, and Sarah was drawn to that famously intense glare by relief pitcher Jonathan Papelbon. After much thought and research, she officially adopted the Red Sox as her baseball team and despite what critics of post-2004 fans say, she's no fair-weather pink hat. "Whenever I commit to something that I'm passionate about, it's really hard to persuade me or change my mind about it," Sarah said. "Once I jump into something, I kind of go all for it."

For Sarah, going all for it meant getting a Red Sox tattoo on her left shoulder blade that September, even though she only had been a fan for a few months. "I had a lot of people that were just like, 'You really don't like them. You don't know a lot about them.' But I did a lot of reading, I thought, for a newcomer," Sarah said. "They had started the playoffs, and I was really excited, and I thought I should do something really big to support them, because I was in Oklahoma and I was so far away." As an added bonus, she said it's a great conversation piece.

A month after permanently inking herself as a symbol of her commitment, she was rewarded with a World Series championship. "I felt like I picked the right team," she said. "I was on top of the world and I felt that it was almost like a rite of passage, like this is definitely the team you need to be rooting for."

And if people still didn't buy into her fandom, Sarah fought dirty. "I was waiting in line to go into this bar, and a guy taps me on the shoulder, the hard, rude kind of tap, and says, 'Is that a real tattoo? Why would you do that? The Red Sox suck!'" The man, of course, was a Yankees fan, so Sarah asked him the only logical question: "I said, 'Where's your tattoo?' He rolls up his pants leg and he has a little New York Yankees symbol the size of a quarter on his ankle. I told him that it was the most feminine place to get a tattoo for a man." If there's ever a way for Sarah to speed up her initiation into Red Sox Nation, embarrassing a Yankees fan in public did it.

But back in Oklahoma, far from the epicenter of Red Sox Nation and anything that's not college football, she was on her own. "You have to explain to people about the Red Sox, because they don't really know. Only the few die-hard baseball fans know what the Red Sox really are. I've had people mistake my tattoo for Christmas stockings several, several times. They say, 'Your tattoo is so festive! You must really love Christmas!'"

The only logical next step was to move to Boston. "What I like about most of New England is that they're so die-hard with their sports teams, you just can't pull them away from it, and if you speak badly about them, it's blasphemy," she said. In May of 2008, she picked up and moved with nothing more settled than a place to live. And while she claims that the city of Boston itself and its history is what tempted her to move east, the Red Sox certainly had something to do with it. "I didn't move for them, but I kind of moved to get closer to them, because it was all so new to me at the time, and I liked the excitement. A small town in Oklahoma doesn't have a lot going on. I'd definitely say the Red Sox were a good portion of the reason why I moved."

And then she looked up Robert, who was back in New England after finishing up in the marine corps. They started hanging out in Boston, and he took her to her first Red Sox game as a surprise. "When you first walk through and you see all the pictures of the past and history, that's exciting," Sarah said. "But when you first walk out to your seat, that moment is as close to indescribable as our wedding." The Sox won that night, and Papelbon pitched—a good omen, especially by Red Sox standards. "The Red Sox were always our go-to conversation or our go-to event in Boston. We had a special bond; we'd go down to Lansdowne Street," she said. "Definitely the Red Sox kind of brought us together."

Their relationship went into extra innings from there, and when it came time to plan the wedding, Sarah got the idea of Fenway stuck in her head, despite the fact that her father, a Baptist preacher, would have much preferred a church wedding. But when Sarah gets an idea, there's really no turning back. Not even the people at Fenway could stop her.

The date was set for the couple to be married on top of the Monster on August 9, 2010 (cleverly 8/9/10). The invitations were printed, but then Sarah got an email. "I had just printed out invitations, and we got an email, saying that they had to reschedule our wedding," she said. "I asked them when could we do it next, and they gave me no answer. We gave up on Fenway because we didn't hear from them for months." Disheartened, Sarah eventually scheduled an interview for another venue. "I got an email [from Fenway], three days before the other interview, that they had an opening in June of 2011. I took it. I didn't ask any questions, but made sure I got a contract this time."

Just the Red Sox being the Red Sox. "We made so many jokes about it. The typical Red Sox—they let you down, pick you up, let you down, but you love them, and that's just so much what it is," she said. "Once I had the vision of the Monster wedding, it was so hard to envision a wedding somewhere else. You look at other places and you're like, 'No, not the one.'"

After putting off their wedding for nearly a year, the couple was finally married on June 26, 2011, overlooking Fenway Park, marking Sarah's first time atop the Green Monster. "Once you're up there, I don't know how I could describe it honestly. It's exciting. There's so much history in that ballpark, and you're standing on top of all of it, and you're getting married," Sarah said. "It's almost like winning the World Series. That's about the only way you can explain it, and we got rings out of it, too."

Sarah may have lost the battle on the groomsmen jerseys, but her wedding was not lacking in Red Sox touches: blue bridesmaids dresses with red flowers; red ties for the groomsmen; and a white bouquet for her with red flowers that were arranged to look like the stitches of a baseball. And, of course, her dress allowed for her to proudly display her Sox tat. Then, for the reception, the wedding party crossed Lansdowne to a most appropriate location, the infamous Sox fan-favorite, the Cask'n Flagon. She printed the table names on baseball lineup cards. Each guest got a personalized baseball, and there were two Red Sox cakes, which were perfected down to the tiniest detail like the Citgo sign in Kenmore Square. The groom's cake was a baseball glove with the writing, "What a catch."

Like most little girls, Penny York may have dreamed of a white wedding growing up, but she has absolutely no regrets that her actual wedding was in blue and red. Not wearing a dress or going to church and having hundreds of strangers show up uninvited for a ceremony, which had to be over and done in a matter of minutes, was all fine by her. York got married in section 43 of Fenway Park during the seventh-inning stretch of a Red Sox game on August 25, 2012. "We just love the game so much and we love the Red Sox so much that we wanted to do it during a game. That was so much more important to us than getting dressed up and having something formal," she said. "There's no way I'd put on a white dress and walk through a church instead of that."

Penny and her husband, Brandon, are both lifelong, die-hard Sox fans. They wore Mr. and Mrs. York jerseys (no, not New York) for the ceremony and were married in front of 42 of their closest friends and family—plus thousands of others. "The feeling of Fenway and the passion of the fans—that's what we wanted to remember," Penny said, "how so many people became a part of our wedding party that weren't invited, how it extended past our friends and family to include 37,000 people. I wouldn't have done it any other way." Unfortunately the Sox lost to the Royals 10–9 in the 12th inning after giving up a 9–3 lead that they had in the fourth. It was also the day that Josh Beckett was scheduled to be on the mound, but then the blockbuster trade that sent Beckett, Carol Crawford, and Adrian Gonzalez to Los Angeles happened first, though Penny said they didn't consider it a bad omen. "We realized, being die-hard Red Sox fans, that heartbreak and happiness go hand in hand," she said. "We knew we couldn't expect it to go perfect, and that's the only thing that could have made it any better."

Well, except for maybe one more thing, Penny half-joked. She had hoped for a little help from the weather gods—just not the kind of help you would think. "It was kind of iffy as far as the weather, so I was really hoping that we would see thunder and lightning and that Bobby Valentine would get struck by lightning, but my wish did not come true," she sighed, though she did get a late wedding present when the manager was fired six weeks later.

It's not surprising that Penny, who grew up on a little island off the coast of Maine, was raised a Red Sox fan, but it is a little surprising that Brandon, who's from Kansas, was also raised a Red Sox fan. More important than the reasoning, however, is that they both relocated to Providence, Rhode Island, to work at the same Bank of America and soon became friends. "The Red Sox were a common bond for us from the very first time we met," Penny said. "They were a uniting factor and something that helped us form a friendship before we had a romance."

One of their first dates was to a game, and the relationship grew from there. After four years, Brandon proposed to Penny on Christmas Day in 2011. "It was just a really fun thing to be so in love with someone and share something that's so important," Penny said. "It seems so funny that something like baseball would be an important part of your relationship, but it was just fun for us."

Even after the couple moved to Charlotte, North Carolina, where they still reside, the Red Sox remained a big part of their life. "It never even stopped us from watching the Red Sox, from finding people locally that love the Red Sox, or even finding a local bar called the Beantown Tavern. We just continued on with our passion for the team," she said. "Even far away, we couldn't go to as many games, but we still go every year for Brandon's birthday over

Opening Weekend. It hasn't changed anything. The fact that we moved away, we don't love them any less."

The couple originally planned a long engagement and set a date in 2013. But the poor health of Penny's mother caused them to move it up. That, and getting married the same year as Fenway's 100th anniversary, was too enticing to pass up. "It was really just so much more important for us to seize the day, to realize how fragile life is and make beautiful memories for everyone there that they could take from that weekend, and oh, we got married too," Penny said. "I couldn't think of a better place to do it. Fenway is magical for us in a lot of ways, and we really wanted to give that magic back to our families."

The group made a whole trip out of the wedding, checking out St. Anthony's feast in the North End, taking a behind-the-scenes tour of the park prior to the game, and eating lunch at Jerry Remy's. That night, Penny said the seventh inning dragged on forever, as the pair anxiously awaited their moment. "It was very tense and exciting. We had people—hundreds and hundreds and hundreds of people—immediately around us that all of a sudden decided they were going to participate in our ceremony," she said. "People were all crowded around, taking pictures of us and coming up to us afterward to congratulate us."

A group of men from Ohio on a guys' weekend played a particularly memorable role in the celebration. "At the end of our vows when she pronounced us husband and wife and we kissed, they started chanting, 'USA! USA!' It was so well-timed, and all kinds of people started participating in the chant," she said. "I asked him why they chose that chant, and one of them said, 'This was like an Olympic-level marriage. There's nothing cooler than what we just witnessed, and the only thing that seemed adequate was to chant USA!'"

There were also tears, and not just the normal bride tears either. The pair agreed to exchange gifts on their big day. Penny was proud to give Brandon cuff links that were made out of retired wooden seats from Fenway. The blue seats were the oldest in Major League Baseball but no longer met size requirements. Brandon, however, had something else in mind. "He told me he had something that didn't cost anything and he was hoping that it meant more to me than anything else," said Penny. In the middle of his vows, Brandon started to recite lines from a poem by Penny's mother, who had passed away prior to the ceremony.

Penny, In time we'll learn each dip and sway
And glide along as one
My darling, won't you dance with me...
Until the music's done?

And then the floodgates opened. "The first three words out of his mouth, I recognized immediately as a poem that my mom had wrote, and it was just really special that he had incorporated that poem into our vows, so it was like my mom was there with us and would be part of that day with me forever," Penny said. "I cried like a baby."

———————

Eric Foley's wedding- and portrait-photography business is based in Connecticut, a state notoriously split between Red Sox fans and Yankees fans. Although Foley is too professional to turn down business just for personal reasons, he doesn't hide which side of the fandom he's on. Walk into his studio and you're greeted with a giant image from one of his engagement shoots at Fenway Park. For half of his clientele, it's often a guaranteed booking.

Foley actually grew up on the wrong side of Connecticut. (The west side of the river is Yankees territory.) His father's love for the Red Sox prevented him from choosing the dark side. However, a defining year in Philadelphia when he was five and just learning about baseball made him a Phillies fan first but not forever. "I was a die-hard fan, but when the strike hit in '94, I lost touch with baseball and I kind of rekindled it when I moved to Cape Cod in 2002 and got back into that Red Sox culture. I could say that, if I had never moved to Cape Cod, I don't know where I'd be."

But there's no mistaking now what a few summers selling ice cream on the Cape beaches did to Foley's temporary baseball apathy. "I'm a blue-collar guy. The culture of the Red Sox was really like my lifestyle, and it was very easy to get engulfed in the spirit of the Red Sox. There's nothing like being in Boston for a Fenway game. When you're in New York, you can be anything. It's a melting pot, but when you're in Boston, everyone's a Red Sox fan, and that's the cool thing about it," Foley said. "You can walk around New York City for five hours and never see a Yankees hat. In Boston, it doesn't matter if it's wintertime, it doesn't matter if it's an off day, it doesn't matter if they're playing in Seattle, you will see everyone wearing Red Sox hats. It's a way of life there. You feel like you're part of the team."

Years later in 2008, Foley was given the proper connections, ironically from a Yankees fan friend who had done a shoot, to photograph clients at one of his favorite places: Fenway Park. "Being a businessman, I wanted to exploit that. It's a unique situation, and nobody else was doing it. I also knew my Yankees fan friend had no interest pursuing it," Foley said. "I've been to Yankee Stadium twice my whole life, and the last time I felt like I was in the lion's den. I felt like I was cheating on my wife. I would never want to go to Yankee Stadium to take pictures."

Now going on five years at Fenway, Foley does six to 10 engagement shoots a year and is well known around Connecticut as "the guy that shoots at Fenway Park." For each shoot the couple gets a few hours to take photos around the park. Sometimes they get the chance to go on the field, step on the warning track, or sit atop the Green Monster. If they're really lucky, they meet players. One of his couples got a photo taken with Carl Crawford. Another couple met Jerry Remy. ESPN once interviewed Foley and his clients.

The couples usually don Red Sox attire, sometimes wearing Mr. and Mrs. jerseys, and prime photo spots are in front of Pesky's Pole, in front of the scoreboard, and even on top of the dugout. He also schedules shoots on a gameday, so that his clients can see batting practice. But more importantly, so he can catch a game.

Foley has stood on Fenway's sacred soil enough times now that he's almost desensitized to the park's knee-weakening charms. But he still enjoys witnessing his clients' reactions. "For me now, it's old hat. I know every nook and cranny at Fenway," Foley said. "But when I have a client who's never been on the field, usually the look on their face is a five-year-old on Christmas morning. It's very gratifying in a sense as well."

Rest assured he hasn't forgotten his first time, comparing it to the scene in *The Natural*, when Robert Redford shatters the lights with his game-winning home run. "It was that defining moment, where I just kind of looked around and realized I was in Fenway, on the field. All the history sort of smacks you in the face, and you realize Carl Yastrzemski stood right here, and Jim Rice stood here, and you can see a million white dents on the Green Monster from where the balls hit the wall," he said. "You visualize all those nuggets of video you've seen, the Carlton Fisk home run, and you sort of walk to that spot, and it's a very nostalgic moment."

The engaged couples he photographs at Fenway are never pink hats. "It's couples that were around long enough to see the Red Sox stink and around to actually appreciate 2004 and 2007. We actually charge a decent amount, so that if somebody is going to do it, they are going to be a die-hard Red Sox fan, somebody who lives and breathes Red Sox like I do," Foley said. "What makes it so unique for us is I'm such a die-hard fan, and I attract these fans, and it's sort of a win-win situation, because I'm getting to shoot someone who loves the Red Sox just as much as I do."

But one time there was a Yankees fan. "The bride was a die-hard Yankees fan, the groom a die-hard Red Sox fan. She showed up with a Yankees jersey on. I get offended by that," Foley said. "I was like, 'No, wait a minute. I am not taking pictures of you wearing a Yankees jersey in Fenway Park.' I think she thought it was funny." For business reasons, though, Foley had to grin and bear it.

Although Yankees fans are usually deal breakers for Red Sox fans, Foley says that 40 percent of his clientele are pairs that support their partner's rival. And whether he understands that or not (definitely not) he does understand the bond between his

When Fenway Park wedding photographer Eric Foley first visited the historic stadium, he thought of Carlton Fisk's memorable 12th inning home run during the 1975 World Series.

Fenway couples. "When you're a Red Sox fan and you're involved in the culture of Red Sox Nation, the Red Sox become part of you, and it really does make you feel like you're part of the team," Foley said. "These people really value that relationship, and maybe it says something about the integrity of their relationship."

And of course, the Red Sox are a huge part of his own relationships with his wife and kids. Foley's wife became a Red Sox fan after meeting him and is now the kind of fan that you can find yelling at the players when they make an error. His kids, though only four and six, are already just as big of Yankees haters as their dad. "I have indirectly, but probably really directly, brainwashed my kids into being Red Sox fans. I had to make sure. If my daughter walks into this house and tells me she's a Yankees fan, she's got to go," Foley joked, sort of. "When my kids see somebody walking around with a Yankees shirt, they automatically say, 'Dad, look, the Stankees.'"

———

Jack Walsh asked Emily Walsh to marry him three weeks after they met at the Axis nightclub on Lansdowne Street, but she declined. (Note: Jack claims not to remember this.) Regardless, 15 years later, Axis had closed down, but the couple finally tied the knot about a first-base throw from where they first laid eyes on each other at closing time on the night of April 20, 1996.

"Got a new boyfriend," said Jack in his thick, Dorchester, Massachusetts accent, convincing Emily to go out with him after the club. "We met and we had the most romantic, instantaneous meeting ever, dancing at a house party until the sun came up. He drove me home, sang me Elvis a cappella, and we fell asleep. Monday, I came home, and on my doorstep, there was a sunflower with a meter tag on it, and it said, 'This flower rocks like you,'" Emily said. "We moved in three weeks later—a wild ride—but it's been 16 years."

Jack did finally and formally propose on their four-year anniversary. But with that, the couple moved from Boston, to Oregon, to California, and to their current home in Idaho. Three weeks into her first pregnancy, Emily had a stroke, and then after the first baby, she had two more babies. Before they knew it, a decade-and-a-half had gone by—enough time for the Boston Red Sox to break The Curse and win not one but two World Series titles. "We were coming up for air for the first time in years and we thought we should be married," Emily said.

They decided on Fenway Park (Emily's idea). It was not just because of their mutual love for the Red Sox (more so Jack's) and not just because they first met next door, but also because Emily says the Red Sox explain them. "We wouldn't have done that with any other team," she said. "The values that the Red Sox team embody, Jack and I are like that. Bust your ass and you'll win. Don't give up. The values that, I think, are associated with the Red Sox and the history of it—that's Jack and I. We have this history and great memories—both challenging and good. That was probably why we found, together equally, the stadium to be the most romantic place to get married."

Emily was told that to get married down on the field it would cost them $25,000 but only $3,000 to do it up on the Green Monster. "He, in that Dorchester accent sass said, 'There's nothing wrong with the Green Mon-stah.'"

Having spent his early years in walking distance from the park, and later in Dorchester, Jack couldn't have dreamt up a better wedding venue. "I was like, 'Wow, usually a guy would think of something like that,'" he said. Growing up, his neighbor, Mr. O'Malley, took Jack and his three siblings to games a couple of times a week. He was at the game, when Yankees star Reggie Jackson and manager Billy Martin got in their famous, nationally televised dugout confrontation in 1977. And even though he was across the country in 2004, Jack flew back for the World Series to celebrate at his friends' old bar, the Eire Pub. "It was misery for us. Every year it would get close, and nothing ever happened. So when we won, it was so great because it had been so long."

Emily, on the other hand, was born in Montana and lived about 10 different places before the age of 12. She moved to Boston in 1994, two years before meeting Jack, and it was the first time she'd had a chance to identify with professional sports. Needless to say, Boston made it pretty easy. "There's no more intimate of a baseball experience I've ever experienced than Fenway Park. I'd go to a million experiences. For him it's more about the team, but for me it's more about the fans. There's so much community in the stadium. You could gag me with a spoon," Emily said. "I'm definitely the person double-fisting the beers in the front row, definitely the cat-calling fan that's right up there in the face of the players that aren't doing well. I'd consider myself sort of a loudmouth, community-supporting Red Sox fan."

And so Emily, Jack, and their three sons took a 42-day trip to Boston to be wed. Jack's father, who had been diagnosed with leukemia, got out of the hospital just one day before the ceremony. The wedding was intimate with just the boys, Jack's father, mother, and sister present. Emily says she will never forget her husband's expression when he first walked into the familiar yet breathtaking park. "To my dying day, I will remember that look on his face. I'm not sure he even cared who he was marrying," she joked. "You're constantly in the context as a couple, constantly an *us*, a what should *we* do? How do *we* move forward? What vacation do *we* take? But if you ever have a chance to see someone you love just stripped of all the outside world…he looked like he was three years old and he's 46. It was so incredibly special, and he was so happy."

Emily dressed the three boys in green argyle Sox hats for the occasion and gave each of them a baseball with a customized message like "What a Catch" and "Home Run." As a surprise, the couple even got to go on the field for photos. "It ruined my shoes, but it was awesome," she said.

Going forward, no matter how good or bad things get, Emily and Jack will continue to keep the faith in both the Sox and each other. "Just like a company or a team or group, the group is defined by its culture, and the Red Sox and New England have a sort of definite 'We'll make it through' culture," Emily said. "Will I lose faith in the Sox after the most terrible season they've ever had? No."

———

When someone calls Cerise Bienvenue's cell phone, they hear Neil Diamond singing "Sweet Caroline," the official song of Fenway Park, where Cerise realized her dream wedding on September 19, 2012. But the die-hard, insanely superstitious Red Sox fan got a little something extra out of her perfect union: Her last name is now (rather fittingly) Boston.

When she met her husband Bobby Boston in 2010, it was as if the Citgo sign was lighting up, signaling that she had found the right partner. "When I first met Bobby, he came to my house, and in every room, everywhere you looked, there was something Boston Red Sox," Bienvenue said. "I asked him, 'Is it weird seeing your name every place that you look?' He said no, but it's kind of weird for me, because now everywhere I look, it's my name, too."

Just don't confuse her Bobby with that one former manager, who shall go unnamed, or else the Sox claws will come out. "I totally do not relate my Bobby to that guy, because I have another name for him. I call him 'the ass clown.' That's the best way I can describe him, and I won't call him by his name, because I don't want to insult my Bobby," she said.

Despite Bobby's surname, he's not from Boston. He's from Las Vegas, where the couple met and currently resides. Luckily for Bienvenue he was still a Red Sox fan. That's not only because of the absence of professional sports in Sin City and his last name, but also growing up during the tantalizing era of Carl Yastrzemski and Carlton Fisk. Bienvenue, on the other hand, is from New Hampshire, which is all you need to know about where and why she waves her flag. She used to sit 10 rows back from the dugout at Fenway. "For me it's a no-brainer. Growing up into it, that's just what we did."

If Bobby's name didn't give him enough of an in with Bienvenue, he also passed her top dating requirement: He didn't root for that team that also shall go unnamed. "One of my only criteria, when dating someone, was that they weren't a fan of any New York team, especially *them*. I don't say those words out loud. It amazes me that people can be Sox fans and marry those...that blows me away. There would never be a moment of peace in my household," she said. "Having a job and being responsible is nice. Those things are important, but being a Red Sox fan is probably most important."

But the real question was—could Bobby hang? "It was in February that we started dating, so people were making wagers, unbeknownst to me, on how long into the baseball season he would last if the Red Sox weren't doing well. I'm as rabid as they come and I get very emotionally invested," Bienvenue said. "Everyone said, 'No one can handle her during baseball season: the good, the bad, the ugly.' We didn't make the playoffs, and they all thought that was it, but he stayed on."

He even stepped up to the challenge, strategically popping the question during a time of Red Sox sorrow for Bienvenue. "He brought home my engagement ring the night before Jason Varitek announced his retirement. I thought I was going to die, and he knew that, so he brought home the ring the night before to try to cheer me up," she said. "Truthfully, he asked, 'Is this going to cheer you up?' And I said, 'Well, no, not really,' but once I had it on my finger, and it was really beautiful, it did help get me through the Varitek crisis. Varitek retiring was the pinnacle worst thing that could happen in my Red Sox world. He'd been my favorite player since he came on board." And after making it through 2012, the worst season in recent Sox history, it was clear that Bobby Boston was a keeper.

Having a wedding anywhere but Fenway was never up for discussion. "About four or five years ago, I was at a game with an old high school friend, and I said, 'I'm not dating anyone right now, but there's no way I'm getting married unless I'm getting married here at Fenway Park, whether the guy is a Sox fan or not,'" Bienvenue said.

Bienvenue wanted to get married during the year of Fenway's 100th anniversary, but her superstitions spurred uncertainty, as the wedding was also coinciding with such a terrible season. Typically, she goes to great, sometimes questionable lengths—cutting her hair or retiring jerseys—all just to help the Sox win. "If I watch a game upstairs and we win, then the next day, that's where I'll watch the game. If we lose, I'll go downstairs. I try to stay in the same habits if we have a win streak," she said. "I'll sleep in certain things. If it's a World Series game, I will or will not go to a certain Starbucks, or I won't get a certain drink. It's almost like OCD with sports. It gets ridiculous even in my own mind. I ask myself, 'Are you seriously even thinking that?' And yep, I am."

Oddly enough, Bienvenue's superstitions didn't carry over to her wedding planning, as she even let Boston go with her when she picked out her dress. But she was still nervous about the implications of her Fenway wedding upon the Red Sox. "I had done all kinds of things to try to swing the tide during the season, and nothing worked. But as it got closer and closer, a lot of people were like, 'This is the best thing that's going to happen at Fenway this year,'" she said. "I had to dig deep and separate my feelings of the Red Sox from my feelings of Fenway Park. The whole day I wasn't thinking about how bad the Sox were doing."

The Bostons had about 50 guests attend their Fenway wedding, which had its own set of surprises in store. Bienvenue found out last minute that they would be able to get married atop the Red Sox dugout, where she ecstatically stepped up, wearing red cleats and baseball socks that she had under her traditional David's Bridal dress. After the ceremony they cued up "Sweet Caroline," and then they also got to go down on the field, which Bienvenue was originally told wasn't possible. "When we were out on the grass in the batter's box, that's when I started to cry. I lost it. I sat down and touched the grass. It was too overwhelming, and I just wasn't expecting it," she said. The couple also had their photo and name displayed on the Jumbotron. An especially quirky moment occurred when Boston touched Pesky's Pole for a photo op and ended up with yellow paint all over his hands because it was fresh and still wet. The reception was also Sox-themed. Tables were named after players, Sox lollipops were in the centerpieces, and, of course, all of the Boston favorites were on the playlist, including "Tessie," "Dirty Water," and "I'm Shipping Up to Boston."

Though untraditional, it was a dream wedding for this die-hard Red Sox fan. "I got married at Fenway Park to a Red Sox fan," Bienvenue said, "whose name is Boston."

—Born in Peabody, Massachusetts, Jess Lander, a writer and dating columnist for the *Napa Valley (California) Register*, is known to preach the gospel of Boston sports to anyone who's listening, and especially to those who aren't.

6

Red Sox as a Muse

Fenway Park exemplifies everything I love about New England: the combination of natural and man-made beauty, the sometimes uneasy but always memorable mix of history and innovation.

—Adam Pachter, introduction to *Fenway Fiction*

Baseball is a game for storytellers. The pace of the action moves leisurely to allow for stories to unravel. It allows you time to relay your favorite baseball anecdote to a friend, family member, or that stranger sitting next to you with whom you may share just one thing in common—you "root, root, root" for the Red Sox. It allows you time to pontificate about the game itself or wax poetic about the national pastime. Other sports are less suited for storytelling. Attending an NFL game in the Northeast can be about just surviving the elements. Basketball and the constant scoring, fan noise, music, and other mindless productions that are part of the NBA experience make it difficult to spin a yarn. Live hockey not only has that edge-of-your-seat, gladiatorial vibe, but is more of a Canadian pastime, hardly the right setting for telling an All-American story.

Many of the greatest storytellers in American literature were either born or spent significant time in New England. Henry David Thoreau. Nathaniel Hawthorne. Emily Dickinson. Henry

Wadsworth Longfellow. Edgar Allan Poe. Anne Sexton. Robert Frost. Edith Wharton. John Updike. As we all know, every story and artist has a muse. When talking about muses, Greek mythology is always a good place to start. After all, what are the Boston Red Sox but New England mythology? The Greek myths had their starting nine muses: Calliope and Polyhymnia (epic and sacred poetry), Clio (history), Erato (love poetry), Euterpe (lyrics), Melpomene (tragedy), Terpsichore (dancing), Thalia (comedy), and Urania (astronomy). It could be said that the Red Sox match the Greek myths muse for muse. Try this starting nine on for size: David Ortiz and Carlton Fisk (epic and sacred home runs), Ted Williams (the best hitter in baseball history), Johnny Pesky (the beloved player), Carl Yastrzemski (Is there a name more lyrical?), Tony Conigliaro (Is there a Red Sox career more tragic?), Jonathan Papelbon (Remember that dance after the 2007 World Series?), Pedro Martinez (a comedic and pitching genius), and Bill "Spaceman" Lee (astronomy, of course). These are not the only Red Sox who have inspired generations at Fenway Park. Each evokes a story: Dom DiMaggio's hit streak, Curt Schilling's bloody sock, Dave Henderson's home run, George Scott's Gold Glove, Bernie Carbo's pinch-hit home run, Tim Wakefield's unselfish relief performance, Dave Roberts' stolen base, Fred Lynn's rookie season.

With players like Trot Nixon fitting the mold, New Englanders love their Red Sox gritty. Author Matthew Mayo literally knows New England grit. He operates Gritty Press with his wife, photographer Jennifer Smith-Mayo, with whom he collaborated on the books: *Maine Icons*, *New Hampshire Icons*, and *Vermont Icons*. In between traveling the world and dismantling old barns, he spins some interesting tales in his critically acclaimed nonfiction books *Cowboys, Mountain Men & Grizzly Bears*; *Bootleggers, Lobstermen & Lumberjacks*; *Sourdoughs, Claim Jumpers & Dry Gulchers*; and *Haunted Old West*. In *Lobstermen & Lumberjacks*, Mayo draws our attention to the time period between 1620 to the 1950s. "Fifty of the grittiest moments" are unraveled as Mayo dispenses tales about she-pirate sirens, man-eating sharks, and the Great Swamp Fight of 1675 between the English and the Narragansetts. "I read everywhere and anywhere," Mayo said, "because I'm hardly ever without a book, be it on my iPad or a ratty paperback in my pocket. A preferred place is stretched out in the shade on our deck, surrounded by books—and no black flies." As you might've guessed—and why would he be in this book if he wasn't?—Mayo is a card-carrying member of Red Sox Nation.

Way back in the 1970s, when I was a kid in Rhode Island, I loved riding my bike and pretending I was a cowboy. But baseball—and specifically the Boston Red Sox—was my abiding passion. Books, hats, shirts, posters, stickers, and baseball cards. I had thousands of baseball cards. My jaws still ache, thinking of all the cracked, flat gum I ate over the years. It powdered when you bit down, and it tasted like peppermint talc.

Each season our Little League team went to see the Pawtucket Red Sox play. And one rainy Saturday a couple of them even came to our practice and gave us pointers. Over the years I was fortunate enough to meet a number of Boston Red Sox players, among them Butch Hobson, Carton Fisk, Jim Rice, Ken "the Hawk" Harrelson, Dennis Eckersley, Bill Lee, and Dwight Evans.

As cool as meeting them was, I remember really wanting to meet Carl Yastrzemski, because he was my grandmother's favorite player. She was a big Red Sox fan. Every day her best friend, Jessie, would visit and they'd play double solitaire for hours, smoking and cursing at each other, watching the games, and snapping down those cards.

They only stopped the action for two things: lunch and when "Yaz" came up to bat. Grandma thought he was the greatest thing since sliced bread, and they both agreed he had "hot buns." I ate my frozen Devil Dog, a grandma specialty, and did my best to pretend I hadn't heard them. Yaz was a Major League Baseball player! Even as a nine-year-old, I knew that important people like Yaz definitely did not have "buns," let alone hot ones.

I visited Grandma often and loved that we had the Red Sox in common. "Of course we love the Red Sox," she, a lifelong Rhode Islander, would say. "They're our home team." And since Yaz was her favorite player, he was mine, too. But for a while there, I was fibbing. Even though I'd seen Yaz play at Fenway, even though I had more cards of Yaz than of any other player, and even though I wore an official Red Sox jersey with No. 8 on the back, I'd never met Yaz. But I had met Butch Hobson, and he'd signed my glove. So for a brief period, I was the world's biggest Hobson fan. I did feel a little like a traitor, but since I hadn't actually met Yaz, still haven't, and I had no interest in his "buns," I figured it was okay to play the field.

When I was 13, my grandma, Arlene Mayo, passed away. All that spring and summer I laid on my bed listening to the Red Sox games on the transistor radio she gave me for Christmas a few years before. I thought a lot about her, about when I used to visit her and we'd watch Yaz hit. I'd sit in front of her TV, glove on one hand, ball in the other, Boston cap on my head, and talk about how I was going to be a major league baseball player one day. "You can be anything you want," she would say. "Just be happy doing it."

I also spent time that summer, trying to figure out the hows and whys of someone so close to me being taken away. I still haven't nailed that one down, but I did vow to her, as I listened alone to the games that season, that I would try to do what she said—be anything I want to be in life, as long as I was happy at it.

That simple but sage advice has stuck with me. And since I can't recall my grandma without thinking of the Red Sox, I gladly make the claim that the Boston Red Sox, via my grandma, had a profound affect on my life. My parents were always hugely supportive of my Red Sox obsession as a kid, and later, of my budding desire to be a writer, but I believe it was my grandmother's laid back fondness for the home team (and perhaps for Yaz's buns), and her love for me, that had as much of a lasting influence on who I've become.

And who am I? I'm just a New England guy who wakes up every day happy as a clam, doing what I love for a living—I'm a writer who still loves my home team.

One doesn't have to search very far in New England to find another author who is a devout Red Sox follower. It's pretty easy to identify writer and editor Adam Pachter as a Sox fan by his wardrobe. If you see him at a book reading, he'll be sporting his Red Sox Hawaiian shirt. The author also owns a well-worn "Sox-Aholic" shirt and a favorite hat that has a distinct vintage look. Says Patcher: "My Sox cap is so faded that my best friend from high school denies it was ever blue."

Pachter conjured the *Fenway Fiction* trilogy with a cast of writers during the past decade. The first in the series, *Fenway Fiction*, was conceived and written prior to the 2004 title and published the following season. Like many members of Red Sox Nation, Pachter counts the '04 World Series victory as his best baseball moment with honorable mention going to beating the Yanks in the American League Championship Series that year amidst a couple of Big Papi walk-offs, capping years of payback. "The Yankees might have won a game or two last century," Pachter said, "but this one belongs to the Sox. And, with apologies to Langston Hughes, a dream deferred, even for 86 years, is not a dream denied." Pachter admits the first book in the trilogy focused on the frustrations that were inherent in being a Sox follower. However, the second book, *Further Fenway Fiction*, delves into the celebratory vibe that followed the cathartic championship and "the consequences of that triumph." For *Final Fenway Fiction*, the final book in the series, Pachter saw a new theme emerge. "*Final Fenway Fiction* explores the theme of Red Sox community, recognizing that a fan cheering from Big Papi's favorite Dominican restaurant has a different perspective than one who signed on after Dice-K joined the team," Pachter said. "And those who root for the Sox in Arlington, Massachusetts, view the team differently than those in Arlington, Virginia, or Arlington,

Texas. In selecting these stories, I hoped to give voice to the vast geographic, ethnic, socioeconomic, and even historical diversity of Red Sox Nation. If the reader leaves with a greater appreciation of that diversity, then I'll have accomplished my goal."

Pachter said he never has played anything in a ballpark tougher than softball, but he explains how he feels forever bonded to America's pastime and the Boston Red Sox. He said, "I attended a game to celebrate my eighth birthday. I saw a player's jersey that read *Adams 8*. I've gone to a baseball game in honor of my birthday every year since. Although I'm a fan of all Boston sports teams, I do prefer the boys of summer to those who play winter ball." For the record *Adams 8* was designated hitter Glenn Adams of Northbridge, Massachusetts. Adams would attend Springfield College in Massachusetts before becoming the fourth overall pick of the Houston Astros in the 1968 secondary draft. Although Adams didn't play in the game, he did swat seven homers that season.

It's the minutiae like Adam's Adams story as well as the plotlines and tension of the game that draw comparisons of baseball to a well-written novel. "A baseball game is like a good book," Pachter said, "something to be savored gradually over the course of a lazy evening or afternoon, while other sports resemble action movies with lots of athletic pyrotechnics. I love movies. Don't get me wrong, but few films can compare to the impact of a truly great read. As a fiction writer, I initially found the Red Sox irresistible because their history was so star-crossed, almost Shakespearean in its ability to come within a game, an out, or even a strike of ultimate victory, only to have that snatched away. I am relieved to discover that even after winning the World Series twice, the Red Sox continue to inspire novelists, poets, and playwrights, because otherwise I'd be out of a job!"

As to why the Red Sox have been an inspiration to legions of writers, Adam answered that query in the introduction to *Fenway Fiction*. "Is it any wonder that the Boston Red Sox have inspired so many writers over the years? Tragedy begets great drama. Tolstoy knew that, even if he was fated to die two years before the Red

Sox moved into a brand new Fenway Park and promptly won the World Series. The Red Sox won four of them, in fact, during that fertile period from 1912 until the trading of the Bambino. And so far as I know, they failed to stir a single novelist or rate a mention in any significant literary work during that whole time…I'm not sure exactly when the Sox made their debut in fiction, but the team's mix of recurring tragedy and regional identity eventually proved irresistible for both writers and Hollywood."

With all the hustle and bustle in the stands and the rush one gets from a big inning, Fenway Park is not exactly conducive to being an ideal place to write. He confesses he doesn't write at Fenway but said, "I do keep my eyes and ears open, because you never know when you'll see or hear something that inspires a story." His story "Green Monster," which appeared in the first book of the trilogy, drew on a number of events that happened at Fenway in the summer of 2002.

When pressed to suggest required reading from the series, Pachter said, "In terms of sheer storytelling skill, my favorite is Bryan Farrow's 'Underneath,' which seamlessly alternates between the modern-day search for Babe Ruth's piano in a Sudbury pond and how it got into that pond in the first place." Pachter claims the trilogy will remain just that, but as any artist or sports fan can tell you, "never, say never." If this is to be the last installment of the *Fenway Fiction* series, Pachter ends it poignantly. The tale "Domo" was inspired by a 2008 Patriots' Day conversation he had with fellow author Bill Nowlin, who published the first two Red Sox fiction anthologies. "Bill told me that his father-in-law had been a World War II prisoner of war in the camp that helped inspire the famous film *Bridge on the River Kwai*," Pachter said. "He said that for many years after the war, his father-in-law had understandably continued to have very negative feelings toward the Japanese. Then he took a trip to Israel and was getting off of a bus in Jerusalem, when he slipped and was saved from falling and hurting himself by a Japanese tourist. And in that moment, all the anger that he'd had toward the Japanese just sort of melted away."

In his tale, Pachter introduces us to Ed Riley, a former prisoner of war who also served in World War II. "Domo" is set during the summer of Dice-K's seminal 18-win season of 2008, when Boston was the defending World Series champs for the second time in the decade. Ed's resentment toward the Japanese, as a result of being a prisoner, creates anxious moments for his daughter, Debbie, and her husband, Tom. Ed not only has difficulty dealing with airplane flyovers, but he's bitter at the fact that the major league season is now opening in Japan. He's also insulted by the use of *banzai* (a Japanese battle cry) on his grandson's gameday poster. To make matters worse, Tom shows up with Red Sox T-shirts and foam fingers from a business trip to Japan. Pachter brilliantly intersperses a memory of Ed's prisoner-of-war time, when saying *domo* or thank you in Japanese was the only means to end torture.

Back in the present day, Debbie rounds up the family for a trip to Fenway, where all Ed wants to do is catch a foul ball. The powerful story reaches its conclusion when Ed is knocked over while reaching for an oncoming foul ball and is saved by a Japanese businessman. "I never met Bill Nowlin's father-in-law," Pachter said. "But my character's journey is similar to his, and the redemptive incident that serves as the climax of 'Domo,' though it takes place at Fenway, was inspired by what Bill had told me. It struck me what an amazing story that was, what it said about the lingering bitterness caused by war as well as the possibility of moving past it, even many years later. And so I was inspired to write 'Domo,' which is dedicated to prisoners of war."

If you're a fan of the Red Sox and *The Twilight Zone*, it's tough not to like Henry Garfield's offering "Beanball" in *Final Fenway Fiction*. Garfield, an avowed fan of science fiction authors, Robert Heinlein and Arthur C. Clarke spins a tale that is reminiscent of Rod Serling's finer lighthearted visits to the "dimension of imagination." Garfield is the author of five published novels, including *Tartabull's Throw* and the historical novel, *The Lost Voyage of John Cabot*. Henry, the great-great-grandson of James Garfield, the 20th U.S. president, teaches English at the University of Maine and writes regularly for

BangorMetro magazine. When he's not writing or teaching, you can find him sailing his 25-foot sloop on the coast of Maine.

Many members started on the path to Red Sox Nation with a dream, an impossible one. The Impossible Dream Team of 1967 to be exact. The moribund 1966 Sox were the last Fenway home team to bring in less than 1 million fans. In '66 Boston averaged a Miami Marlins-like 10,014 fans per game. The 1967 Impossible Dream Team created a bounce that the Sox are still profiting from, as they were first in the American League with 92 wins and attendance with an average of 21,331 fans per game. Garfield is one of those fans who was inspired. "I am a Red Sox fan today because of the Impossible Dream Team," he said. "In 1967 I was nine years old, and my family moved from Philadelphia to Maine. I had vaguely been a Dodgers fan because of Sandy Koufax, who retired that offseason after the Dodgers were swept by the Orioles in the World Series. But the 1967 Red Sox were the first team I followed, day in and day out, over the course of a season. My dad grew up in Concord, Massachusetts, and followed the Red Sox without much hope, as they had been terrible for many years. He and I took a trip to Maine in April to look at the new house we would move to in June, when the school year ended." He fondly recalls how a busy New England workday could go from productive to unproductive, depending on the Sox. "Some guys were outside working with a ballgame on the radio," he said. "Work came to a halt when Billy Rohr took a no-hitter into the ninth. I remember other games over the course of the summer—Conigliaro erasing a 1–0 deficit in extra innings with a two-run homer, Conigliaro's beaning, the 'Tartabull's Throw' game that would inspire my novel of the same name, the last two games against the [Minnesota] Twins. By October I was in a new school in Maine, and kids were ferrying World Series scores to the classroom from the principal's office. I was hooked for life."

Garfield explains the "secret origin" to his short story "Beanball." "[It] came out of a novel in progress about baseball on Mars," he said. "In college I wrote a paper for an astronomy course on the physics of baseball on several different worlds in the solar system. I had an idea that Earth had descended into war and anarchy, and that much of our cultural heritage, including baseball, had been kept alive on Mars. Originally, the story didn't have a Red Sox angle, but when Adam [Pachter] was putting together the anthology, I thought I'd try to work the Red Sox into it somehow."

His work takes place in 3004, the 1,000th anniversary of the 2004 World Series. "I had to allow enough time to pass—1,000 years—for terraforming Mars to be realistic," Garfield said. Norton Anderson, president of the local chapter of the Baseball Revival Association, leads a team of actors to perform a reenactment of the Great Comeback. Baseball is now thriving on Mars, which has undergone terraforming, while Earth has been besieged by biological wars and the American Middle Ages. This leads Norton to cast Hilo Mattamuru as Dave Roberts in hopes that this "reconstituted myth" will re-spark interest in America's former pastime. Throughout the short story, Hank pokes good-humored shots at the New York Yankees' own myth. For example, the name of the Bronx Bombers shortstop seems to be lost to history, while Roberts', Kevin Millar's, and David Ortiz's namesakes are well preserved. "I couldn't resist the urge to tweak Yankees fans and their self-importance," Garfield said. "Derek who? I love it that Mark Bellhorn was the hero of the 2004 ALCS—our answer to Bucky F. Dent. I think I began to hate the Yankees in the 1970s. It was okay that the Red Sox lost the 1967 Series to the [St. Louis] Cardinals. The pennant race was thrilling enough, and they were beaten by the better team. But they should have won in 1975, and they surely should have won in 1978, when they were the best team in baseball."

Another poke at the Yanks and a clever spin takes place while discussing the wear and tear of fireball pitchers in the 21st century. The characters in the story remember Tommy John as a surgeon and not the former Yankee who won 288 games during his major league career. "[He's] not in the Hall of Fame," Garfield said. "But you hear the phrase 'Tommy John surgery' almost every time you turn on a ballgame." The Martians, who seldom have difficulty defeating any opponent, see the game more as a cultural exchange and are perplexed at the Boston-New York rivalry of 10 centuries ago, which "hardly seemed like a clash of cultures." Garfield notes that after winning the 2004 championship the Sox "beat Yanks silly for the next 100 years."

Considering he wrote a Sox-centric short story titled "Beanball," Garfield is a good source to discuss the most fearsome Red Sox hurlers. "The most intimidating Red Sox pitcher of all time is probably Pedro Martinez circa 2000, but I'd like to give a nod to Luis Tiant as the most underrated," he said. "People forget that the Red Sox picked him up off the scrap heap after arm trouble nearly ruined his career. I think he belongs in the Hall. In 1968, the year Denny McLain won 30 games and Bob Gibson posted an otherworldly 1.12 ERA, Tiant won 21 games for a mediocre Cleveland Indians team with an ERA of 1.60. After his arm trouble, he won scads of important games for the Red Sox, and he did it with élan. He had another sub-2.00 ERA season for the Sox." Tiant did in fact lead the American League two times in ERA (the aforementioned 1968 Indians season and 1972 Boston season with a 1.91 ERA and 15 wins). El Tiante, forever beloved in Boston, picked up Game 1 and Game 4 victories in the 1975 World Series.

One could fill a volume of books on the experiences of Red Sox Nation during the 2003 and 2004 seasons. It's easy to see how the '04 squad might inspire a sci-fi story commemorating their 1,000[th] anniversary. Like many other Fenway Faithful, Garfield experienced a roller coaster of emotions both in his life and as a fan. He said, "In many ways the Red Sox salvaged the year. The war in Iraq was raging, George W. Bush looked likely to be re-elected, and in September, I had to fly out to San Diego to bring my daughter home from college because she was gravely ill. I remember watching a game against the Yankees in a hotel room the night before our flight back with the sound off. The Red Sox scored two runs off [Mariano] Rivera in the ninth to win it. By October my daughter was in the hospital in Maine, and I was driving all over the state to two teaching gigs and a newspaper job as well as to see her and the woman who would become my second wife." Although he's since divorced, Henry fondly recalls proposing during the '04 playoff run. "I asked her to marry me as the Red Sox were getting pounded

CS. Her son was undergoing treatment for
I didn't watch the ALCS because I could not
uma." He remembers saying something to the
now what's going to happen with either of our
try, or the baseball season, but I want us to be
d caved during a moment of weakness and turned
on u.   e perennial playoff participant, Kenny Lofton, hit a
home run tha. made it 7–0 Bronx Bombers.

A few days later, Garfield recalled the low point of his year. "I remember sitting at a traffic light, waiting to turn in to the hospital, where my daughter was, the day after the 19–8 blowout in Game 3," he said. "A storm had blown through and knocked most of the leaves from the trees. Winter was coming. My daughter wasn't getting better." But every valley has a peak, and the eventual World Series title played out well. "I heard Johnny Damon's grand slam in Game 7 on the car radio while driving to my fiancée's house after covering a political event for the newspaper," he said. "I think that was the first time I believed they might actually win. Even so, I didn't want to jinx it by watching. We went to bed. Much later, she got up and went downstairs. I knew what she was doing, but I didn't join her in front of the TV until the ninth inning. We watched the postgame show on NESN [New England Sports Network] until there was no more show to watch. The next day I drove to the hospital to pick up my daughter, who was being released. 'The Red Sox did it,' I told her. 'They beat the Yankees when it counted. They came back from three games down. They're going to the World Series.' We hugged. 'You must be so happy,' she said. She wasn't out of the woods yet, and the Red Sox still had to beat the Cardinals, but for the first time in months, I felt hopeful."

Storytellers aren't the only ones who can…uh…tell stories. As many photojournalists and artists will tell you, a picture is worth a thousand words. For Neal Portnoy, that rings true. Portnoy, a Red Sox lifer who used to play and coach sports regularly, is a self-professed jock who can draw well…really well. If Portnoy had his own baseball card, his stats would feature a who's who of sports talent he's drawn—from Larry Bird to Drew Brees to Pedro Martinez to Sox rival, Derek Jeter. He's drawn Kanye West and Jerry Garcia. His original works have been used as part of a campaign to raise funds for the Children's Miracle Network, the Dana Farber Cancer Research Institute, the Doug Flutie Jr. Foundation for Autism, and other charitable organizations. His illustrations have been included in more than 700 programs and media guides as well.

Portnoy, though, was a jock first and continues to be. (He's a private pitching instructor for Extra Innings in Auburn, Massachusetts.) Portnoy has been a college pitching coach for a number of schools since 1982, including Worcester State University and Assumption College. "My abilities as a former pitcher and my personality have coupled with my being able to work with kids," he said. "My knowledge of the game over the years has been extremely beneficial as an instructor." Knowing the game and the players so well has helped Portnoy master his artistic craft—a style that developed over the years as he played sports and coached. "I now work exclusively with felt-tip markers and pens. I've been doing this since 1974," he said.

While he draws numerous sports figures, Portnoy, of course, finds the most joy in inking Red Sox players. His love for the Sox increased just as his art career took off. He said: "[It] became even stronger as I became older, when I had the opportunity to get involved with Jimmy Fund golf. I had the thrill to be in events supporting the Jimmy Fund with Red Sox alumni such as Bob Stanley, Luis Tiant, Rich Gedman, Bill Lee, Jerry Moses, Russ Gibson, Mike Andrews, Yaz, Rick Miller, Jim Lonborg, and others!" One of Portnoy's favorite stories to tell is one in which he presented David Ortiz with a lithograph of his likeness that Portnoy showed him at a signing. "Papi said, 'This for me?'

"Like you," Portnoy said, "this is how I make my living. It wasn't free."

Fenimonial: My Day as a Batboy

The father of my best friend in high school worked for the Red Sox. I don't remember in what capacity. But one day in the fall of 1964, my friend asked me, if I wanted to be a replacement batboy for the Sox during a weekday, day game. Of course, I said yes, and we skipped school and went to the park. The Sox gave us uniforms and the second baseman, Chuck Shilling, loaned me a glove, and I went out to the right-field line to collect foul balls during the game. The Sox were playing the Kansas City Athletics. The only ball hit toward me landed in the stands and bounced into right field, where I went after it, but the Kansas City right fielder, Rocky Colavito, picked it up and threw it to me. The Sox won the game 10–1.

After the game I went into the tunnel to go back into the clubhouse and I was stopped by a player named Tony Horton. He was a rookie that year and he wanted me to go out in the field and shag balls while he took batting practice. I couldn't believe how hard he hit the ball. But I was out there, catching fly balls off the Green Monster and throwing them back in to the pitcher. When he was done taking batting practice, I went back into the clubhouse and changed clothes. Most of the players were still there. Carl Yastrzemski, Tony Conigliaro, Dick Stuart to name a few. It was a great experience.

—Lou Frissore, a retired systems analyst and photographer from Boston

7

The Invisible Line
in Connecticut

*To be loyal to rags, to shout for rags, to die for rags—that is a loyalty
of unreason. It is pure animal; it belongs to monarchy, was invented by
monarchy; let monarchy keep it.*

—Mark Twain, *A Connecticut Yankee in King Arthur's Court*

There is a schism in the great state of Connecticut. When it comes to sports in the Constitutional State there are two kinds of state residents: those who root for the New York Yankees and those who cheer on the native New Englanders from Boston. Somewhere in the middle, though actually not exactly geometrically centralized, the state is divided, and many have written about where exactly the two sides meet.

Some say Red Sox Nation and Yankee Nation meet midway in Hartford, but *The New York Times* dug deeper. In an August 2006 piece, Harvard College Sports Analysis Collective's Ben Blatt tried to determine the exact location of this line of demarcation. Using Facebook, the research coordinator looked at more than 150 Connecticut towns to see what percentage of fans rooted for which home team. The results came down to the cities of Guilford and Middletown. In those areas, Blatt theorized it to be an approximate

50/50 split between fans of the Yankees and royal Sox rooters. According to that *Times* piece, midway may actually be New Britain, with the midway point between Fenway Park and Yankee Stadium being Rocky Hill. With a rivalry so rich in feuds, follies, and crushing losses—and in 2004, the sweetest victory of all—it's nice to know Connecticut is a wonderful walking contradiction: a house divided that has managed to stand for aeons. Sure, there's a fictional line, but where it starts doesn't matter. The line gets blurry.

Jared W. Kupiec is chief of staff for the city of Hartford's mayor, Pedro E. Segarra. He's a longtime Red Sox fan, but his boss, the mayor, roots for the Yankees. Segarra follows the Bronx Bombers because he grew up in the South Bronx. On the other hand, Kupiec cheers on Boston because he was raised in northeastern Connecticut. "There have been a number of surveys and polls conducted to try and quantify this phenomenon over the years," he continued. "There is no definitive line, so to speak." He said, "Most use the Connecticut River as a good barometer. For example, if you live east of the river, you're a Sox fan. If you live west, you love the Bronx Bombers."

With the exception of residents like Segarra, whose Bronx roots make him an interlocking *N* and *Y* lifer, logic is the best way of figuring out this fictional line business. You don't really need to be a genius to figure out that in southern Connecticut, you're likely to see more Yankees caps than farther up on I-95. Yes, the closer you are to New York state, the more likely you are to be rooting for the pinstripes. On the flip side, the deeper you get into Connecticut and farther you get away from the Empire State, the more likely you are a Sox fan. However, Joseph DeMartino, a UConn alum who serves on the town council for Fairfield, which is in the southern part of the state, is the exception to that rule. "As a die-hard Sox fan now living in lower Fairfield County but that grew up in Danbury and went to school in Storrs, I can assure you that the line is somewhere north/northeast of the Fairfield County border," DeMartino said. "If I were to guess, I would draw a diagonal line, dividing the state from Salisbury in the northwest corner to Madison and conclude that the lower half is 45 percent Yankees, 35 percent Mets, 20

Although Hartford, Connecticut, mayor Pedro Segarra, pictured during a 2010 gala, is a New York Yankees fan, his chief of staff, Jared Kupiec, remains a Red Sox loyalist. (Getty Images)

percent Sox. Those above the diagonal line are likely 65 percent Sox, 20 percent Mets, and 15 percent Yankees."

Michael Tretreau, the first selectman for the town of Fairfield, echoed those sentiments. "There is no defined boundary, but as you enter Fairfield County there tends to be an increasing focus on New York," he said. "I would definitely say that in the county there are more New York team fans than Boston-area team fans. And just by way of trivia, the New York Giants used the train in the town of Fairfield during the late 1950s and early 1960s."

Fellow Fairfield County native Sherri Marshall Hill concurs. Football allegiances, however, are a different story. "Here in southwest Fairfield County, I'd say Yankee fans prevail," she said. "Surprisingly, a lot of these same folks seem to like the [New England] Patriots. I don't get that. [New York] Giants all the way!"

Fairfield County's Jason Jacoby further illustrates the area's pull for the Yankees. "Fairfield County basically treats itself like a suburb of New York," he said. "You get a lot of people, like Westchester, who work in the city and commute in every day. There were some Red Sox fans thrown in, but the majority of people are Yankees fans."

Jacoby said that changes the deeper you get in the state. "It's a very similar experience in New Jersey actually. Northern Jersey—you will find all New York team fans. Once you get to central/southern Jersey, you find more Philadelphia and even D.C. fans." Jacoby's grandfather, however, was a huge Yankees fan despite living in Hartford. He gravitated to his grandfather's team since his parents weren't big fans. Plus, he loved Don Mattingly.

Major League Baseball has its own rule regarding the diving line. "Whether [the Red Sox] win or lose, I am still a fan. However, MLB makes it hard for me to actively follow the team, because I live in a certain county in Connecticut," said Bryan Lizotte, a Shelton resident. "According to MLB rules, NESN [New England Sports Network] is prohibited from broadcasting in Fairfield County, because it's Yankees territory…NESN can broadcast in *all* of Connecticut except for Fairfield County. It really makes me mad, since I actually live only three blocks away from the city of Derby, which is in New Haven County and can receive NESN."

Lizotte actually called MLB a few years back to see if he could get that changed. "They told me that I could watch the Yankee games…huh? I just feel that I am being discriminated against because of where I live. MLB wants me to buy the MLB package on cable, so I could watch *all* the games. I don't want to watch *all* the games. I just want to watch my favorite team: the Boston Red Sox. Besides, for NESN games broadcast on MLB, you don't get the pre and postgame show."

Even though the cable restriction still irks Lizotte, the Red Sox loyalist admits he is on the minority side of the game's best baseball rivalry. "There are a lot of Sox fans in Fairfield County," he said. "[But] they are definitely outnumbered by the Evil Empire fans. I'll never forget, soon after the World Series win in 2004, I was wearing my Red Sox jacket—I always wear it, whether they win or lose—and went into an office building, and this middle-aged woman behind the counter said, 'The Red Sox *suck*!' I told her, 'I guess 'suck' must mean good, since they embarrassed the Yankees on the way to winning the World Series.'"

Joseph A. Geary, a Red Sox fan, is the chief of staff for the mayor of Waterbury, a city divided pretty much 50/50, like many other towns and cities. "It's that close," he said. Neil M. O'Leary, the mayor of Waterbury, concurred on the percentages but will not endorse his coworker's personal choice, "I am a die-hard Yankees fan, but I truly believe that the city of Waterbury is evenly divided between Yankees and Red Sox fans. This makes for some very interesting debates between families and friends in Waterbury."

Chris DiMauro grew up on the southeast city of East Lyme, where he said the breakdown is 60 percent Sox, 30 percent Yankees, and 10 percent for the Mets or another team. "I would say the invisible line on the coastline starts around New Haven but does not go straight up…more diagonally up through Waterbury and then Torrington," he said. "I hope everyone to the left of that line gets a paper cut today."

8

A Tale of Two Twitties

Dear baseball gods PLEASE let #Beckett have a good day. Even if we just get out of the 1st scoreless. Thank you, die-hard #RedSoxNation fan!

—Christi Wolfe@cwolfe56

It's the morning of October 26, 1986, and Red Sox first baseman Bill Buckner pours a cup of coffee, tries to digest some breakfast despite his churning insides. He turns on his iPad. Twitter, Facebook, and Tumblr are tearing him a new one. After skimming the angry vitriol, he can take it no longer and goes outside to walk the dog. Normally he would grab the morning paper, but he can't bear to read more scathing headlines. As soon as he walks out the door, TMZ is there, and flashbulbs go off like he just walked the red carpet of a Hollywood premiere. "Billy, how'd you let that ball go through your legs?" one reporter cries out as he clicks on his camera as fast as he can. Another cries out "Can the Sox win tonight after this?"

Buckner slams the door immediately, stands by it for a minute to process it all, when all of a sudden, his BlackBerry, which had been vibrating all morning long, starts buzzing yet again. He just received yet another text from Marty Barrett. He walks slowly to the kitchen counter and throws the phone against the wall. It shatters into pieces.

Considering the anachronisms of the above scenario, of course, it never happened. Sure, "Billy Buck" likely felt like crap the morning after he let Mookie Wilson's dribbler pass through his legs during the New York Mets' 10-inning win against the Red Sox in Game 6 of the 1986 World Series, but in some ways he is lucky that it happened then. Could you imagine how much more different it would be in our digital world?

On August 19, 2012, the Twittersphere was ablaze during the final game of a three-game series between the Red Sox and the New York Yankees. The 2012 Sox team had struggled mightily all season long, and many still had not shaken the bad taste in their mouths from the final game of the 2011 campaign. Red Sox Nation remembers it all too well. The Red Sox were well on their way to the postseason, but then came September, when a few losses snowballed into more losses and culminated with a regular season-ending loss to the Baltimore Orioles to knock them out of the playoffs. The Sox went home; closer Jonathan Papelbon, who gave up that hit to the Orioles, signed with the Philadelphia Phillies; beloved manager Terry Francona was tossed out of town; and wunderkind general manger Theo Epstein fled to Chicago to try to bring his Bostonian magic to a Cubs franchise that hadn't won the World Series since 1908. Perhaps 2012 was less painful, but the end result was even worse. Pitchers may not have been throwing down beer and chicken during games, but a player reportedly text messaged Sox brass, asking them to fire Tito's replacement, Bobby Valentine.

Even though the 2012 Red Sox made more headlines off the field than on it, the Boston Red Sox and New York Yankees rivalry has historically been the biggest, baddest, most entertaining, and riveting in all of sports and for good reason. Babe Ruth turning in socks for pinstripes. Carlton Fisk exchanging punches with Thurman Munson. Bucky Dent replacing our hopes with tears. Pedro Martinez serving up Don Zimmer a plate of grass. From Aaron Boone's heroics to Johnny Damon's defection, the rivalry is the best there's ever been in the history of any game. "There's more high energy during a Yankee/Red Sox game," former Red Sox pitcher Bronson Arroyo said. "I've never felt anything like that.

You go back and you watch on tape or see a special on HBO, and there's just so much scrutiny. It's ridiculous how many people's lives depended on whether we won or lost."

In the olden days, Sox and Yankees fans would clash at Fenway, Yankee Stadium, local pubs, and anywhere, really, debating whose team was better and which respective player was a bum. Arguments still ensue at those places, but now they also take place in accordance with the digital world. Because we live in a world of social networking, social media, and antisocial socializing, we decided to take a different approach to the Yankees/Sox rivalry. What better place to gauge the pulse of a team's fan base in 2012 than to turn an eye or iPad to Twitter for ESPN's *Sunday Night Baseball*, featuring the two rivals on August 19, 2012.

Red Sox Nation is not a united front these days and it's playing at the field, in the stands, and most certainly on the Internet. There's disdain for some players—notably Josh Beckett (more on him later), free-agent bust John Lackey (thankfully, no more on him later), and Jon Lester for their reported disregard of Francona last season and their ho-hum attitude in the clubhouse. To put it mildly, many fans have cried foul with the hiring of Japanese royalty and snarky baseball mind Bobby Valentine as Tito's replacement, while others blame the ownership for the failings of the team.

Brian Smith, @bgssmithdc
Bobby Valentine is as "big in Japan" as Matt Dillon's band was in Singles…too bad neither translated to the US #firebobbyv #RedSox

Pregame

It's gametime on ESPN, but conversation about the game to be played hasn't been discussed. The coverage so far has centered on the buzz that several Sox players had texted ownership for a meeting to complain about Valentine. Banter also focused on whether free-agent bust Carl Crawford would undergo season-ending Tommy John surgery, basically ending any chances that the current sub-.500 team could make a miraculous playoff run. Since Beckett was on the mound this evening, commentors wondered if he would resemble the vintage lights-out performer or the player who sported an ERA of over 5.00.

Meanwhile, the ESPN telecast of American League East of the struggling Sox and playoff-bound Yankees opened hot on the heels of an epic 19-inning game between the defending World Series champs the St. Louis Cardinals and the Pittsburgh Pirates. Clearly, the 2,112[th] regular-season game between the Red Sox and Yankees wasn't anything to write history books about.

> *Ryan New @TheNewStyleUES*
> At this point I'd rather watch an 85 year old 350 pound woman undergo hemorrhoid surgery than watch another Yankees/Red Sox game...

Game On

The highlight of the 100th celebration of Fenway Park has arguably been when a certain ESPN analyst and former Red Sox manager, Francona, hesitatingly returned to Fenway for the first time since getting the hook. With Boston's winning percentages of .500 (April), .517 (May), .556 (June), .462 (July), and—as of August, 19—.353 through August, it's easy to see why the Sox are chasing the Yankees by 12.5 games, despite scoring two less runs than the Bombers (593 to 591). These Sox also trail the newly minted second wild-card spot by seven games.

> *Stuart Bristow @stuartsoxfan13*
> At this point I have become more realistic, part of me wants to believe that they can win 30 of these next 40 but it may be too late

Heading into August 19, 2012, Valentine never figured the Red Sox would fail to rise higher than third place, but staring at a 59–62, fourth-place record is exactly where Boston found itself. Valentine, hired after the disastrous 7–20 September 2011 skid, faced criticism throughout the season. No reports were harsher than the Yahoo! story, revealing the Red Sox players held a meeting with the owners to discuss replacing Bobby V.

Valentine, who essentially swapped jobs with Francona (more on that later), is beloved in Japan after winning the Japan Series in 2005 with his Chiba Lotte Marines, who swept the Hanshin Tigers in four games. But that was the Land of the Rising Sun. Boston is the Land of the Rising Media. "As far as my job is concerned, I'm not doing a good job," Valentine said. "I didn't get paid to do anything other than get to the playoffs and win a lot of games. The team I'm managing is not there."

In a weird twist of fate that basically became a lopsided trade, last year's *Sunday Night Baseball* announcer, Valentine, is in the dugout for the Sox, while Terry Francona joined ESPN as an analyst after he lost his job in Boston. In the announcers' booth, Francona responds to Dan Shulman's question about the good and bad of managing the Red Sox. "The pro's the passion, and the con's the scrutiny," Francona said.

Meanwhile, the Twittersphere buzzes about a pending Kelly Shoppach trade. He allegedly was the player who texted ownership about a meeting to oust Valentine. Others circulate rumors or wishes for a Valentine replacement, including former pitching coach and Blue Jays manager, John Farrell, and recently retired and beloved catcher, Jason Varitek.

The Yankees, owners of the best AL record on August 19, have 10 players with at least 10 home runs. Conversely, Bobby Valentine has yet to be able to write a lineup with the following five names listed together: Ellsbury, Crawford, Pedroia, Gonzalez, Ortiz. Instead he sends the following lineup card to the umpires for the Sunday night affair:

1. Jacoby Ellsbury CF
2. Carl Crawford LF
3. Dustin Pedroia 2B
4. Adrian Gonzalez 1B

Scott Lauber @ScottLauber
Adrian Gonzalez before All-Star break: 6 homers in 339 at-bats. Adrian Gonzalez since All-Star break: 9 homers in 129 at-bats #RedSox

5. Ryan Lavarnway C
6. Jarrod Saltalamacchia DH
7. Scott Podsednik RF
8. Pedro Ciriaco SS

Boston Red Sox @RedSox
Ciriaco matched career-high w/ 4 hits yesterday. 1st Sox w/ multiple 4-hit games versus Yankees since Boggs '89. What will he do @ plate tonight?

9. Nick Punto 3B
Josh Beckett P

NESN @NESN
If Josh Beckett's ERA were a mortgage rate...well, you probably wouldn't want that rate.

Shelley @shelley1005
Ah Becks.....it wouldn't be a 1st without allowing a run to score, eh?

Scott Lauber @ScottLauber
One strike from getting out of first inning, Josh Beckett instead gives up RBI double to Curtis Granderson. Story of his season #RedSox

Kevin Daly @dailyboxscores
Can we get Beckett surgery on Tuesday to remove his head from his ass?

Alex Speier @alexspeier
21 starts, 23 1st inning runs allowed by Beckett.

Michael Berger @MichaelSBerger
Amazingly Josh Beckett's first inning ERA for 2012 actually dropped from 9.90 to 9.86. #stillawful

Sox Fan @MissingFenway
My prediction: Beckett traded to TOR in the off-season,
John Farrell straightens him out, we regret it. #RedSox

Olde Towne Team @OldeTowneTeam
One thing ESPN is great at is slow motion, just like Josh
Beckett #RedSox

Pete Abraham @PeteAbe
I always bring my iPad to the games Beckett pitches. Just
watched a season of Mad Men.

Pitcher Hiroki Kuroda, seeking his 12th win and owner of two
summer shutouts, quickly induces three straight ground-outs, much
to the delight of the Yankee Stadium crowd and to the dismay of
Red Sox fans at the game and following on Twitter.

M Keel @CrashFDavis
Surely Red Sox hitters lead the league in worms killed in
the infield. Kings of groundouts.

As the first inning comes to an end, Terry Francona states on
the ESPN telecast, "With losing, comes some drama in Boston,
that's just the way it is." The 2012 Red Sox knew a thing or two
about first-inning deficits. It seemed as if every time one tuned in
to watch them, they were in a 3–0 hole. In just 11 games against
the Yankees leading up to August 19, they gave up 19 runs. This
late summer night would be no different. Derek Jeter leads off with
a double, hit No. 3,249 and the 311th off of Boston, but who's
counting? A couple of batters later, Jeter crosses the plate on a Curtis
Granderson double to shallow right. This early setback is another
remainder of Josh Beckett's struggles in 2012. The Sox have just
seven wins in his 20 starts up to this point. (They are also 10–15 in
games started by Jon Lester, leaving them 42–34, when anyone not
named Beckett or Lester gets the starting nod).

kdawg @kdawg0113
I'm so sick of Ellsbury. I'm sick of Ortiz and Beckett and Salty and Lester too. So sick of them they made my list ahead of Matsuzaka

Against the other seven junior circuit teams that were members of the eight-team AL, the Red Sox have losing records against just two of those teams—the Cleveland Indians, and you guessed it, the Yankees. Their record against the dreaded Yanks is 958–1139.

Nilson Pepén @JuniorPepen
The #RedSox are 17–15 at the new Yankee Stadium. They are the only American League team with a winning record in the park. #RedSoxNation

Kuroda has taken the sizzle out this game, retiring the side quickly again in the second. Four up, four down. Five up, five down. Six up, six down. A Red Sox batted ball hasn't left the infield yet.

Michael LaPayower @BigYankeesFan
There is no #Rivalry the #redsox sucks

An intended throw to third base by Red Sox catcher Ryan Lavarnway is airmailed to left fielder Carl Crawford.

Red Sox Monster @redsoxmonster
Around the horn to the left fielder.

Jared Carrabis @Jared_Carrabis
For being a former Gold Glover, Carl Crawford often looks like a shaky, ungraceful outfielder. #RedSox

It used to be that the Red Sox would bat former hit kings at the bottom of the order. (See Mueller, Bill.) Now the Sox have to settle for serviceable utility men in the eight and nine spots. With that said, third baseman Nick Punto, the No. 9 hitter, records the Red Sox's first hit of the evening during the top of the third inning. Beckett opens the third inning with a strikeout off of Casey McGehee. However, the Yankees captain, irritating Jeter, unloads another double for hit No. 3,250. This is followed by an always Swishalicious walk. After a Robinson Cano out and a Yankees double steal, Curtis Granderson is walked to load the bases for A-Rod fill-in, Eric Chavez. An ESPN graphic notes that 50.3 percents of the Yankees runs this season have come from home runs, a perfect time for a grand slam. Fortunately, Beckett strikes out the former All-Star.

Becca Black @becca_black424
I enjoy the red sox whether they're winning or losing but I usually have to settle for losing and I'm okay with that #redsoxnation

As the game rolls into the fourth, more discussion surfaces about Valentine's tenure and Crawford's pending surgery. Then Ichiro Suzuki, just acquired by the Yankees, chimes in with a blast.

Domination Official @AmusingApparel
Only thing better than beating Red Sox, is beating 'em when Beckett is the starter. Love it.

Derek Lowe, 2004 Boston Red Sox hero, was added to the Yankees roster weeks ago. Francona speaks admirably about his former starter, who performed on short rest during the curse-breaking playoffs. He informs the audience about what he might bring to a Yankees pennant chase, especially after a recent four-inning save early in his Yankees career. On the field Cano misses tagging Saltalamacchia.

Michael Berger @MichaelSBerger
Even the NFL replacement referees could have told you that Saltalamacchia was out.

Jeter records the 3,251st hit. In light of recent suspensions of former Yankees teammates Bartolo Colon and Melky Cabrera, ESPN's Skip Bayless will make national headlines by insinuating that Jeter might be using performance-enhancing drugs.

Jon Chattman @AsidesMusic
Pete Rose just bet against Derek Jeter surpassing his hit total. #tooeasy #redsox #yankees

Beckett walks Granderson on a full count to load bases. On a 3–0 count, Chavez pops up as the game nears the brink of unraveling. For the time being, the Sox keep it interesting.

Jared Carrabis @Jared_Carrabis
Eric Chavez swinging on 3–0 with the bases loaded? That would have been a great idea ten years ago. #Yankees

Gary Marbry @nuggetpalooza
@bradfo @alexspeier #RedSox had not recorded an out on a 3–0 pitch since last Sept 3 until tonite. 1st time w/2 in a game since 2004.

An ESPN poll shows that 75 percent of those polled think Beckett will not be back with Boston next year. Kuroda finishes off the Sox for another 1–2–3 inning, and the shutout prevails through six.

Pesky Martinez @RedSoxTriumph
#LittleLeague WS talk might be a cheapplug BUT shows how incompetent Sox bats have been

Ichiro hits his second homer of the game (for his seventh multi-homer game of his career). Jeter is finally retired, but he and Ichiro will finish with six of the Yankees' eight hits and all four of their runs. In just 12 games vs. Boston, the Yankees have tallied 31 homers.

Enter Junichi Tazawa to face Russell Martin.

Alex Speier @alexspeier
Random but awesome stat: Junichi Tazawa, with 1.64 ERA, .311 BAA, has a shot to be 2nd pitcher in ML history w/sub-2 ERA, BAA > .300.

Alex Speier @alexspeier
Tom Browning (1.54 ERA, .303 BAA in 23 1/3 IP in 1984) the only pitcher ever to pull it off (min 20 IP)

Heading to the ninth, former AL saves leader and Mariano Rivera insurance policy Rafael Soriano enters in a bid for his 31st save. Crawford bounces a ball up the middle for his potential last at-bat of the season, but Dustin Pedroia bounces into a double play. That woeful play is symbolic of the Red Sox's performance on the national stage.

Not Jackie Jensen @JJensenRF
And this is like watching Thelma & Louise head off toward the cliff... #RedSox

A. Rodriguez @nyyhater
This is slow torture. #redsox

Mikey D @mikeyd0611
So serious when I say this.... But at what point do you think for 2013 ? #RedSox

Steve Berthiaume @SBerthiaumeESPN
#RedSox have become the Larry Brown/sic (Isiah) Thomas Knicks circa 2006.

Pesky Martinez @RedSoxTriumph
tough night looking bleaker and bleaker...still ill be at fenway next weekend and thats always a good thing

A September *Sports Illustrated* cover displaying Bobby Valentine in a Macaulay Culkin-esque, *Home Alone* pose accompanied by the words *dysfunctional, broken,* and *unprepared* was not what Red Sox Nation had in mind for the 2012 season. Unfortunately the Red Sox celebrated the 100th anniversary of Fenway Park and the Titanic season with a shipwreck of their own. Possibly the only saving grace to the season was shortly after the game on August 19, general manager Ben Cherington jettisoned Crawford, Beckett, Gonzalez, and Nick Punto to the suddenly ready to spend again Los Angeles Dodgers. Boston could thank their longtime rival Magic Johnson, the former L.A. Lakers point guard and current Dodgers minority owner. He relieved the Sox of $270 million. While announcing the deal at a press conference, Cherington stated, "We recognize that we are not who we want to be right now." Shortly afterward, the L.A.-bound quartet tweeted their grins onboard a plane to the West Coast.

L.A. floundered to a 17–18 finish with their high-priced additions. Beckett won two of his seven starts, and Gonzalez hit three home runs in 36 games. Boston received James Loney, Ivan DeJesus, Allen Webster, and two players to be named later, as well as much-needed flexibility in the offseason. Unprecedented injuries left Boston with a 69–93 record, the worst record since 1965. The most humiliating loss occurred on August 31, when the Red Sox lost to the Oakland A's, 20–2. The Sox finished the season, getting swept by the Baltimore Orioles and Yankees, and Valentine was fired the day after.

9

A Tale of Two Bartenders

There is no private house in which people can enjoy themselves so well as at a capital tavern.

—Samuel Johnson

Whether it's wearing a golden thong like a former New York Yankees first baseman supposedly did or eating chicken prior to each game start like former Red Sox third baseman Wade Boggs, superstitions run supreme in our national pastime. But prior to 2004, one curse ran supreme over all others: The Curse of the Bambino. As folklore went, the curse started the day the team sold the immortal Babe Ruth to the Yankees during the 1919 off-season.

As history will tell you—before the Babe was sent packing, the Sox had won five titles, including winning the very first World Series. But after Ruth left town, the Sox would go on an 86-year drought that ended in 2004, when the Red Sox came from a 0–3 deficit to beat the Yankees in the American League Championship Series in four straight games. The Curse officially ended once the Sox swept the St. Louis Cardinals to win it all that same year.

Historically, however, the Red Sox have been symbolic in the other direction. They have been a team that let their fans down in agonizing fashion. Yet despite all of this, the fans would come back stronger and more devoted, year in and year out, even following heartbreak on their very last game of the season. There's a bitter taste, but the "There's always next year" mantra was adopted by the fans.

Fans came back following the Bucky Dent homer. They came back following the Game 7 loss in the 1975 World Series, featuring Carlton Fisk's iconic game-winning dinger. There are countless games and highlights that personify the team and their fans. But three particular games in the Sox's recent past define the franchise, and who better to paint the picture of Red Sox Nation than bartenders throughout New England?

They can tell you how it feels to watch their fears become reality, and on the flip side in recent years, their dreams come true. Ask any bartender in any New England city, and they'll all tell you similar stories of watching their clientele cheer the Sox on and cover their eyes as their season slowly unravels. To chronicle three franchise-defining games, we went to the two rival cities that were—for those three nights (and countless other times)—united at the keg.

It Wasn't 2003

The 2003 campaign was supposed to be the year in which Boston would finally shake the monkey off their back and overcome the Evil Empire. Pedro Martinez dominated once again, and the tandem of Manny Ramirez and David Ortiz seemed unstoppable. The Sox didn't place first in the American League East (finishing behind the Yankees by six games) but cruised to a wild-card berth. Poised for their first championship since that dreadfully chanted year of 1918, the Sox's season ended with a season-long hero becoming the goat. In 2003 you arguably couldn't find a more lights-out, clutch pitcher than longtime Sox knuckleballer Tim Wakefield. A stud all season and reliable as ever in the playoffs, Wakefield headed into Game 7 of the American League Championship Series as a potential series MVP. He was that good, but unfortunately, on one pitch to Bucky Dent 2.0 (Aaron Boone), the Sox season ended. Just as they so often had done, the

Sox let the fans down and echoed a sentiment of "there's always next year." But when you dissect the promise this 2003 team had, this one stung arguably more than any other loss in decades. The Sox had forced the series to seven games, smacked more homers (12) than any other team had in the ALCS, and had it won, but manager Grady Little left in Martinez long enough to allow the Yankees to tie the game during the late innings. It shouldn't have happened, but as history has repeatedly told Beantown fans, these things happen to the Red Sox.

Joe Donovan, a bartender at the Baseball Tavern in Boston since 1991, has seen it all too well. The server was praying to the baseball gods that—just this once—the Sox wouldn't doom themselves and fall into bad habits of losing in heartbreaking fashion. That night in October, he recalled, was wonderful—at first. "It was a great night for business. The place was packed, and everyone was looking for a huge win after Game 6," he said. And how could they not! The Red Sox had their ace, Martinez, on the mound, ready to fire away. The Sox led late—until Little left Pedey in a little too long, as any longtime fan will tell you. "When we took the lead late, there was a hum in the bar that was incredible," Donovan said. Optimism abounded. Customers were exuberant, believing this would finally be the time the Sox bested the Yankees for the first time since the pre-1920s. That euphoria, that optimism, that excitement faded once Boone hit the homer off of Wake. "It was ugly," he said. "People were sick, walking out with their head down. The bar was empty in 10 minutes."

It had happened again.

On the flip side was Chris Wertz, who left Boston after high school to attend college in Connecticut. (He moved to New York City to pursue acting.) The long time bartender wasn't tending pints and bottles that night. Instead he was in the upper deck of Yankee Stadium. "The Red Sox were the best team in baseball in 2003," he said, "and that had seemingly been undone by a force beyond their control." Yes, forces—the forces of the goats, as we like to call it. The Red Sox, no matter how close they could get to winning a championship, for some reason couldn't overcome themselves or the circumstances that led them to unravel more than Lindsay Lohan at a city bar.

A year later, Wertz was at the Riviera Café in the West Village, and Donovan, of course, was at the Tavern. What a difference a year makes.

2004...This Is Next Year

Say what you will about the Red Sox—no matter how ugly it gets, the fans keep coming back year after year with natural, raw optimism. Going into the 2004 playoffs, the Sox were no doubt a contender to go the distance, but would past failures cloud any momentum? When it came down to another ALCS between the Sox and the Yankees, sports lovers and writers wondered if Boone's home run off of Wakefield would negatively carry into the series. Down by three games, the Sox came back and forced another Game 7, but this year was different. Well, not at Donovan's bar.

The atmosphere was rocking at the Baseball Tavern, a Boston bar, as the Red Sox celebrated their first World Series title since 1918. (Getty Images)

"People were all around Fenway to watch the game…the Tavern was packed again," he said. "Even though we fought back after getting our asses kicked—there was still the feeling that it was going to happen again." Customers were waiting for the inevitable doom to fall upon the Red Sox just as it had the year before. "Every pitch was a torcher," he said, "just waiting for the shoe to drop."

But that "feeling" faded once the Sox recorded the final out, creating the biggest comeback in sports history. "When the final out was made and the Sox were going to the World Series, it was completely out of control," Donovan said. All that optimism that crashed and burned a year prior was ignited tenfold that night. On a personal note, Donovan, who was raised just south of Boston in Milton and became a fan thanks to his father and grandfather's love of the team, cherished the moment. "It's something that when some out-of-town fans ask about it, you still get chills," he said.

The atmosphere was amazing. "Beer and drinks went into the air. People were hugging, crying, and making phone calls," Donovan said. "The bars emptied along with all the dorms in the area—about 200,000 people in the Kenmore/Fenway area. It was an awesome night!"

Back in New York, Wertz had a case of déjà vu—except he wasn't in the upper deck. He was at that café in the West Village of Manhattan. Oh, and the end result was totally different. "There really was no more pressure," he said. "The same momentum that had carried an Aaron Boone home run barely out of the ballpark one year before swung and was lifting dingers easily out of Yankee Stadium for the Red Sox…Game 4 of the 2004 World Series felt a lot like Game 7 of the ALDS. To me it felt like it was already won before the game started. I think I spent most of the game waiting to celebrate. Of course, we were going to win; we knew that. Fate had been shown to be on our side for over a week, and there was no need to worry anymore. So we watched and we waited. I rarely challenge the jinx. But during Game 4, I openly spoke about how it felt to finally win the big one. And yet we still won. It was a whole new way of thinking.

"I swapped stories with other fans about where we were during Game 6, 1986 and other importantly disappointing games. I think we were trying to build a justification for the celebration we were about to have. True Calvinist New Englanders sometimes feel guilty being happy. But if this was truly achieved through the power of faith, as had become the motto of the 3–0 uprising, then to hell with guilt. We were celebrating faith rewarded.

"When the final pitch came, we screamed, we yelled, we hugged. We called friends and family and shared the moment as much as we could."

2007…Phew, That Was Easier

Something happened after the Red Sox won it all in 2004, and it wasn't just an end to those "1918" chants that Yankees chuckleheads used to shout. The post-2004 world is one in which Red Sox fans stopped fearing the worst would happen and expected to compete for a title each year like their Yankees counterparts. General manager Theo Epstein brought in many big-ticket stars along with a homegrown base of stars like Jacoby Ellsbury and Dustin Pedroia. These Sox were the same old Sox—scrappy grinders—but with a twist: they were free of any curses and superstitions. And there was a more optimistic tone in Donovan's bar during Game 4 of the 2007 World Series between the Sox and the Colorado Rockies than in postseasons of the past. The Sox had won the first three games, and as Donovan will tell you, there was no expectation by any of the social sceners that night that the Sox would implode. "It was almost like people expected it now, and the 2004 anticipation was gone," he said. This time with 600 people packing the bar, which had moved to a much larger location since 2004, fans felt comfortable celebrating the inevitable. What a relief it was for Sox Nation to not have to feel as if a Buckner ball or Boone bomb was on the horizon. "When [Paplebon] made the [last] out, it was crazy, but not at all like it was in 2004," Donovan said. "2004 changed people's lives. It brought them back to their childhood. You would see World Series champ flags on gravestones everywhere. I know I did it to my dad's."

Wertz, like Donovan, was tending bar that evening—only he was working in New York at the Boston fan-run bar, Professor Thom's, in the East Village. While the night (thankfully) failed to provide many gut-wrenching, heart-in-throat moments, Wertz said it's all pretty damn memorable to him, especially considering he almost missed it—well, almost. "I had finally recovered from the endless heckling I received for being foolish enough to get married and go on a honeymoon during the beginning of the playoffs. In my mind it didn't matter. Either we lost, and I missed the agony, or we won, and I'd be back for the more important games," he said.

That's how he rationalized it. Regardless, by the time the Sox defeated the Cleveland Indians in the ALCS in seven games, Wertz was back in town to serve cold beer for that series and watch and work the entire World Series. "I wasn't about to attend any more weddings, mine or otherwise, until this thing was done. So my wife went without me to Nantucket for a friend's wedding while I tended bar." That's the true devotion of Red Sox Nation—a newlywed putting his team before his new bride.

Game 4 of the World Series that year provided a new and unique feeling for Sox fans: it was a feeling that it was all in the bag. They were a confident bunch. "The crowd—more than 200 strong at Thom's for Game 4—certainly never felt that there was a chance the Sox would blow it. The Rockies were playing [Washington] Generals to a team whose fate was suddenly the expectation of victory. Ironically, just three years before, the opposite was still true. It seemed like no lead was ever safe, that any Red Sox pitch at any time could result in a 15-run home run," he said.

After the first three games, the Red Sox had outscored the Rockies 25–7. "That old notion of self-doubt was gone from the room completely. The talk was only of 'when we win.' I tell you, it was a nice change."

Once Jonathan Papelbon came in to save the game, Wertz cued up "Shipping Up To Boston" on the stereo and "it was Irish jigs and shots on the bar until the wee hours of the morning." Like Donovan, he said the "level of elation and relief" was nowhere near 2004 levels. He also said it "never quite erased the pain of 2003.

But it was a hell of a run and for us dispelled the argument of dumb luck on which some hung the 2004 win. To us, this was the beginning of something. Great ownership and solid management had created a winning formula, which should have been able to repeat itself for a long time."

10

Legion from the Region

New England has a harsh climate, a barren soil, a rough and stormy coast, and yet we love it, even with a love passing that of dwellers in more favored regions.

—Henry Cabot Lodge

Winning begets winning, and conversely losing begets losing. It seems cliché, but the New England region has proven this axiom true since the 1980s. After the Celtics won their 16th title in 1986, they were pretty much lost the rest of the century due to Larry Bird's ailing back and the premature deaths of Len Bias and Reggie Lewis. The Boston Bruins (1988 and 1990) and the New England Patriots (1985 and 1996) played the role of bridesmaid in each of the century's last two decades. And we all know how 1986 ended for the Boston Red Sox, so no point in opening old wounds. The '86 Celtics notwithstanding, the New England region mostly settled for runner-up status.

New England's end-of-20th century blues, however, gave way to a 21st century sports renaissance. Essentially, the city of Boston became the first city to win a championship in all four major North American sports in this century. The early 2000s saw the Bill Belichick/Tom Brady-led Patriots put their stamp on the NFL with three Super Bowl championships. This feat was followed by two Boston Red Sox World Series sweeps, leaving no room for error or anguish. The Celtics' 2008 NBA title behind the "Big Three" plus Rondo finally ushered in a new era for which Celtics fans had been hungering. Shortly after, the Bruins claimed their sixth Stanley Cup title in 2010. The 2006 Portsmouth (New Hampshire) Little League team grew up in the shadow of the 2004 Sox world championship, as it would launch an 83-game high school-win streak. Clearly, when winning is in the ether, it even trickles down from professional franchises to high school programs and little league sandlots.

On July 9, 2011, the Portsmouth High School Clippers were recognized by the Boston Red Sox. The high school heroes were celebrated not only for their four straight Division II New Hampshire state titles, but for their national-record, 83-consecutive-game win streak. Earlier that spring they broke the record of Homer (Michigan) High. The pregame ceremony took place behind home plate, moments before the Sox took the field against the Baltimore Orioles. The late-Carl Beane, Boston's public address announcer from 2003 to 2012, informed Red Sox Nation of the team's incredible accomplishment as Wally the Green Monster peppered the Clippers with high-fives and hugs. Several of the players on the field have since moved onto Division I college ball.

Coach Tim Hopley, who played center field on Portsmouth's Division I championship team in 1988, became the team's coach in 1996. Coach Hopley made sure to invite the team's bus driver Joe Dubois, who not only took the team to all of their road games during the four years, but also drove 12 of the 14 players and their families to Fenway Park for the ceremony. Mike Zhe covered the streak for the *Portsmouth Herald* and also contributes to the *New England Baseball Journal.* "They've just had a series of good classes of baseball players. In the spring of 2012, six Portsmouth alums —Ben Hart (UMass), Mike Fransoso (Maine), Nate Jones (Wake Forest), Mike Montville (Maryland), Aidan O'Leary (Manhattan), and Keegan Taylor (Northeastern)—were playing Division I college ball," Zhe said. "The first guy to come through the Little League program and go somewhere was pitcher Chris Anderson, who was drafted by the [Minnesota] Twins in the 18th round in 2006 and knocked around the minors for a couple years. In addition Jordan Bean and Steve Hemming played on that 2006 Little League World Series team and attended St. Thomas Aquinas. St. Thomas Aquinas not-so-coincidentally was the nearby private school that ended the Portsmouth win streak in 2012 and ended up winning the D II title."

From 1957 to 2000, New England Little League teams competed in the East region of the Little League World Series. During that span Connecticut was not only the most successful New England state, but it also surpassed New York, New Jersey, and Pennsylvania with 10 East region championships (and two Little League World Series championships). During that same 44-year span, all but Vermont won at least one East region title. New Hampshire has three, Massachusetts two, Rhode Island two, and Maine one. Beginning in 2001 the East region was split into the Mid-Atlantic region and the New England region. The New England regional headquarters are located in a place familiar to sports fans, Bristol, Connecticut, which is also the home of ESPN. Vermont remains winless in this smaller region, while Massachusetts leads the way with four New England regional championships. Connecticut and Rhode Island have won three apiece, while Maine and New Hampshire have each won the New England region once. This lone New Hampshire entrant, however, has enjoyed the most success in the larger tournament. Portsmouth Little League has represented New Hampshire six times in the New England tournament, including its 2006 run, when they played in the shadow of Red Sox twin peak titles of '04 and '07. Portsmouth defeated Glastonbury, Connecticut, 3–0 in the New England championship behind a 13 strikeout, three-hitter from Bean. Taylor drove in all of his team's runs, as Portsmouth blanked their Connecticut opponents in front of a crowd of 8,000 mostly pro-Connecticut fans. Ironically, Bean and Taylor later became rivals in their high school careers. Taylor pitched an amazing 25–0 record during his time with the Portsmouth Clippers.

Impressive facilities and a former Red Sox player helped Portsmouth become a power. "Another factor to consider is the opening of USA Training Centers in Portsmouth about a decade ago," Zhe said. "[The] big indoor complex with fields, batting cages [is] a convenient place for local guys to work out and hit in the winters, which last pretty long here in New Hampshire. Bob Stanley was on board for a few years as the pitching coach before taking a job with the Blue Jays in 2012." Although the training center has since moved to the nearby town of Newington, it helped Portsmouth form its dominating squad.

With a national record in its reach, the entire community rallied around the team. "Everybody around the team downplayed the streak, as it got closer to the Homer [Michigan] mark of 75 in 2011," Zhe said. "The day they went for the record breaker was at Pembroke Academy, about an hour away, and it seemed the whole community was there, which is something you might see for high school basketball or football in these parts but is very rare for high school baseball. After the game there was a big celebration and some parents brought out a big banner they had made with *76* on it and *record breakers*, so, it was obviously a bigger deal than they let on."

Just breaking the record, however, was the easy part. The Clippers had to sustain the win streak, as another high school was in the midst of its own. Because high school baseball does not always run concurrently across the nation, Martensdale (Iowa) High's win streak snuck up on the Portsmouth community. "We got word in July that there was a school in Iowa that was getting close to breaking the mark of 83 that Portsmouth finished the year with," Zhe said. "That was surreal to everyone. Nobody knew there were still schools playing high school baseball. It wasn't that Portsmouth was upset their mark could get broken, but they thought they'd at least have the offseason to enjoy it. The two coaches, Hopley of Portsmouth and Justin Dehmer of Martensdale, have been communicating since July 2011, sending congratulatory texts after big wins and speaking by phone at least once. It never got to an us-vs.-them thing, more like a mutual appreciation."

Hopley, an assistant coach for the Clippers football squad, is a modest guy. He'll be the first to tell you the streak has been helped by the Clippers' demotion in class levels, allowing Portsmouth to play smaller schools. "One of the most important things to recognize about the streak is that it began after the team dropped in classification from Division I to Division II before the spring 2007 season, due to enrollment," Zhe said. "Instead of playing all their games against the city schools like Concord, Nashua South, Manchester Central, Keene, and good programs from the big suburbs, they're in a league where they don't get tested day in and day out. There are a handful of good teams in Division II each year, but the league doesn't have the depth of Division I." That said, winning 83 games in a row at any level in baseball is worthy of a commemoration at Fenway Park.

Fenway hosted recreational league and high school baseball games, including state and regional tournaments, All-Star, and park league contests, until the 1950s. More recently, it has played host to the annual Boston City League baseball All-Star Game. The game features select high school student-athletes from the North and South regions of Boston. The 10th edition of the game (won by the North 11–5) returned to Fenway in 2012 for the first time since 2008.

The Boston Red Sox know a thing or two about streaks in the 21st century. The Sox are currently in the midst of an eight-game World Series winning streak. Hardly the mark of what for generations, was a hard-luck, curse-ridden franchise. The Sox started off even more spectacularly last century before the franchise endured a historically long drought. As tough as this might seem for New York Yankees fans to believe, it's the Sox who own the World Series record for most titles before losing a World Series. They won five titles—in 1903, 1912, 1915, 1916, and 1918—before losing a Fall Classic. After that, however, they only played in the play-offs sporadically, starting in 1946. Considering the many Game 7 heartbreakers, it's understandable that they've never been swept. In retrospect maybe a sweep would've been easier to take, but then again hardened losses built strong character throughout the New

England region and made those two recent World Series titles even sweeter.

We have to look back to the Red Sox's American League pennant-winning team of 1946 for the longest Boston winning streak. The streak began early in the season, when the Sox were just 6–3; at that point the Red Sox had been outscored 49–48. That would all change from April 25 to May 10. With bookend wins against the Yankees, the Red Sox would win 15 consecutive games. When the streak was finished, they would stand at 21–3, having outscored their opponents by 59 runs and posted a 5.5-game lead over the second-place Yankees. Boston ultimately would win the pennant by 12 games over the Detroit Tigers, posting a 104–50 record. The Red Sox enjoyed a winning record each month: April (11–3), May (21–6), June (18–10), July (20–10), August (21–11), and September (13–10).

New England Natives

New Englanders not only have filled the Red Sox but also squads throughout the major leagues. There have been 191 major leaguers born in the "Nutmeg State" of Connecticut. There are three Hall of Famers who played in the 1800s: Ned Hanlon, Roger Connor, and Bridgeport's Jim O'Rourke. O'Rourke has a statue, outside of the Bridgeport Bluefish ballpark, honoring him. The Nutmeggers have accounted for 40,913 major league hits and 2,106 home runs. On the pitching side, Connecticut natives have amassed 1,620 wins and 13,816 strikeouts. Stamford's own Bobby Valentine was hired before the 2012 season, but his first year hardly made anyone forget the reign of Terry Francona, and he was fired the day after the season ended. Twenty Connecticut-born players have suited up for the Red Sox: pitcher Pete Appleton (1932), shortstop Jack Barry (1915–17, 1919), outfielder Darren Bragg (1996–98), pitcher Craig Breslow (2006, 2012), first baseman Walt Dropo (1949–52), second baseman Billy Gardner (1962–63), first baseman Candy LaChance (1902–05), catcher Roger LaFrancois (1982), outfielder Joe Lahoud (1968–71), pitcher Brian Looney (1995), second baseman Dick McAuliffe (1974–75), pitcher John Michaels (1932), pitcher Kevin Morton

(1991), second baseman Al Niemiec (1934), outfielder Jim Piersall (1950, 1952–58), pitcher Rollie Sheldon (1966), third baseman Earl Snyder (2004), first baseman Mo Vaughn (1991–98), pitcher Gary Waslewski (1967–68), and pitcher Pinky Woods (1943–45).

As one of the country's least populous states, it's not surprising that Vermont has produced just 37 major leaguers, the most recent being Oakland's Daric Barton. The legendary "Pudge," Carlton Fisk, is the only Hall of Famer born in the Green Mountain State, but that's because it was the closest hospital to his home in nearby Charlestown, New Hampshire. Catcher Birdie Tebbetts, who played with the Red Sox from 1948–50, is the only other Vermont native to make the All-Star team. There have been 8,461 hits and 568 home runs by Vermont batters and 621 wins and 4,295 strikeouts by Vermont pitchers. Other Vermont-born Red Sox include: pitcher Ray Collins (1909–15), pitcher Jean Duboc (1918), third baseman Larry Gardner (1908–17), second baseman Amby McConnell (1908–10), and pitcher Steve Slayton (1928).

Though the smallest state in area in the United States, Rhode Island has actually produced 75 major league ballplayers, dating from 1878 with Fred Corey of the Providence Grays to 2012 and the Chicago Cubs' Jeff Beliveau. The Ocean State has produced three Hall of Famers (Gabby Hartnett, Hugh Duffy, and Nap Lajoie) in addition to four more All-Stars (Paul Konerko, Davey Lopes, Clem Labine, and Dave Stenhouse). Eleven Red Sox were born in Rhode Island: outfielder Rocco Baldelli (2009), shortstop Jimmy Cooney (1917), pitcher Ray Jarvis (1969–70), pitcher Ed Kelly (1914), first baseman Rick Lancelotti (1990), pitcher John LaRose (1978), pitcher Bill Lefebvre (1938–39), pitcher Chet Nichols (1960–63), pitcher Ken Ryan (1992–95), pitcher Joe Trimble (1955), and pitcher Dan Wheeler (2011). Major league Rhode Islanders have slapped 20,173 hits and slammed 1,316 home runs. On the mound they have tallied 687 wins and 5,630 strikeouts.

Known for its primary, which signals the start of the United States presidential campaign and its well-quoted motto "Live Free or Die," New Hampshire also has produced 51 major leaguers (eight of whom called Fenway home at some point in their career).

The eight New Hampshire Sox are: pitcher Ray Dobens (1929), third baseman Bernie Friberg (1933), pitcher Rich Gale (1984), outfielder Phil Plantier (1990–92), outfielder Kevin Romine (1985–91), pitcher Bob Smith (1955), pitcher Stan Williams (1972), and pitcher Rob Woodward (1985–88). Frank Selee, who won five pennants with the Boston Beaneaters and had a hell of a mustache, is the only Hall of Famer born in the state. Players born in the Granite State totaled 7,760 hits, 307 home runs, 928 wins, and 8,663 strikeouts.

The commonwealth of Massachusetts ranks 14th in U.S. state population, but only six states (California, New York, Illinois, Pennsylvania, Ohio, and Texas) have produced more major league athletes. With 650 ballplayers born in Massachusetts, the total surpasses all five other New England states combined. Hall of Famers from the "Bay State" are Rabbit Maranville, Pie Traynor, Joe Kelley, Wilbert Robinson, Leo Durocher, Tim Keefe, Mickey Cochrane, Tommy McCarthy, John Clarkson, Connie Mack, Jack Chesbro, and Candy Cummings. Twenty-three members of the Red Sox were born in Boston. According to *Red Sox Threads* by Bill Nowlin, they include: catcher Jack Slattery (1901), outfielder Paul Howard (1909), catcher Bunny Madden (1909–11), second baseman Walter Lonegran (1911), third baseman Herb Hunter (1920), outfielder Shano Collins (1921–25, 1931–32), outfielder John Donahue (1923), outfielder Sy Rosenthal (1925–26), outfielder John Freeman (1927), second baseman Bill Marshall (1931), pitcher Jud McLaughlin (1931–33), second baseman Andy Spognardi (1932), pitcher Ed Gallagher (1932), shortstop Eddie Pellagrini (1946–47), pitcher Mike Palm (1948), pitcher Dick Mills (1970), pitcher Skip Lockwood (1980), pitcher Matt Murray (1995), pitcher Carlos Castillo (2001), second baseman Mark Bellhorn (2004–05), pitcher Manny Delcarmen (2005–10), and pitcher Rich Hill (2010–12).

Although many of the Bostonian Boston Red Sox were fringe part-time players, there have been some Red Sox All-Stars from Massachusetts. Bill Monbouquette (1960, 1962–63), Jeff Reardon (1991), Rich Gedman (1985, 1986), Tony Conigliaro (1967), and

Jerry Remy (1978) all made appearances in the Mid-Summer Classic as members of the Red Sox. Cy Young winners Tom Glavine and Steve Bedrosian contributed to the 6,415 wins from Massachusetts products, while former Red Sox pitcher Wilbur Wood and former phenom Mark Fidrych contributed to the strikeout total of 55,498. Former Red Sox prospect Jeff Bagwell added to the Massachusetts totals of 105,064 hits and 4,230 home runs.

The scenic state of Maine, which seceded from Massachusetts in 1820, has never produced a Hall of Famer, but 76 major leaguers have been born in the Pine Tree State. Catcher Bill Carrigan (1906–16) was the player/manager of the 1915 and 1916 World Series-champion Red Sox. The catcher known as "Rough" was born in Lewiston. Maine's second largest city prints *The Farmers' Almanac* and was the site of the famous Muhammad Ali-Sonny Liston fight in 1965. The only All-Star ever born in Maine was Bob "the Steamer" Stanley who pitched his entire career (1977–89) with Boston. Other not-as-notable Red Sox born in Maine include: pitcher Clarence Blethen (1923), pitcher Curt Fullerton (1921–25, 1933), third baseman Harry Lord (1907–10), outfielder Charlie Small (1930), and catcher Squanto Walker (1914). Maine has "mashed" for 10,742 hits and 225 home runs. On the hill Maine pitchers have tallied 598 wins and 5,388 strikeouts.

The All-New England Red Sox Team
Catcher—Carlton Fisk (Charlestown, New Hampshire)
"Pudge's" Hall of Fame plaque in Cooperstown, New York, appropriately reads: "His dramatic home run to win Game Six of the 1975 World Series is one of baseball's unforgettable moments." Born in a Bellow Falls, Vermont, hospital but raised in Charlestown, New Hampshire, Fisk had 164 regular and postseason Red Sox home runs, seven Sox All-Star nods, and the 1972 American League Rookie of the Year and Gold Glove Awards. As the star of Fall Mountain High School basketball team, the 6'3" Fisk hoped of one day getting drafted by the Celtics. But with the fourth overall selection in 1967, the Boston Red Sox were the New England team to come calling. Wearing the now-unfamiliar No.

40, Fisk made his debut on September 18, 1969, going 0–for–4 in a late-season loss to the pennant-winning Baltimore Orioles. After that cup of coffee, Fisk donned his now-retired No. 27 for a 14-game call-up in 1971, when he batted .313. By 1972 he was well on his way to legendary status, as he earned the AL Rookie of the Year trophy while leading the league in triples with nine. With 1,078 games played in 11 seasons for the Red Sox, Fisk had a 37.2 WAR (wins above replacement), which ranks ninth among all Sox position players. Similarly he is ranked ninth in defensive WAR as well at 9.3. The original—and in the minds of New England… only—Pudge was followed by Worcester, Massachusetts' own Rich Gedman, who occupied 857 games behind the plate, giving the successive Sox backstops almost 2,000 games by New Englanders.

First Baseman—Mo Vaughn (Norwalk, Connecticut)

The nickname "Mo" in Boston Red Sox circles has taken a different turn in the late 1990s and 2000s. The moniker is synonymous with the greatest closer in Major League Baseball history, Mariano Rivera, a hated Yankee who used to flummox the team for years. But before the feared closer took flight in the Bronx and made us absolutely hate the Metallica classic, "Enter Sandman," a different Mo, who was beloved by fans and teammates for his larger-than-life personality and his heroics at the plate, reigned in Beantown.

For eight years he was the city's biggest star. He was a home run threat at the plate—arguably the most feared hitter in baseball for most of the 1990s—and a lovable presence in the clubhouse and the community. Plus, he was literally a hometown hero. Born in Norwalk, Connecticut, and raised in Easton, Massachusetts, the Seton Hall grad burst onto the scene.

Vaughn was born on December 15, 1967 to educators Leroy and Shirley Vaughn, who taught and supported their son's interest in the great game of baseball from an early age. Young Maurice played ball at every level as a kid, and by high school he received the nickname "Mo" from a coach, who—as the story goes—couldn't say "Maurice." At Seton Hall, Vaughn established himself as "Hit Dog" by breaking the school's record for dingers with 57. In 1989 the Red Sox drafted the All-American, and he quickly worked his way through the system.

Vaughn was in the majors by June of 1991 and starting by 1992. While he struggled that rookie season and was subsequently demoted to Triple A Pawtucket, Vaughn worked out his kinks with hitting coach and former Sox player Mike Easler and never looked back. A refined stance, swing, and outlook turned Vaughn into a superstar. In 1993 he smacked 29 homers and 101 RBIs. The following year, he knocked 26 out of the park and plated 82 runs during a strike-shortened season. In 1995 and shortly thereafter, the big man and eventual three-time All-Star arguably carried the team on his mighty back.

He led the team to the AL East title with a season that would earn him the AL's Most Valuable Player and Silver Slugger Awards in 1995. That year, he batted .300, smashed 39 homers, and plated 126 runs. But Vaughn wasn't just known as an intimidating, powerful force in the lineup. A true New Englander, the player was renowned in the community for his many charitable contributions. He supported the Jimmy Fund, formed his own youth-development program in Dorchester, Massachusetts, made countless appearances at schools, and became a role model for area youth.

In a nutshell, Vaughn was a fan favorite who cared deeply about the team and region for whom he played. In 1996 he reached a peak with 44 home runs and 143 RBIs. He also batted .326, an impressive average for a home run hitter. Vaughn helped the team reach the postseason in 1998. He never won a World Series ring with the team but was arguably one of the most recognizable players in franchise history, though a falling out with the media and public feuds with management tainted his Sox legacy. Following 1998 the Sox couldn't let Mo leave soon enough, and he signed with the Anaheim Angels for a then-record $80 million, three-year deal. While he hit well in Anaheim, he was plagued with injuries and wore out his welcome there. After missing the entire 2001 season, the first baseman was traded to the New York Mets in exchange for pitcher Kevin Appier. Despite hitting 26 homers in his first year in Queens, he never really took flight. An injury-plagued 2003 campaign was unmemorable, and Vaughn retired shortly thereafter. Since his retirement, he's made a name for himself in the housing industry, forming a company that worked in New York state and, of course, Massachusetts.

In 2007 he was linked to performance-enhancing drugs in the Mitchell Report, but he's never addressed it. Although his Boston legacy was tainted with those allegations and his ugly exit, he was a real hometown hero who made his mark on the field and within the community.

Second Baseman—Jerry Remy (Fall River, Massachusetts)

All-Star. Author. Announcer. Much beloved Jerry Remy has done it all in his home state of Massachusetts. The Somerset High School grad was originally drafted in the 19th round by the second incarnation of the Washington Senators. He, however, never played for those ill-fated Senators, waiting instead to sign a pro contract after the California Angels selected the left-handed hitter in the eighth round of the 1971 secondary amateur draft. The "Rem Dawg" made his big show debut in 1975. After three seasons in Anaheim, the Sox came calling for the New Englander in winter of 1977. In a swap that landed Remy back in Fenway forever, relief pitcher Don Aase and some cash were sent packing to the West Coast. Remy proceeded to make his only All-Star appearance that first year with the Sox in '78. Although he hit just two home runs during his Red Sox career, the second baseman ranks 50th in Red Sox career hits with 802. In the 1990 Hall of Fame voting, Remy received one vote (or 0.2 percent) and was removed from the ballot. He, though, was inducted into the Red Sox Hall of Fame in 2006. As fortunes would have it, Red Sox Nation is treated to hearing his voice as color commentator each night on NESN (New England Sports Network) broadcasts. In addition Remy keeps busy, having authored children's books about Wally the Green Monster and *Red Sox Heroes*.

Shortstop—Lou Merloni (Framingham, Massachusetts)

A product of Framingham South High School who eventually starred and set several records at Providence College in Rhode

Island, Lou Merloni was drafted in the 10th round of the 1993 amateur draft. He made his debut on May 10, 1998, going 0–for–3 while batting ninth for Jimy Williams' Red Sox. Five days later in his first Fenway at-bat, he swatted the first home run of his major league career. He, though, popularized the "Merloni Shuffle" for his frequent trips from the farm system to the big show and vice versa. Sweet Lou made eight plate appearances in the 1999 playoffs, including two hits and one RBI in a Game 3 AL Divisional Series start vs. the Cleveland Indians. Following that postseason he signed with the Yokohama Bay Stars of the Japan Central League only to return to the Red Sox the following July. Merloni was selected off waivers by the San Diego Padres in March 2003 but once again headed back to New England later that summer via trade to the Sox. He left the Sox prior to their World Series season, though he has returned to the Boston area. This time it was on the radio waves via WEEI's morning show, *Mut and Merloni*. In his six years with the Red Sox, Merloni played in 273 games (with 75 games at shortstop), totaling a .269 batting average with 194 Sox hits, 60 of which were for extra bases.

Third Baseman—Larry Gardner (Enosburg Falls, Vermont)

For decades, the hot corner has been a position synonymous with power numbers. From Mike Schmidt to Chipper Jones to Adrian Beltre—but not necessarily poultry king Wade Boggs—big numbers have typically come from players manning third base. That wasn't always the case especially during the early years of last century—a time, when power numbers arguably weren't as important as solid fielding and base knocks. Larry Gardner, a fixture in Boston for 10 seasons, was a fine example of this. Never a power threat, the infielder, who shined at second and third for the Sox, was a solid hitter with decent speed and fine defense. More importantly, as the history books will show, he was an integral part on championship Boston teams. Case in point: this member of the Sox from 1908–1917 had three World Championships (1912, 1915, and 1916) under his belt by the time he retired. Take that, Jeter.

Although Gardner put together a fine career (.289 career average with 1,931 hits and 165 steals), one game stands out.

During the 1912 World Series against the New York Giants, Gardner had the game-winning, World Series-winning sacrifice fly in the decisive eighth game of the series. (Yes, we said Game 8.) Christy Mathewson had walked Duffy Lewis intentionally to face Gardner in the 10th inning of the game. Gardner responded by driving in Steve Yerkes with the winning run, and the Sox won it all. Although he played with other teams in his career (the Philadelphia Athletics and the Cleveland Indians), New England—specifically the "Maple Syrup State"—was always his home. When he retired he even returned to the University of Vermont to coach their baseball team. Gardner was posthumously inducted into the Red Sox Hall of Fame in 2000.

Left Fielder—Phil Plantier (Manchester, New Hampshire)

The term "one-hit wonder" gets bounced around a lot—especially if your name is Right Said Fred or the Baha Men. That term also applies to countless Major League Baseball players who make their mark for one magical season. When it comes to New England native Phil Plantier, the term definitely applies and—to take a page from the infamous one-hit band the Baha Men—he let the dogs out in 1990.

Drafted in the 11th round by the Sox in the 1987 draft, Plantier showed great promise for becoming a fixture in the BoSox lineup. His successes in their minor league system propelled him from Single A ball to Triple A, and by 1990, he was called up to the big show. After spending some more time in the minors, he was promoted to the majors in 1991, and right away, Plantier took off like Ichiro Suzuki on roller skates in the rain.

In just 53 games that year, Plantier smashed 11 taters and knocked in 35 runs. Best of all, he hit .331 and was a huge bright spot in a season during which the Sox finished second to the mighty Toronto Blue Jays. That season was the lone highlight for the Manchester, New Hampshire, native, who failed to live up to that promise the next year. After a so-so 1992 campaign, the outfielder was sent to the San Diego Padres and flourished there. In 1993 he smacked 34 home runs with 100 RBIs.

But like in Boston, Plantier's San Diego success was a one-year deal. After batting just .220 in 1994, he was one of 12 players involved in a trade between the Padres and the Houston Astros. For the remainder of his career, Plantier bounced around to several teams, including the Detroit Tigers, Oakland Athletics, St. Louis Cardinals, and a second tour of duty with the Padres.

Center Fielder—Jim Piersall (Waterbury, Connecticut)
Center fielder Jim Piersall vaulted from the Leavenworth High School New England Basketball Championship in Waterbury to a 17-year major league career. Signed as an amateur free agent in 1948, Piersall made his debut on September 7, 1950 as a pinch-runner for Ted Williams in a late-season win against the Yankees. Piersall spent the first half of his career (eight seasons) with the Red Sox, for whom he made both of his career All-Star appearances. The Nutmeg State native scooped up a Gold Glove in 1958, but left Boston that offseason via trade to the Cleveland Indians. His 66 home runs rank 42nd, and his 919 hits rank 38th in Sox history.

Right Fielder—Tony Conigliaro (Lynn, Massachusetts)
For a team like the Boston Red Sox with a rich history of sluggers, it says a lot when you have the 11th highest slugging percentage in franchise history. Tony C is also tied with Carlton Fisk for 14th in team history with 162 regular season home runs. The St. Mary's High School student-athlete was signed by the Red Sox as an amateur free agent in 1962. Manager Johnny Pesky inserted him in center field for the season opener at Yankee Stadium on April 16, 1964. During the next year, he became the youngest player in AL history to lead the league in homers. It was the same season the Sox drafted his brother and future teammate, Billy, in the first round. Among his astonishing long ball feats, Tony Conigliaro was only 22 years old when he reached the 100-homer plateau.

Sadly, Conigliaro was struck in the face by a pitch from California Angels pitcher Jack Hamilton in 1967. The Impossible Dream Team managed to make it to Game 7 of the World Series even without him. And Tony C came back to set career highs with 36 home runs and 116 RBIs in 1970 and won the Hutch Award, which is given to the major leaguer who best exemplifies the fighting spirit and competitive desire of Fred Hutchinson. While most ballplayers are preparing for a life in coaching or broadcasting, Tony's life tragically was cut short when he suffered a heart attack in 1990 at the age of 45.

Pitcher—Bill Monbouquette (Medford, Massachusetts)

The same year Gardner joined the Red Sox elite in their Hall of Fame, another native New Englander had his day in the sun. Bill Monbouquette joined that infielder in the Hall of Fame class during 2000, and like Gardner, this hometown star shined for nearly a decade in Boston.

Yes, long before Jarrod Saltalamacchia challenged letterers to fit his surname on the back of a jersey (and fans to pronounce his name correctly), there was Monbouquette, a stud pitcher on a mostly forgettable Sox contingent from 1958–1965. A native of Medford, Massachusetts, this right-handed pitcher held American League batters at bay with his amazing control and poise on the mound. "Monbo" had many career highlights, including a 17-strikeout game against the Washington Senators in 1961 and a no-hitter tossed against the Chicago White Sox a year later. He was also selected to the All-Star team three more times than Wily Mo Pena. Although he was traded to the Detroit Tigers following the 1965 season and spent a few years on other teams including the rival Yankees, Monbouquette will always be associated with the Red Sox.

Relief Pitcher—Bob Stanley (Portland, Maine)

It's been replayed more than your favorite *Seinfeld* episode. We've seen it and relived it more times than any of us care to remember. It's October 1986, and the Boston Red Sox are just one strike away from winning the World Series, but they...um, yeah...they don't. Two key events within the same inning with the same batter tarnished the Sox for the rest of Game 6 of that series and helped set the stage for a New York Mets World Series victory in Game 7.

It all started when Bob Stanley entered Game 6 with the Sox just one out away from winning it all and shutting up all the chants of "1918." But the right-hander tossed a wild pitch to Mookie Wilson, which allowed the Mets to tie the score. In the very same at-bat, the speedy outfielder smacked a slow duck fart that went right through Bill Buckner's legs. As Vin Scully famously said, "Little roller up along first…behind the bag! It gets through Buckner! Here comes [Ray] Knight, and the Mets win it!"

That call from the iconic Los Angeles Dodgers announcer plagues New England to this day. Anyway, it wasn't exactly over for Game 7, but the emotional roller coaster that crashed like Lindsay Lohan lingered into Game 7. The Sox lost Game 7, and their curse continued. History has labeled Buckner a goat and ditto for Stanley. But that's unfair. Billy Buck was a solid hitter. Plus Wilson may have beaten him to the bag anyway. As for Stanley, his career is better than one pitch, and most fans agree or should agree. "The Steamer" was a rock star in Boston for a long time before a guy named Mookie stepped up to the plate.

A native New Englander born in Portland, Maine, Stanley was the go-to guy in the Sox bullpen for most of his decade-plus in a Sox uniform. Playing his entire career with the team from 1977–1989, the former first-round pick shined in part because of his great sinker. Before and after that aforementioned wild pitch, Stanley was a workhorse for the Sox. He set an American League record for relief innings with 168.1 in 1982 and led the league the preceding and following year. Stanley also pitched in the starting rotation when needed and remains the team's all-time leader in pitching appearances. A member of the Sox Hall of Fame, he ranked first on the all-time Sox saves list with 132 until Jonathan Papelbon took his place in 2009.

Bulldog Battery

Throughout their history the Sox have some connections to New England's esteemed universities. In 1883 Litchfield, Connecticut, native "Jumping" Jack Jones pitched his only season in the major leagues, going 11–7 while splitting time with the Philadelphia

Athletics and the now-defunct Detroit Wolverines. A teammate of his (although for just slightly more than a cup of coffee) was catcher Al Hubbard from Westfield, Massachusetts. On September 15, 1883, Jones pitched to Hubbard in a game that was lost to the record books. Fast-forward to the 21st century, and Boston Red Sox battery mates Craig Breslow and Ryan Lavarnway took the field together on August 18, 2012. What the four men have in common is that they all attended Yale University. When asked how Lavarnway caught, Breslow commented, "I guess Ryan caught like a Bulldog."

The recent graduates, Breslow in 2002 and Lavarnway 2008, both played for John Stuper, who pitched in the NL from 1982–85 and compiled a 32–28 record, including a Game 6 complete-game victory for the St. Louis Cardinals against the Milwaukee Brewers in the 1982 Fall Classic. Breslow was the captain of Yale's 2002 squad, and Lavarnway was the 2007 NCAA batting and slugging percentage champion taken in the sixth round of the 2008 Major League Baseball draft.

The Sox not only have an Ivy League connection, but also a military link. Few American cities go as far back to the roots of our country as that of Boston. Therefore, it's no surprise that the patriotic city that served as the flint of the revolution fielded a baseball team known as the Boston Americans. The Americans won the first World Series in 1903; by 1908 the franchise was known, then and forever, as the Boston Red Sox. Despite the name change, no Red Sox team (or any Major League Baseball team for that matter) was as patriotic in service to the United States as the 1942 team that finished second in the American League.

Ted Williams is often regarded as the greatest hitter of all time. With 31 home runs in his 1939 rookie season and 29 home runs in his 1960 swan song, he remains the only man to hit at least 25 home runs in a season in four different decades. Despite all of his baseball accomplishments, Williams' most admirable feat may be his patriotism on the battlefield. The Splendid Splinter missed the entire 1943–45 seasons and substantial time in other seasons while serving as a U.S. Navy flight instructor during World War II and a Marine bomber jet pilot during the Korean War.

Fellow Hall of Famer Bobby Doerr entered the military after the fourth of his nine All-Star seasons in 1944. Doerr rose to the ranks of staff sergeant but did not go overseas to Japan, as President Truman's actions brought the war to an end. After his rookie season in 1942, in which he led the league in hits (while setting a rookie record) with 205, shortstop Johnny Pesky proceeded to serve three years in the military. Upon his return to action in 1946, he helped the Sox to the World Series by leading the AL in hits once again with 208. Pesky turned the trick one more time in '47, pacing the junior circuit with 207 hits. In the navy Pesky met his wife, Ruth, and even played some ball, appearing in an AL vs. NL game in Honolulu in 1945. After his second All-Star season, Dom DiMaggio

One of the greatest hitters ever, Ted Williams, grins as he stands before a Marine Corps recruiting poster bearing his picture. He missed the 1943–1945 seasons while fighting in WWII and is one of the many Red Sox with connections to the military.

left Fenway Park for three years of service with the United States Coast Guard. While serving overseas he managed to play some baseball at the Norfolk Naval Training Station in Virginia. Like for Pesky, a potential Cooperstown career was hampered by missing so many prime years in service of the country.

Several of the lesser known members of the 1942 Sox were members of the military. Catcher Bill Conroy, who played with Red Sox from 1942–44, missed the 1938–41 seasons while serving in WWII. Conroy joined the Sox after his discharge and batted .200 in close to 300 plate appearances. "Rawhide" Jim Tabor patrolled third base at Fenway, averaging 15 homers while batting .273 during seven seasons. Tabor entered the Army at Fort Devens, Massachusetts, in the fall of 1944. After missing the entire '45 season while at Camp Croft, South Carolina, he was given a dependency discharge in the winter of '46. When he cleared waivers later in the winter, however, Tabor was sent to the Philadelphia Phillies and missed out on the Sox's '46 pennant. Paul Campbell entered games mostly as a pinch-hitter in his 44 Red Sox plate appearances in 1941–42 and 1946. Those baseball years enveloped three years of military service. Infielder Tom Carey served in the navy from 1943 to 1945. Like many other ballplayers in service, his role was to add morale. Therefore, he spent most of his time as a baseball coach at an upstate New York training base. Carey was a Red Sox role player in 1939–41. His final two seasons with the Sox were brief appearances with just one hit in one at-bat in 1942 and only five at-bats upon returning in '46.

As for the pitching staff of the 1942 Red Sox, Tex Hughson missed the 1945 season as he fought in World War II with a bat and a glove. Like Carey, he improved military morale through baseball at various military outposts, but Hughson's service areas ranged from Texas through the Pacific. Hughson was a three-time All-Star whose breakthrough season came in 1942, when he led the AL with 22 wins. Tex finished with a .640 win percentage in eight seasons with the Sox, totaling 96 wins. Joe Dobson missed 1944–45 after being inducted into the Army on December 22, 1943. Dobson became the 17th player the Red Sox lost to World War II service.

Fresh off a career high 14-win season in 1942, "Broadway" Charlie Wagner joined the navy for three seasons. Not only was Wagner the roommate of Ted Williams, but he also served as assistant director of minor league operations for the Red Sox from 1947–60. As if that wasn't enough time with the Sox, Wagner scouted for them from 1961–69 and 1971–92. Wagner did not scout during the 1970 season, because he was the Sox pitching coach. Right-hander Bill Butland won seven of his nine major league victories for the 1942 Red Sox, and the Indiana native served the U.S. Army. After leading the league in games pitched in 1943, Mace Brown, the one-time All-Star and pitcher who gave up Gabby Hartnett's "Homer in the Gloamin'" while with the Pittsburgh Pirates, served in the U.S. Navy from 1944–45. Brown won nine games for Sox in 1942.

New England product, first baseman Tony Lupien, played in 1940, 1942, and 1943 for the Red Sox. As a baseball captain for Harvard—see, the Ivy League connection comes full circle—he batted .442 as a senior. He spent 1941 in the minors because Hall of Famer Jimmie Foxx was the Sox first basemen. Lupien, however, became the Sox's regular first basemen in 1942, when Foxx was sold to the Chicago Cubs. After spending some time on naval bases, he fought for the rights of players returning from service. *The Sporting News* even covered his quest to see ballplayers-turned-servicemen treated fairly. After a premature end to his career, Lupien went on to a 21-year coaching career at Dartmouth University.

Outfielder Lou Finney voluntarily retired from baseball after being inducted into the army. At the age of 32, Finney stayed on his farm in White Plains, Alabama, with his wife, Margie, where he grew food, which was crucial for the country's war effort. So Finney, who sat out the entire 1943 season and parts of the following year, accumulated only 13 home runs in six seasons but struck out just 60 times in 1,930 Red Sox at-bats.

Pitcher Earl Johnson was the most decorated military man in the team's history. Johnson fought in the Battle of the Bulge and received the Bronze Star, a Bronze Star with clusters, and the Silver Star. He pitched for the Red Sox in 1940–41 and 1946–50 while compiling a 40–32 record. Other Sox who served the conflict but did not play on the 1942 squad: pitcher Emerson Dickman (1936, 1938–41), catcher Frankie Pytlak (1941, 1945–46), catcher Danny Doyle (1943), pitcher Dave Ferriss (1945–50), first baseman Al Flair (1941), outfielder Andy Gilbert (1942, 1946), pitcher Mickey Harris (1940–41, 1946–49), catcher Roy Partee (1943–44, 1946–47), and catcher Hal Wagner (1944, 1946–47).

Patriots' Day

The Red Sox are aligned with the military and its Revolutionary War history, which is perhaps best demonstrated by the commemoration of Patriots' Day. The day is a tribute to the anniversary of the first battles of the American Revolution in Lexington and Concord on April 19, 1775. At Fenway at 11:05 AM, it is the one fixed date on the Sox's schedule and the only morning game. On the third Monday of April and timed to end just as Boston Marathon runners are moving through Kenmore Square, the Fenway game occurs during the state holiday that Massachusetts and Maine have honored since 1894. The Boston Marathon, which was first held in 1897, is one of the oldest races in North America. (They started officially crowning a woman's champion in 1972.) The Boston Marathon has been won by a New Englander man or woman 37 times, including victories by marathon greats like: Joan Benoit (Cape Elizabeth, Maine), Alberto Salazar (Wayland, Massachusetts, by way of Cuba), Bill Rodgers (Hartford, Connecticut), and seven-time winner Clarence DeMar (Massachusetts by way of Ohio).

"Marathon Monday" is also a day for reenactments and Fenway Franks. Prior to 1953 the Red Sox and Boston Braves (formerly the Beaneaters) alternated the Patriots' Day home gate. But when the Braves fled for Milwaukee, the Sox took ownership of the day. The last time the Sox did not play in Boston on Patriots' Day was in 1958, when they were at Yankee Stadium. Three Red Sox have hit three home runs on Patriots' Day: war veteran Ted Williams, Jim Rice, and Dick Gernert. Since 2000 the Red Sox are 9–4 on Patriots' Day, including 7–1 while playing under Terry Francona—the same Francona who owns an 8–0 World Series record. Four of Cy Young's 511 victories came on Patriots' Day for the Sox.

The following pitchers won Patriots' Day games during the 21st century: Frank Castillo (2001), Derek Lowe (2002), Mike Timlin (2004, 2006), Curt Schilling (2005), Josh Beckett (2007), Clay Buchholz (2008), Justin Masterson (2009), and Daisuke Matsuzaka (2001). Manny Ramirez and Jason Varitek have each belted two Patriots' Day blasts, while Mark Loretta, David Ortiz, Jeremy Hermida, Jacoby Ellsbury, Kevin Youkilis, and Jed Lowrie have blasted one home run. From 2000–2012, 12 Red Sox have at least five Patriots' Day hits: Ortiz (14), Varitek (12), Ramirez (11), Dustin Pedroia (8), Trot Nixon (7), Shea Hillenbrand (6), Youkilis (6), Bill Mueller (6), Julio Lugo (6), Ellsbury (5), Lowrie (5), and Johnny Damon (5).

So there you have it...the Red Sox are a franchise rich in hometown heroes, patriotism, and a strong connection to the student-athletes of New England.

11

Plan 9 Innings
from Outer Space

The most important thing about Spaceship Earth—instructions didn't
come with it.

—R. Buckminster Fuller

Planet Earth, September 27, 2012

Bill "Spaceman" Lee has gained a reputation as being one of the greatest eccentrics in baseball history. But what also makes him so quotable and endearing to listeners is that—despite his moniker—he is as down-to-earth an athlete as you'll ever meet. The peculiar left-hander has pitched in just about every country that has a pitcher's mound. The Boston Red Sox record holder for most games pitched by a lefty (321) even ran for president, with his platform vacillating between being an instigator and an iconoclast. If you love talking baseball, metaphysics, literature, life, and serendipity, then pull up a chair and ride the cosmic wheel with "Spaceman" Lee, a mind-altering human. You'll begin where you end and be all the better for it.

Lee cuts no corners and gets right to the point when explaining the inhabitants of his second home in America's great Northeast, saying "New Englanders are pretty provincial. They don't go really outside their borders. No one seems to be tough enough, like a New England Yankee with their stick-to-it-tiveness. You have to put your nose to the grindstone and be tightfisted and survive the winter. Most of the ballplayers that come here are not of that cast. They are more of a Southern gentry and they can't handle the toughness, the tight corners, the driving that you have to do, the—you-can't-get-there-from-here type of mentality. It kills a lot of guys that come to New England. These New Englanders are set in their ways, and they are not gonna change. They're Yankees. They dig the hole for their horse in the fall, just in case he dies during the winter. And they have a place to bury him, so they won't have to cremate him at the cost of $500." The unfiltered trailblazer explained the contradictory nature of the Red Sox and Yankees rivalry, "The New York Yankees are really a metropolitan team that really have no Yankee values whatsoever," he said. "That's the whole trouble with that schizophrenic relationship between Red Sox fans, where the Red Sox are actually the Yankees, and the Yankees are actually the flamboyant urban dwellers. It's confusing to people who don't understand New England values."

Swampscott, Massachusetts, August 20, 2012

Johnny Pesky served as broadcaster and first-base coach for the Red Sox during the Spaceman's tenure with Boston. To demonstrate the amount of love pointed in the direction of the former shortstop, the *Lynn (Massachusetts) Sunday Post* wrote in 1985 that Pesky led the majors in "most friends." When the Boston icon passed away on August 13, 2012, several former Red Sox made the trek to fondly recall "the Needle." Left-hander Bill Lee was among them. The one-time All-Star recalled, "I told all the people at Johnny Pesky's funeral that if they look up at the wall, they see four men up there. And all four of them are West Coasters: Bobby Doerr, Johnny Pesky, Ted Williams, and Dominic DiMaggio. It was the nucleus of that bunch in '46, and they were all West Coasters."

Many Red Sox—before, during, and after the Spaceman took flight from Burbank, California, to Fenway Park—have been fellow

West Coasters: Williams, San Diego; Doerr, Los Angeles; Johnny Pesky, Portland; DiMaggio, San Francisco; Dennis Eckersley, Oakland, California; Dwight Evans, Santa Monica, California; Rick Burleson, Lynwood, California; Nomar Garciaparra, Whittier, California; Jon Lester, Tacoma, Washington; Jacoby Ellsbury, Madras, Oregon; and Dustin Pedroia, Woodland, California. Bill offers why he was able to adapt quickly and survive in New England after being selected in the 22nd round of the 1968 draft. "I was quick-witted and I could handle it, but it took you a while. You had to almost completely dislearn everything you had learned west of the Mississippi to survive east of the Mississippi," he said. "You had to have patience. You had to have a temperament to allow people to cut you off, and then you finally found you had the right of way. Everyone gets their turn in New England. It's not a law-and-order type of place. It's more of a cooperation place. People tend to tolerate other people cutting them off, and it's something we just didn't understand, coming from the West Coast."

Boston, Massachusetts, June 25, 1969

With the Red Sox trailing the Cleveland Indians 6–3 in the top of the fourth inning, Boston manager Dick Williams called the bullpen for William Francis Lee. With that, Lee's career went into orbit—well, that is, after he issued a walk to left fielder Duke Sims, the first batter he faced. Lee walked two more, gave up two hits and one run, while striking out in his first at-bat in the pre-designated hitter American League era. A globetrotting life in professional baseball was now in full throttle, and the best was yet to come.

The Spaceman charted his course to the show and explains how he appreciated the path from the back roads of Boston to the star-crossed bright lights. "I won the national championship in 1968 and I went right to Waterloo, Iowa," he said. "I got into a fight with my manager and was benched. I ended up going to Winston-Salem [North Carolina], and did well under that manager. Then I went to Double A for a month. Then I was up to the big leagues. When I first arrived, I didn't have anyone close that led me. I just kind of winged it and learned from rote. I got along and met people. The guy who was my best friend was a bleacher creature that was out there, and I started hanging out with the real common clave of New England: the Somerville crowd, the little mill towns. [I] kind of learned the Yankee values that way. It wasn't the 'Boston Brahman,' which every Red Sox aspires to be, that stay at the Park Plaza. That wasn't my upbringing. My upbringing was back alleys and pool halls."

By the end of 1969, Dick Williams, the man who skillfully maneuvered the Impossible Dream Team through the epic 1967 season, was sent walking. The Hall of Fame manager, however, left an impression on Lee, which lasts to this day. Lee says, "I loved Dick Williams. Dick Williams brought me over to Montreal. He was the greatest manager from the seventh inning and on. He could handle pitching really well. He was a cantankerous kind of a mean guy, but he really had the respect of his bench and all of his players. He was a manager who used them all. Like Casey Stengel said, 'The key to managing is keeping the 17 people that haven't made up their mind away from the six that hate you.'"

Boston, Massachusetts, October 26, 1973

The 1973 Boston Red Sox finished 89–73 and in second place, eight games behind the Baltimore Orioles. Reggie Smith led the team in batting at .303. On the surface of things, the center fielder had done well in Boston—two home runs in the 1967 World Series, two All-Star Game appearances, and one Gold Glove. Boston, however, sent Reggie Smith and pitcher Ken Tatum to the St. Louis Cardinals for pitcher Rick Wise and outfielder Bernie Carbo. Future coconspirators of the Spaceman were now on board. The one-of-a-kind hurler revealed that not everyone was cut out to play in Boston and that Smith was most likely a casualty of that mold. Lee said, "Reggie Smith just crumbled. Like guys like who lived out in the suburbs, he isolated himself back and forth. He was frustrated by that provinciality. He was from Los Angeles, and that really ate him up. No one really thrives under that type of upbringing."

Boston, Massachusetts, July 31, 2004

With the 2003 defeat fresh in every New Englander's mind, general manager Theo Epstein reshaped the roster with a four-team trade at the summer deadline. The 1999 and 2000 batting champ Nomar Garciaparra was shockingly sent to the Chicago Cubs, while the Sox received shortstop Orlando Cabrera from the Montreal Expos and first baseman Doug Mientkiewicz from the Minnesota Twins. Reggie Smith might have had difficulty playing in the city of Boston, but a player who thrived in New England, according to Lee, was fellow Expo, Orlando Cabrera. "Cabrera did fine, but Edgar Renteria, who was from the same town—Cartagena, Colombia, did not survive," Lee said. "If you lack communicative skills, you'll get friggin' hammered here. Cabrera was a street wise-type kid who got along fine."

The Spaceman once again points out that New England is not for everyone and that money plays a big role. "Manny [Ramirez] was a Ritz-Carlton guy. Those are the guys that had a lot of money. Back in our day, we only made $9,500 or $11,000 per season. We would stay in cheap little apartments out on the North Shore and carpool together. That's the only way we survived. Dustin Pedroia, what did he do? He embraced it. 'I'm not gonna get into this rat race. I'm gonna live right next to the ballpark.' He walks to work. You've either got to be an urbanite or a country boy. The suburbanite mentality just doesn't work well in Boston."

Baltimore, Maryland, September 18, 1977

Memorial Stadium was filled with 51,798 fans for "Thanks, Brooks Day," celebrating the 23-year career of Orioles third baseman Brooks Robinson. The Yankees were on their way to their first World Series championship since 1962. Used as both a starter and reliever and always prepared to pitch, no matter what calamities took place the night before, Lee was in the midst of a modest season. "I was not a fan of Don Zimmer," he said. "I like Zimmer as a baseball man. He's a typical middle infielder that does not appreciate pitchers. We formed an anti-Zimmer group called the Buffalo Heads. Fergie

Jenkins was one of the Buffalo Heads with Rick Wise, Bernie Carbo, Jim Willoughby, and I."

The Spaceman sensed the impending "breakup of the band" looming. "The Buffalo Heads realized we weren't going to be together again, that the Red Sox were going to break us up, and they did," Lee said. "They broke us up really big. Carbo was gone. Wise was gone. Jenkins was gone. I was the last one left." But they went out on a bang. "On Brooks Robinson Day, we had a big party and we drank quite a bit," Lee said. "Carbo slept underneath the massage table. The rest of us were in the bullpen hungover and sleeping. Jenkins was asleep in the golf cart. I more or less ran six miles because I knew I may get a chance to get in the game. I used to get hammered, but if I punished myself in the night, I punished myself in the daytime. The phone rang in the second inning, because rookie Mike Paxton got lit up like a Christmas tree. They said, 'Get Jenkins up.' And there's Jenkins asleep in the cart. Walt Hriniak did not want to go wake him up. I was looking over, going, 'Who wakes up a Hall of Famer on the last day of a nothing game to pitch?' That was Zimmer calling down. Jenkins never got into that ballgame. He never got out of that golf cart."

The Sox would rebound from the 4–2 hole that Paxton dug. Bob Stanley ably navigated through five scoreless innings, and Bill Campbell picked up the 27th of his league-leading 31 saves. The Hall of Fame 3-4-5 combo of Rice, Yaz, and Pudge (Fisk) combined for seven hits and four RBIs to power the Sox to a 10–4 victory against the O's and their legions of Robinson fans.

Boston, Massachusetts, June 21, 1972

It's hard to fathom that the Boston Red Sox gave former third basemen Butch Hobson a shot as skipper, but Hall of Famer Ted Williams had to travel to the nation's capital for a chance at managing in the big leagues. Hobson was the Sox manager from 1992 to 1994 who suffered through a 207–232 record during a dismal stretch for Boston.

After an 86-win season as the manager of the Washington Senators in 1969, The Splendid Splinter had a less-than-splendid lineup card for the 1970 to 1972 seasons. His swan-song season as a manager was the first season of the Texas Rangers. En route to a 100-loss tally, Ted Williams brought his Rangers to a half-filled Fenway. Texas sent Oshkosh, Wisconsin's own Bill Gogolewski to the mound, while BoSox manager Eddie Kasko sent fading All-Star Ray Culp to the hill. The game was hardly a pitchers' duel, as neither man made it past the fifth inning. Gogolewski's line was: 4⅓ innings pitched, nine hits, five earned runs, one walk, two wild pitches, and one hit batsman. Culp was culpable for 3⅓ innings pitched, six hits, six earned runs, and four walks. Rangers Jim Panther and Horacio Pina, along with the Red Sox's Gary Peters, were equally ineffective. Sox pitcher Don Newhauser retired the only batter he faced. The only two pitchers who earned their pay for the day were Luis Tiant (who earned the win out of the pen in the 11th) and Bill Lee (who pitched a scoreless ninth and 10th inning.) Second-year outfielder Ben Oglivie hit the second home run of his career in the wild 10–9 affair.

"An intellectual that people didn't know was Ben Oglivie. He went to [four different colleges] and could do a crossword quicker than anybody I ever saw," Lee said. "There were other players that read, but they did not read the type of stuff I read. They read fiction and bad fiction." Lee is one of the game's most well-read ballplayers, "My ideal place in New England to read is right here in Craftsbury, Vermont. I'm surrounded by books and I just sit on a hill in Vermont and read," he said. "I read about discourse, beat poet Gary Snyder, T.C. Boyle, Malcolm Gladwell. I read everything that comes out. I read everything Gore Vidal wrote. I didn't like his fiction, but I loved his essays. Christopher Hitchens' *God is Not Great* was just hilarious. I read Rene Descartes. He was the same way on discourse. There is something out there that creates mathematics. He proved logic, which kind of disproves a lot of the things on Earth. But there is still that uncertainty, when you get into quantum mechanics. You've gotta have faith in something."

San Rafael, California, August 23, 2012
Rousing applause is par for the course wherever and whenever Lee pitches. He pitched and hit the San Rafael Pacifics to a 9–4 win

against Maui Na Koa Ikaika. On a clear night in Albert Park, he threw to catcher D.J. Dixon, who was born the year that Lee played his final major league game, and the Spaceman was in the zone. Management looked brilliant, because the Pacifics would win the North Division of the NABL by one game over Maui. Lee said, "I told them, 'You fly me out and bat me ninth. You don't have to pay me. That's all you have to do.' I ended up pitching nine innings. I went 1–for–3. It was one of those days of perfection: 'days of light gravity,' as Kurt Vonnegut used to say."

Adam Smith could not have been more economical that night. Lee's line was 36 batters faced, 94 pitches, 69 strikes, nine complete innings, eight hits, four runs, and no walks or strikeouts. "I have the largest file in the Hall of Fame as far as archival information," Lee said. "Now with these games where I just pitched and hit, I have two hats in the Hall of Fame, along with two uniform tops, two baseballs, and a baseball bat—all of them are from the age of 60 on. Isn't that amazing?…I've had good days. I've had these remarkable little vignettes of superior full-of-myself stuff, but I get out of the tub now and I have to use two hands. I can see gravity just start to eat me up as I reach 67. That's what puts you in your place."

Atlanta, Georgia, August 24, 1979

In front of 6,757 Atlantans at Atlanta-Fulton County Stadium, back when games took about two hours to play, the Expos defeated the hometown Braves. It was one of those rare seasons, when the Expos drew better at home, as they surpassed the 2 million-mark later in the summer for the first time. Hall of Fame knuckleballer Phil Niekro, who was well known for his complete games, was on the mound for Atlanta. He took the loss and dropped to 16–17 on the season. Opposing him on the hill and no stranger to complete games himself, with 72 in his career, was Lee.

The Spaceman would improve to 12–10 on the season, as the Expos were en route to a franchise-record 95-win season. Hall of Famer Dick Williams' Expos lineup card read: "Warren Cromartie, Rodney Scott, Andre Dawson, Tony Perez, Rusty Staub, Gary Carter, Larry Parrish, Chris Speier." And batting ninth—was

Lee. To recap, that's three Hall of Famers, three All-Stars, two solid ballplayers, and one Spaceman. The 2–0 victory moved the Expos to within two games of the eventual 1979 world-champion Pittsburgh Pirates. Parrish and Carter supplied the home run fireworks, while Lee singled in the top of the seventh off of the knuckleballer.

Further demonstrating that pitching was not his only skill, Lee hit .364 in 1981. "I could hit the knuckleball, I could hit off speed, and I could hit anyone, I thought," Lee said. "I hit .241 for my career in the National League. I didn't get to swing the bat in my prime. In my greatest three years of baseball, I never got to swing the bat. The DH is the most ridiculous statement that was ever created. It's Buckminster Fuller: 'All forms of specialization bring extinction,' and that's why I hate it."

Montreal, Quebec, September 6, 1981

Three years after hosting the summer Olympics, 47,193 Montreal fanatics filed into Olympic Stadium. They witnessed Lee single to left in the fifth inning before leaving the game in the seventh of the 4–3 loss to the Houston Astros. Lee's hit was off of Joe Niekro, who like his brother, served up the knuckleball for more than 20 major league seasons. From 1979 to 1983, the Expos had the highest winning percentage in the National League. Yet despite all the success on the field, they could only muster one playoff appearance in the pre-wild-card days of 1981. The loss on this date was followed by an impressive run by the Expos, who played at a .607 clip in the final 28 games.

At any given time in Major League Baseball, there are typically two to three knuckleballers. The Niekro brothers combined for 539 wins, and in the 1980s they were joined in the knuckleball fraternity by Charlie Hough and Tom Candiotti. Most recently Boston's own Tim Wakefield and the 2012 NL Cy Young Award winner R.A. Dickey dazzled fans and perplexed hitters with the cruel dodginess of the knuckler. Wakefield earned 186 of his 200 career victories for Boston and added three postseason wins for good measure to go along with his two World Series rings. In 2012 the well-traveled knuckler/author R.A. Dickey became the first 20-game winner for the Mets since Frank Viola won 20 in 1990. "Wakefield is a great guy. Think about him. He was one day away from being released, and R.A. Dickey was one yard away from not crossing the Missouri River," Lee said. "Those two guys have had tremendous success, but on the cusp of failure and almost oblivion, where they would've died. It's amazing the fickleness of a knuckleball. Tim Wakefield had a great foundation and body mechanics. He was never one who had that kind of stuff from the waist up. He didn't have the sinker or command of the curveball, but he could do the mechanics of throwing the ball right down the middle. But by throwing the ball right down the middle, you cannot throw the ball right down the middle as a knuckleballer. That's the serendipitous nature and irony of the knuckleball. It doesn't go where you want it to go; it goes where it wants to go.

"I never wanted to be seduced by the knuckleball, even though I've always had it in my repertoire and I've always saved it for old age. I will use it for three innings. But I don't put all my eggs in the knuckleball's basket. It's so unpredictable and so hard to control. It's body mechanics. You have to have a release point that is almost perfect every time. And you have to repeat that. That's Malcolm Gladwell's 10,000-hour rule. You've got to put in 20,000 hours to be a knuckleball pitcher.

Boston, Massachusetts, September 26, 2012

To say the Fenway 100th celebration did not go as planned would be an understatement. While the 2011 Braves suffered a collapse just as bad, they kept their coaching staff and team intact and were headed to the 2012 playoffs. As for the Sox, the highlight of their 2012 September was naming and honoring the All-Fenway team. The starting lineup as voted by the fans: C Carlton Fisk, 1B Jimmie Foxx, 2B Dustin Pedroia, SS Nomar Garciaparra, 3B Wade Boggs, LF Ted Williams, CF Fred Lynn, RF Dwight Evans, P Pedro Martinez, P Lefty Grove, P Jonathan Papelbon, manager Terry Francona, pinch-hitter Bernie Carbo, pinch-runner Dave Roberts. First reserve honors were given to: C Jason Varitek, 1B

Mo Vaughn, 2B Bobby Doerr, SS Johnny Pesky, 3B Mike Lowell, LF Carl Yastrzemski, CF Dom DiMaggio, RF Trot Nixon, P Roger Clemens, P Luis Tiant, P Tim Wakefield, P Dennis Eckersley, P Dick Radatz, and manager Joe Cronin. The second reserve squad included: C Rich Gedman, 1B George Scott, 2B Jerry Remy, SS Rico Petrocelli, 3B Frank Malzone, LF Jim Rice, CF Reggie Smith, RF Tony Conigliaro, P Babe Ruth, P Smoky Joe Wood, P Curt Schilling, P Jim Lonborg, P Bill Lee, and manager Dick Williams. As for the exclusion of Manny Ramirez, Lee suggests why his play didn't resonate with New Englanders, "Manny was tolerated, but he was never accepted because he didn't have that work ethic."

Still one of the game's colorful characters and still throwing strikes, Bill "Spaceman" Lee points to the dugout during a 2012 Red Sox-Yankees game. (Getty Images)

For the Spaceman it was mostly pleasantries and catching up with other revered figures of Red Sox past. When asked about his Hall of Fame teammates, Lee prefers to talk about their lives away from the game. "Yaz, I was just with him. He looked really good," Lee said. "He's working in the garden, taking long walks, and he looked a lot better than he has in years. He's becoming a little bit nicer and mellowing into his old age a little better. Carlton Fisk was there too. He's a cantankerous Yankee, a tough kid. Marichal, Cepeda, and Aparicio—I was with all three of them. I played for Luis Aparicio in Venezuela. Orlando Cepeda, Juan Marichal, and I are very close friends." Lee also described his favorite current Sox, including how much he enjoyed Pedroia. "I like Alfredo Aceves, even though he's had a hard time with the manager. I worked with him," he said. "I like Andrew Miller, the left-hander. I like the way Clay Buchholz pitches. I'm a big Buchholz fan. I like the little wiry guys that overachieve…I love Jose Iglesias. I got to work with him on getting him to hit a little better. He's got some kind of beautiful hands. Pedro Ciriaco has got potential. I like Cody Ross, but the other guys seem to be going through the motions. Bobby Valentine can curb the enthusiasm of Forrest Gump."

Kansas City, Missouri, July 24, 1973

Fenway Park has hosted the All-Star Game three times (1946, 1961, and 1999). The Kansas City Royals hosted their second All-Star Game in 2012. And after five years of at least six Sox stars, Big Papi was the lone Red Sox player. During the previous All-Star Game in Kansas City in 1973, Kauffman Stadium (then called Royals Stadium) opened and hosted its first Mid-Summer Classic. Bill Lee was joined by fellow Boston All-Stars Carlton Fisk and Carl Yastrzemski. The game provided another opportunity for the Spaceman to be managed by Dick Williams, who was now with the defending World Series-champion Oakland Athletics. The game, however, was disappointing for Lee, as he never entered, and Sparky Anderson's National League crew trounced the AL squad 7–1 behind home runs by Bobby Bonds, Johnny Bench, and Willie Davis. Nonetheless, Lee was excited enough that even a chance encounter with a rival couldn't ruin his All-Star Game nod. "I was at the game in the bullpen. It was a big thrill to go the All-Star Game," he said. "I was pretty excited. I stayed at a nice hotel. It was special, except I had to ride in a cab with that asshole…Reginald Martinez Jackson."

Boston, Massachusetts, May 20, 1975

Seven starts, one relief appearance, six wins, five complete games, two shutouts. May 1975 was just another month for the hardworking pitcher. Lee pitched his first of two consecutive Fenway shutouts against the Oakland Athletics. The second followed four days later against the California Angels. The Spaceman held Reggie Jackson and the A's to two hits over nine innings on 78 pitches. In one hour and 51 minutes, only three A's reached base, while Jim Rice and Tony Conigliaro rocked Vida Blue in the 7–0 rout. Four days later, Lee allowed five hits and five walks in a shutout. May was Lee's best month, evidenced by his 33 career wins in the second month of the baseball season. "I remember always getting off to a good start. The years I didn't, I came back right away," Lee said. "I kind of struggled in the late summer, but the weather started getting crisp again, and the ball started not carrying as far. I was a guy who pitched to contact. That was basically my career." However, when you look at his monthly ERA averages, it's hardly a roller coaster ride: April (3.90), May (3.37), June (4.07), July (4.16), August (3.42), and September/October (3.13).

"You had to pick your days when the wind wasn't blowing out and you'd get lucky," he said. "Games when you'd score six, seven, eight runs, because you were gonna give up four. For sure, your ERA was always a point higher at Fenway Park. I had a 3.62 lifetime, but it was more like 4.00 [3.90 to be exact] at Fenway. You had to keep the ball in the ballpark. Don't walk anybody. That was the key to pitching at Fenway."

Brockton, Massachusetts, September 5, 2010

In between minor league stops for the Pittsfield Red Sox of the Double A Eastern League in 1969 and the Brockton Rox of the

Canadian-American Association in 2010, Lee pitched anywhere a ball was handed to him. A throwback to the times of Bob Feller, Satchel Paige, and other noted barnstormers, the Spaceman points to Fenway's first famous resident for barnstorming inspiration, "Babe Ruth used to barnstorm," he said. "They barnstormed around the world. In New England the last guy to barnstorm was Birdie Tebbets." On this particular day, Lee would marvel the 6,126 fans in Campanelli Stadium by pitching 5⅓ innings while allowing two runs and five hits to the Worcester Tornadoes. The crafty lefty left everyone amazed, just as he has did on pitching trips to Cuba, China, and Russia. Lee has no qualms pulling up a chair, pouring a cold one, and settling in for some storytelling while savory a victory, "I continue to play as a ringer. People fly me in, and I pitch games all over the place. That allows me to stay in the ballgame. That's why all these archives end up in the Hall of Fame. They may have run me out, when I was 35 years old, but I've played more after they've run me out. I'm still continuing to play on my own terms."

New Bedford, Massachusetts, June 9, 2012

As the New Bedford Bay Sox prepared for the 2012 NECBL (New England Collegiate Baseball League) season, they played one last exhibition game. Their opponents, the U.S. Military All-Stars, received a larger ovation than the home team, which delighted Bay Sox president Pat O'Connor, who comes from a strong military background. A highlight of the game was the one inning pitched by Lee against former NFL quarterback Doug Flutie and the Army. Manager Rick Miller, Lee's former teammate, dragged Lee, who had driven 400 miles to throw one inning, off the mound. The Spaceman had to make decisions like that for a brief period of time when he served as the manager of the Winter Haven Super Sox of the Senior Professional Baseball Association in 1989. Lee was replaced after seven games as the player/manager but managed to pitch in 22 games. He threw 103⅓ innings for the short-lived Sox. (And by short we mean one of the two seasons of the league's existence.) The counter-culture hero finished with a 3–9 record for the last place Super Sox.

Montreal, Quebec, May 7, 1982

Montreal Expos general manager John McHale and manager Jim Fanning released Lee shortly after his three-inning relief appearance against the Los Angeles Dodgers. It was a bitter end to The Spaceman's career. "Every lefty pitches in the majors until they are 50," he said, "unless they are named Bill Lee." Lee, however, remains optimistic about the game he loves and has even mended some fences. "I patched things up with Jim Fanning this year, when we did the Gary Carter tribute. We tried to get some enthusiasm for the Expos. He has a 21-year-old son that looks just like me. It's the most ironic thing you'll ever see. They may run me out of baseball, but I'm going to continue to play baseball. The funny thing is the venues opened up for me more and more. And I have more wins after the game than I had in the game and I surpassed Satchel Paige." Eddie Feigner of the King and his Court is the only pitcher with more wins, 9,743.

East Brookfield, Massachusetts, September 15, 2012

Cornelius McGillicuddy, born in East Brookfield, Massachusetts, and better known as Connie Mack, spent 50 years as the manager of the Philadelphia Athletics, recording 3,582 wins, nine pennants, and five World Series. Those numbers earned the former catcher enshrinement into the Hall of Fame in 1937. The Tall Tactician, who wore business suits instead of a uniform, was also the owner of the Athletics, while his son Earle played sporadically for the team and served as manager during Connie's illnesses. Grandson Connie Mack III served as a member of the U.S. House of Representatives and Senate, and his great-grandson Connie Mack IV was a member of the U.S. House of Representatives. While Connie Mack Stadium was last used by the Philadelphia Phillies in 1970, Connie Mack Field in East Brookfield was rededicated in 2012 during the 150th anniversary of Connie Mack's birth.

To commemorate the game, East Brookfield battled North Brookfield in honor of Mack's first championship game. The ageless Bill Lee, approaching a 50-year career in baseball, led East Brookfield to a 27–7 victory in the vintage baseball game.

The Spaceman took to the mound and totaled eight RBIs, a result of two run-producing singles and a grand slam over the right-field fence. Lee, who can play center field, right field, and a pretty good first base, sums up his final exploits of the 2012 summer by saying "I hit a grand slam in a vintage game in the presence of Connie Mack the third, fourth, and fifth on their great-grandfather's field. [During] my last at-bat on the field—I hit a grand slam. I'm almost thinking of hanging 'em up. It gives you the bite that you can [still] play…It's the days like that that make the game interesting."

12

Growing Up Pesky

In 2007 I was hired by NESN to write and direct a documentary on the 1967 Impossible Dream Red Sox. So I headed to Fort Myers with my brother to procure some interviews. We were staying at a drab Best Western not too far from the park. And the first morning we came downstairs to find Johnny Pesky sitting in the lobby, drinking coffee from a Styrofoam cup.

"Hey Johnny, you need a ride to the ballpark?"

"Sure, if you're going that way."

Cut to my brother, Scott, and I in our rental Buick, with Pesky in the back seat. Upon arriving at the park, he offered, and we accepted a detailed tour of the Red Sox facility. He kindly offered that we could "take a shit" in the locker room if we were so inclined. Hospitality at its finest! He spit on the ground the whole time…a ballplayer to the end.

—Brett Rapkin, a documentary filmmaker
whose works include *Spaceman: A Baseball Odyssey*

Johnny Pesky will always be known as "Mr. Red Sox." He played stellar ball in Boston for years, managed them for a year and even called their games. The Portland, Oregon, native, who passed away at 93 on August 13, 2012, stood for the best of this great game of baseball. He played the game hard and with heart and remained loyal to the organization that gave him his start in 1940.

Even up to his very last days on this earth, he was seen at Fenway Park, tearing it up with the players. "I used to love to sit and talk to Johnny all the time, as if he was my own grandfather and not Johnny Pesky," pitcher Bronson Arroyo said. "I loved to hear his stories and pick his brain to see where he's been in life...He called everybody 'peckerhead.'"

Since that character resided on the north shore of Massachusetts, it was very common for David Pesky to be interrupted when he was out in public with his father. Fans would come up to their table while they were dining and ask for an autograph, picture, or a simple handshake. "Most people waited for my dad to be finished eating before asking," David said. "Johnny loved it. We used to tease him about it...It was always like a receiving line, and Johnny loved it all—especially the kids. He'd ask the little girls, 'When are you getting married?' and ask the boys, 'What do you play?' He was just so grandfatherly."

For his entire life, David Pesky shared his father with the sport he loved so deeply, its fraternity of players, and all of New England. "I didn't mind sharing my father," he said in an interview just a month and a half following his father's passing and days after a Fenway Park memorial service. "I'm proud of everything my dad did."

In a way the Sox legend, born John Michael Paveskovich, was more of a mascot than Wally the Green Monster. After all, Wally was named after the Green Monster—not the other way around. In contrast, the Pesky Pole was just another foul pole before it was renamed in the player's honor. As the story goes, former teammate Mel Parnell dubbed it the Pesky Pole while calling a game in which the slap-hitting Pesky actually smashed a shot down the right-field line—one of just a handful of dingers he hit at Fenway.

What Pesky lacked in the power department, he made up with solid defending and a reliable bat. Until 1997, when Nomar Garciaparra hit 209, Pesky held the team record of most hits by a rookie. Off the field, Pesky earned arguably even more respect for the way he carried himself and for the service he gave his country. (Like his teammate Ted Williams, he left baseball to serve three years in the navy during World War II.)

Pesky was eventually traded to the Detroit Tigers and later played with the Washington Senators, but he'll always be a Red Sox. He managed the team from 1963 to 1964 and stayed in baseball long after he retired, coaching various minor league teams. For David Pesky, there was never a life without baseball in it. And while he was born in Boston, he said, "I was raised all over the place." His dad would move the family each time he landed a different minor league gig, including places in Michigan, Texas, Arizona, and North Carolina. The Peskys even moved to other countries. "When you're a baseball family, you move," David said. "I remember when I was seven years old. We were in Nicaragua. There we were with a Nicaraguan army major driving us around in a jeep. I remember we used to just drive up a volcano. It definitely wasn't your typical childhood…It wasn't a very glamorous lifestyle, when you're in the minor leagues, and Johnny did his time. We lived in Knoxville Tennessee, and in Lancaster, Amish country. We lived in a trailer."

Eventually, the Peskys settled in Gloucester, Massachusetts. Pesky had spent many years living in Swampscott and always had a strong connection to the north shore. David, now 59, aspired to be a ballplayer but learned fairly quickly that he couldn't follow his father's mighty big footsteps. "I just could never see the fastball," he said before chuckling. "I tried a little bit, but I was a lost cause. And I'm pretty athletic—just with kayaking and hiking—outdoors stuff." David Pesky, however, said his father hated the outdoors. "Here he was with a profession, which he spent his whole life under an open sky, and he didn't like the outdoors at all. Every autumn, a leaf would fall on he ground, and he'd say, 'Take a look at these damn leaves.'"

David didn't follow his dad's baseball footsteps, but he and his dad did play catch all the time. Because of his dad, he also acquired some interesting friends, Pesky's minor league players. "These 18- or 19-year-olds were my playmates," he said.

David said the man behind the "Needle" was one in the same. In other words, what you saw in the media was exactly what you got from Johnny. "He was a good guy. Sure, he'd get angry, but he'd be angry for a total—and I'm being literal—of four or five seconds. He'd just say 'Argh' and smile. He never held a grudge. He was just a sweet, sweet guy. He had a temper, but it just went so quick," he said.

For example, Johnny had just managed a tough game for the Red Sox, and he was livid about losing it. David Pesky recounted, "He had all of the players lined up and he was giving them hell. You could hear a dime drop. I came in at a moment of the highest tension, and I just said, 'Hi, Dad, who won?' and then just ran around. I hadn't been paying attention. Like most kids I wasn't focused on any one thing. Well, Johnny said everybody broke up laughing after that."

David said he's been left with so many great memories of his father, and the various tributes that have been pouring in since his passing have been cathartic. "He was just such a good-hearted man. He was very human. I mean he used to cry at *The Sound of Music* on TV," David said. "He was an emotional guy...an innocent guy. David Halberstam got it best when he said Johnny was an innocent. You'd talk to him for an hour or so, and you just felt he didn't have a mean bone in his body."

And he always wanted to help. "Dustin Pedroia really loved Johnny and took a lot from him," David said. "When [Pedroia] came up and was struggling, Terry Francona told Johnny to go over and talk to Dustin and calm him down. By God, he did. Lo and behold, he broke out and never looked back. Every time they'd get together, they would kid each other. Johnny would say, 'If I had your skills, I'd have hit .400.' He'd play the same game with other pitchers. 'I could hit that softball of yours,' he'd say. The banter was fun, and I noticed, when a new person was on the team, they'd always come up to Johnny. They'd sit next to him and say, 'Hi, Mr. Pesky, I just joined the team.' He'd just say, 'Oh, hey kid, don't call me Mr. Pesky. Call me Johnny.'"

But clearly there must've been some darkness behind the light Pesky shined, right? He must've gotten angry? This Red Sox franchise with a history of crushing losses must have taken it's toll on him. "He'd be down for a couple days, and it wouldn't last. And when they were bad, he'd take the stance: 'Well, we're not a good team this year. We'll get 'em next year. He was just extremely accepting of what the baseball gods presented him," David said. During a typical offseason day, David said, "he'd sit down in his chair, watch hockey or cowboy movies. He loved cowboys. He'd go to a few dinners, various hot-stove league events…the New Hampshire baseball dinner was one of his favorites. Basically, he'd just wait for the baseball season."

During a 2006 ceremony celebrating his 87ᵗʰ birthday, Johnny Pesky stands near the right-field foul pole named in his honor.

His benevolence even extended to the Evil Empire. "He didn't buy into hating the Yankees. They were a professional team, and he respected them. You know Derek Jeter said some beautiful things about Johnny [after his passing]. He loved Jeter," he said. During 2004, when the Sox finally conquered Jeter's Yankees, Pesky, though, played a special role. "To the Red Sox's credit, he was a big part of both championship seasons in 2004 and 2007," David said. "He raised the flags, and it was the right thing to do. He was a fabulous ambassador of the Red Sox."

During that 2005 Opening Day ring ceremony, which preceded a game against those Yankees, Pesky was announced last and, of course, got the biggest hand. "They did it in reverse order of service. They started with the guy that reported last week, and the very last person was Johnny. It was very moving," he said. So what was Johnny's take on finally getting a World Series ring after 60 years in baseball? Well, true to form Johnny walked into the clubhouse, locked eyes with David and his wife, Alison, glanced at the ring, and said with child wonderment, "Look at that!" That was Johnny Pesky. "He was simple. He was not an intellectual person," David said, "but he was very smart at what he did...not so much about other things, and we loved him for it."

David planned to take some infield dirt from the shortstop position at Fenway and plant it within the gravesite of his father. It's a fitting tribute to Mr. Red Sox, who will always have his permanent Fenway Park fixture. "He loved Pesky's Pole," David said. "He used to say, 'It's the best thing that ever happened to me.' 'Ink is good' he'd always like to say, and he wasn't a vain man. But he knew this is a performance business."

But that pole is not his only legacy. "The place Johnny holds in New England is very interesting. He's going to live for the ages, and that's a good thing," David said. "The Red Sox treated him well, and we're all going to miss him. The one consolation of all of this is I know he will never be forgotten."

Johnny Pesky Eulogy

The passing of Johnny Pesky is a profound loss for the family that loved him so dearly and for the team he was so loyal to and that, most notably in the last decade, treated him with such loyalty and affection. On behalf of all of us who loved him, thank you. His passing is a great loss for all his friends and for the millions whose lives he touched.

But weren't we blessed to have such a luminous presence in our midst for many years?

Johnny never aspired or expected to be the celebrated figure that he became. In his mind he was just an undersized kid from Portland, Oregon, the fifth of six children born to hardworking immigrant parents, the visiting clubhouse boy for the Portland Beavers of the Pacific Coast League who wanted nothing more than to be a ballplayer himself someday.

Part of his special allure was that he was a direct connection to a bygone baseball age. He broke in with the Red Sox at a time, when no night baseball game had ever been played in Boston. He played in the World Series in 1946. That was not even on television. As a player he never made as much as $20,000 a year. Nowadays, pitchers are routinely paid much more than that for a single inning. But he was also a reminder that, as much as the trappings around it have changed, baseball is, at its essence, still the same game that it always was: three strikes and you're out; 90 feet from home to first; 108 stitches in every baseball. And the hardest thing in sports is still to hit a round ball squarely with a round bat when it's coming at you at speeds of 95 miles an hour and more.

Other former players have lived to ripe old ages and never became quite as beloved as Johnny. There was never a campaign to make him beloved, never a marketing strategy. It just happened. People came to realize that it wasn't because of what he had been or when he had played. It was because of who he was at his very core.

There was no guile in him. He had very little ego. That isn't to say that he didn't know he was a terrific player. He possessed the competitive fire that is part of the makeup of every elite athlete.

He loved to tell the story of his first day in spring training as a rookie with the Red Sox. He was still a shy kid and was somewhat nervous about how he'd be treated by some of the star players whose socks and jocks he'd washed in the clubhouse back in Portland. He was especially edgy about meeting up again with Ted Williams. Ted was just a year older but had already become a baseball colossus. He'd hit .406 the season before, and his larger-than-life persona and primal animal magnetism had taken the baseball world by storm. Johnny was sitting with some other players that first day, when into the room came Ted, filling it, as always, with his very presence. He pulled up a chair next to Johnny and pronounced, "So you're going to be the new shortstop? You can help us, if you can hit .280." Johnny surprised even himself when he blurted out to the great Williams, ".280? Hell, I can bunt .280!"

And he could. That first season of 1942 he hit .331 and led the league in hits with more than 200 of them. The next season he was in uniform again but not that of the Red Sox. He was in the uniform of the United States Navy. He remained in that Navy uniform throughout the 1943, '44, and '45 seasons. In 1946, after the conclusion of World War II, he was back in his Red Sox uniform and he once again led the league with more than 200 hits. In 1947 he again led the league with more than 200 hits. It is by no means a stretch to assert that, had he been playing ball in '43, '44, and '45, he'd have had 200 hits in those years, too. Six consecutive seasons with more than 200 hits would have punched his ticket to Cooperstown, New York, and the National Baseball Hall of Fame. But Johnny never once complained or regretted that World War II had cost him that chance. The fact is he was even prouder to wear the uniform of his country than that of his baseball team.

Besides, it was while in the navy that he met a beautiful, perky young woman, Ruth Hickey of Lynn, Massachusetts, who was also in the navy. Ruthie was a machinist's mate in charge of starting up the engines of airplanes. She started up Johnny's engine, too. They fell in love and got married. And they stayed in love and stayed married for 60 years, until Ruthie passed away in 2005. She had loved tweaking Johnny that he was nothing special, but she knew, of course, that he was. She adored him, as he did her. After she died he soldiered on, but it was never quite the same for him.

People talk about Joe DiMaggio's 56-consecutive-game hitting streak. That was nothing. Johnny Pesky signed about 560,000 consecutive autograph requests. He never turned one down.

I had a phone call a day or so after his passing from a fellow I had not seen or talked to in more than 50 years. He had never even met Johnny Pesky, but he knew that I was fortunate enough to have known him, and he just wanted to talk to someone about how much Johnny had meant to him. There are thousands of stories just like that.

Pesky was especially close to Dom DiMaggio, who after baseball was even more successful in business than he was on the field. He knew that jobs as a minor league manager or coach did not provide much in the way of either income or security. So on several occasions he offered Johnny the opportunity to join him in his business. But the answer was always the same: "Dom, I couldn't love you more if you were my own brother, but I'm a baseball lifer. They'll have to cut the uniform off me."

He remained in that uniform even after his days as a player, coach, and manager were over, hitting hundreds of fungoes, signing thousands of autographs, and telling what seemed to be tens of thousands of stories about Ted, Dom, and Bobby Doerr. He was a constant reminder of why baseball is the greatest game and of why we all fell in love with it in the first place.

His No. 6 is emblazoned above the right-field grandstand in Fenway Park alongside the retired numbers of other great Red Sox players. Those others are all in the Baseball Hall of Fame. Not Johnny. But in a real sense, he has achieved an even higher station. He is in the heart of everyone who has ever rooted the Red Sox and who loves baseball.

When the Red Sox finally won that historic World Series in 2004, the great moment for many, if not most, of us was not the final out; it was not the celebration on the field. It was not even the grand parade that wound through the streets of Boston and out onto the river. The moment that is seared in our memory is of an exultant Curt Schilling charging into the clubhouse, spotting Johnny, sweeping him up in a giant bear hug, and whirling him around like a rag doll as Johnny wept for joy.

Johnny was always an emotional man. It was said of him that he'd cry at rain delays. As he got deeper into the winter of his life, those emotions tended to bubble to the surface more easily. Two weeks ago Friday, he was at Fenway Park for a luncheon at which the newest members of the Red Sox Hall of Fame were inducted. The room was filled with great old Red Sox ballplayers. Many of them were fluttering around Johnny, like moths around a flame. No one loved him more than the players. He had mentored so many of them. He was somewhat overwhelmed by all the fuss, and sitting in his wheelchair, he was weeping softly, again with tears of joy. When I spotted him, I spontaneously spouted out a couple of verses of a little poem I had written for him some time ago for one of his birthdays. He always got a kick out of it, so I would update it over the years to fit other occasions and recite it to him again. When I finished my recitation two weeks ago, I leaned down and kissed him. I never imagined that I was kissing him good-bye. It's just as well, because then two of us would have been weeping, and there is no crying in baseball—except on that rare occasion when a magic, bright beacon, such as that which was the life and the spirit of Johnny Pesky, fades out of sight.

With your forbearance, this is another updated version of that little poem Johnny liked so much, one last time, just for him.

Here's to you, Johnny Pesky,
You're baseball in this town.
You played, you coached, you managed.
You never let us down.
Two hundred hits a season,

When you played, How's that?
You hold the all-time record
For swings with a fungo bat.
They named a foul pole after you.
The reason, it is clear,
Is you could hit the ball that far
Once or twice a year.
You saw them all, from Ted and Dom,
To Yaz, Big Papi, too.
Seventy years of players
All learned a thing from you.
You're Mr. Red Sox. You're the man!
You're in our Hall of Fame.
You understood this basic truth,
That baseball's just a game.
The game of life counted with you.
To know you, was a pleasure.
Farewell, we love you, Johnny.
You're a Boston treasure.

—Dick Flavin
St. John the Evangelist Church
Swampscott, Massachusetts
August 20, 2012

13

Here Yesterday, Gone Today

by Jess Lander

There's no way I can go play for the Yankees, but I know they are going to come after me hard. It's definitely not the most important thing to go out there for the top dollar, which the Yankees are going to offer me. It's not what I need.

—Johnny Damon, Boston Red Sox (2002–2005),
New York Yankees (2006–2009)

Every sports fan knows that saying good-bye to their favorite players due to trades or free agency is all part of the game, part of the sports circle of life. But it still can hurt. Outsiders might find it ridiculous how attached fans get to people with whom they will never meet in person, never shake hands, or go to dinner. Like movie stars, they hardly seem real at all. But in truth, it's hard not to fall in love with someone that's on your television screen for more than 150 games a year, especially when that person brings you one of the greatest joys in life: victory.

In the initial stages, there's sadness and even anger. After years of undying loyalty, sticking up for them when they made mistakes or when others were doubtful, how could they just leave? But like any breakup, the wound eventually heals. New players come in and shatter the records of the old legends, winning over previously broken hearts. And then after a while, sometimes all is forgiven. Like one's high school years, fans selectively remember the good times—not the bullying, the teasing, or the acne. Even Cleveland will one day get over the night that LeBron James stomped on its heart, crushed its dreams, and spit in its face on live national television. And when that day comes, they'll build him a statue. Well, maybe.

Yet if there's one tribe of fans that has an especially tough time parting ways, whether it's with players they love or players they hate, it's Red Sox Nation. Sox loyalty is like that of your most trusty companion, man's best friend, the canine. But if a player turns on the Sox, it's all over. It doesn't matter if they were a driving force on the World Series team that brought the first championship to Boston in 86 years. "It's pretty clear-cut in our town. If you play well, they love you, and they can be hard on you if you don't, and they think you aren't giving maximum effort. It's not always easy here, even with the best ones," said Dan Shaughnessy, a legendary reporter for *The Boston Globe* and the man who coined the phrase, "The Curse of the Bambino."

Joe McDonald, born and raised in Rhode Island and a Red Sox beat writer for ESPNBoston, said that some players just can't cut it in such a passionate city. "Red Sox fans are extremely loyal, and the one thing they know is they're not casual fans. Everyone talks about the pink hats and stuff, but really, with Fenway and the Red Sox, you don't have casual fans. These people know their baseball. They're passionate about it. There are some players who can handle the pressure of playing in Boston, and some players who can't. Over the years, it's been quite evident, which players can and cannot."

Handling them anything but gracefully, Red Sox fans take breakups personally. It's about so much more than the inconvenience of having to buy a new jersey. But it's not like anyone can blame them either. Known as the most die-hard fan base in baseball but also sometimes as the most obnoxious or rowdy, it can all be traced back to one terrible managerial decision in 1919. It's a decision that took the fall for nearly a century of misery and left a bad taste in the mouths of Red Sox fans, that not even two championships in four years time could erase, though that helped. It all started with The Bambino.

The Curse of The Bambino

George Herman Ruth Jr. was not the kind of player you get rid of. He was the kind of player that comes along once in a lifetime. He was the greatest baseball player of all time, the athlete of the 20th century. But the Boston Red Sox were stupid enough to send him packing, and they paid for it greatly.

The Red Sox won World Series titles in 1915, 1916, and 1918 with Ruth in the Sox rotation. In 1918 Ruth's power at the plate got him a regular place in the starting lineup, and in 1919 he set the single-season home-run record with 29 dingers. On December 26, 1919, it was all over, just like that. Sox owner Harry Frazee sold the Babe to the New York Yankees for $100,000 in cold, hard cash that was rumored to have helped him fund a Broadway play. The baseball gods had seen enough.

In 1920 Ruth nearly doubled his record with 54 home runs. He hit 59 the next year, in addition to driving in 171 RBIs, scoring 177 runs, and batting .378 with an .846 slugging percentage. That was just the beginning. The previously championship-less Yankees grabbed a hold of seven pennants and four World Series titles with Ruth on their side, and the Evil Empire was born. The Red Sox, on the other hand, wouldn't reign again for almost nine decades. This one trade would forever cast a shadow over Red Sox Nation, serving as a painful reminder of what can happen whenever another player flew the clubhouse, whether it was the decision of the player or a bad move by the organization.

It was the start of the greatest rivalry in sports. "The Red Sox gave up their only greatest player in history for basically nothing. That really kicked off the rivalry, and fans never forgot that," McDonald said. "The story became bigger. It became mythical." It became The Curse of The Bambino and it carried on for 86 years. "There is nothing like it in all sports," he said. "When it comes down to it, you really have to say it probably dates back to Babe Ruth, but it's not just all him and that trade." McDonald is right. A lot more has gone on between the two cities to fuel the fire that Babe Ruth ignited.

Red Sox fans know that their players will be tempted by the promise of more money or a new opportunity. Usually it's just business and not personal. But there is a line. To Red Sox fans, leaving Boston and signing with a division opponent is worth a few strikes and boos, but no amount of money is worth crossing enemy lines and signing with the Yankees. That is unforgivable, especially after what happened with the Babe. "The worst thing you can do as a free agent in Boston is sign with the Yankees. There is no greater betrayal," said journalism professor Mark Leccese, a 27-year-season-ticket holder at Fenway Park who grew up in the Boston suburbs. "We realize that players are going to be free agents. We sort of understand all that. Just don't go to the Yankees. We understand it unless you go to the Yankees, and then we don't."

McDonald straddles the line of fan and reporter and sees both sides of the argument. "It takes a lot of courage for a player who plays for the Red Sox to go then play for the Yankees and visa versa, but only because each fan base is so passionate about their players, and they've all been superstars." he said. "To see a fan favorite go to the other side, and in their mind become a traitor, it's tough for fans. They don't let those players forget it."

It's personal, Leccese said, because the rivalry dates back way before baseball. It's so much more than a game. It's economical. It's a defense of turf. It goes all the way back to when there were colonies and when this was a rivalry between the Dutch and the Puritans. The Babe trade was just another instance in the tale, when New York grew bigger and better than Boston. Boston was once the leading U.S. city along with Philadelphia, before New York began to grow, opened the Erie Canal, and eventually took over the No. 1 spot by the late 19th century. "In baseball the rivalry goes back a century, but the rivalry between the cities goes back three centuries," Leccese said. "Boston became a second-tier city, and because of the proximity, it's just always been a contentious stare across Connecticut at each other. There's a long history of rivalry between us and New York. But then baseball was the perfect place to encapsulate it, heighten it, and focus it."

The heated baseball rivalry is well known by even the most casual of baseball fans. It's to the point where, for Red Sox fans, beating the Yankees comes second to almost nothing, including rings. "Like everybody else here, I waited a lifetime for 2004. I waited a whole lifetime, and the sweetest part of 2004 was not necessarily sweeping the Cardinals. It was the unbelievable—you couldn't believe it, even as it was happening," Leccese said, "the Yankees being up 3–0 in the American League Championship Series, and then the Red Sox winning 4–3. The Yankees can have their 27 championships. That series means more to me, means more to a Red Sox fan, than 27 means to a Yankees fan. It was the day you finally slayed the dragon. Eighty-six years of the dragon breathing fire on you, and you finally slayed it, and not just slayed it—but humiliated it."

Yet some Sox supporters believe the rivalry is a bit over the top at this point. Shaughnessy called the way that Sox fans handle their players going to the Yankees "immature," noting that the Babe trade happened nearly 100 years ago. Mike Moran, a Swampscott, Massachusetts, resident with encyclopedic Red Sox knowledge, also believes it's a thing of the past, or at least it should be. "All the Red Sox fans can think of is we used to have Babe Ruth, and then we got rid of him, and he went to the Yankees and became the greatest player that ever lived. But that's not always how it happens. Now [that] that's not happening, we can't blame the Yankees anymore," he said. "No one likes to be abused, and we were abused in that trade. But I don't think there are any more steals. I don't know if anyone really gets outsmarted anymore."

Whether Red Sox fans' hatred for the Yankees is reasonable or not, the hatred is well known to players on the Red Sox roster. One would figure they would think twice before stepping foot into the land of fire-breathing dragons. But that hasn't always been the case.

With Babe Ruth in the rotation, the Red Sox won World Series in 1915, 1916, and 1918. But after trading him to the Yankees, a Sox title drought ensued for the rest of the 20th century known as "The Curse of the Bambino."

The Chicken Man

Third baseman and Hall of Famer Wade Boggs was a repeat offender. He stuck the knife in and then turned it. He threw Red Sox Nation a hook followed by an uppercut. After 11 seasons in a Red Sox uniform from 1982–1992, Boggs signed with the Yankees, won his one and only World Series, and then moved on down the AL East division to the Tampa Bay Devil Rays.

Boggs, given his nickname by Jim Rice for his odd, superstitious ritual of eating chicken before every game, had a strong career in Boston, winning several batting titles and recording seven consecutive 200-hit seasons. But it was also clouded over with a very public extramarital affair with Margo Adams. There were other incidents, including a spat with Roger Clemens over the difference between a hit and an error in one meaningless game. In his final Beantown season, Boggs slumped to .259, a rare dip below .300 for him. Sox fans packed his bags and were ready for his departure. "The fans were sort of done with it," said Shaughnessy, though the famous *Globe* writer noted that watching Boggs win a World Series in New York was a tough pill to swallow.

In fact, Red Sox fans will never be able to rid themselves of the symbolic image of Boggs, the traitor. He made sure of that when after the Yankees won the 1996 World Series, he jumped on the back of a police horse and rode it around the field with his finger pointed to the sky. "Jumping on that horse was like taking the noses of Red Sox Nation and rubbing them in the poop of that horse," said Kevin Hassett of Pembroke, Massachusetts, who's worked in media relations in the sports industry.

Ted Doyle from Hingham, Massachusetts, a former press agent for Ted Williams among other players throughout the years, once had the opportunity to meet Boggs at an All-Star Game in San Diego. Introducing himself as a Boston guy, Doyle didn't expect the cold shoulder that Boggs gave him in place of a handshake. "Boggs, he was always kind of a jerk. I'll never forget meeting him at the All-Star Game. I'm just standing there, and he's waiting to take batting practice. I walk up to him, tell him I'm from Boston, and you would have thought I'd asked him for a loan. He barely murmured anything at all, and that was the end of the conversation," Doyle said. "He was a difficult guy to like and he didn't do himself any favors."

Then, in Tampa Bay, Boggs collected his 3,000th hit, launched the first home run in Rays history, and had his No. 12 jersey retired. In a final act of betrayal, the cut that severed the cord, Boggs tried to wear his Tampa Bay cap when it came time to be inducted into the Hall of Fame, despite having played with them for just two seasons. And it didn't end there. McDonald said that anytime he's seen Boggs at a Red Sox event, he was flashing around his Yankees World Series ring. "Even when he was inducted into the Red Sox Hall of Fame, he had his Yankees World Series ring on," he said. "It's like, 'Oh, come on, are you kidding me? You're going to wear a Yankees World Series ring to a Red Sox event?'"

It's safe to say that the majority of Red Sox Nation didn't mourn Boggs' departure. "For Boggs, as good of a hitter as he was, it was time to go," Moran said. "He was the perfect Fenway hitter, though—a lefty. We were lucky to have him, and you have to sometimes just put these things in the rearview mirror and move forward."

The Rocket

Long before the 11-time All Star, two-time World Series champion (none with the Red Sox), and seven-time Cy Young winner became a poster player for the steroids controversy, Red Sox fans hated Roger Clemens. To Boston, the steroids thing was just another checkmark on the list of why Clemens will never be warmly welcomed back in the Bean, and why his departure was for the best. Guilty or not guilty of steroid use, Clemens will forever be guilty on all counts as a traitor in a New England courtroom.

Clemens' 13 years in Boston from 1984–1996 were supposed to be so much more. He was supposed to be a Tom Brady, a Larry Bird, or a Bobby Orr. He was supposed to stroll into Fenway Park, put the Red Sox up on his back, and carry them to victory over and over again. But that's not how things turned out. The Rocket heated up but never fully launched.

It's not that there weren't good or even great times, because there were. Clemens was, without a doubt, a hero. He nabbed 192 wins in Boston, won three of his Cy Youngs there, and had a World Series appearance. He struck out 20 batters against the Seattle Mariners, the first pitcher ever to record that many in a game. And then he did it again against the Detroit Tigers in his final weeks with Boston. Moran fondly remembers the day Clemens broke the strikeout record. "I was doing work outside, and my father was watching, and he'd come out every 10 minutes and say, 'He struck out another!'" Moran said. "When he came on the team, he was unbelievable. When you talk about greatness, that was greatness."

But then there were the not-so-good times. Game 6 of the 1986 World Series, the game in which Bill Buckner let a ball go through his legs in the 10th inning, might not have even gone to extra innings had it not been for Clemens leaving after the seventh, with the Sox leading 3–2. Though there are multiple accounts of the story, one version is that Clemens asked to be pulled due to a blister on his finger. There were also the prima donna moments, like getting ejected in just the second inning of Game 4 of the 1990 ALCS against the Oakland A's for cursing at umpire Terry Cooney. (That incident would foreshadow his famous bat-throwing episode in 2000, when Clemens was with the Yankees.) The Sox lost that 1990 game and were eliminated from contention. For Moran and many fellow Sox fans, the Oakland ejection was a big sign for concern. "That's not how an adult acts in any situation," said Moran, noting that it's not the kind of thing he even sees from the young players he coaches. "It was so much the opposite of what you'd expect from a professional athlete, especially a great one. There's no reason. There's no excuse, and after that I think everyone thought he was a little bit crazy." Clemens also had a losing season in 1993, never really showed up in the playoffs, and never lived up to his future title as the Greatest Pitcher of All Time while in Boston.

So it wasn't exactly a surprise when Clemens announced he would be leaving Boston in 1997 when Red Sox ownership refused to match his perceived worth, and general manager Dan Duquette made a comment about Clemens being in the "twilight of his career." Signing with the Toronto Blue Jays, a division opponent, for the price tag of $28 million stung a bit, especially after the Texan had expressed interest in playing closer to home as a reason for leaving. The pain sharpened, when the previously plump Clemens shaped up and went a spectacular 41–13 in his two seasons with Toronto, earning the Cy Young Award in both years. Leccese attended Clemens' initial return to Boston, when the pitcher was first with the Blue Jays. "I was there at the game when he first came back, and a lot of us were startled at how different he looked. He'd shed a lot of weight and he got a very mixed reaction—a bunch of boos and a bunch of cheers," Leccese said. But the real traitorous nature of Clemens came full circle in 1999 when Clemens went to the Yankees. "When he went over and signed with the Yankees, it was just all boos all the time," Leccese said.

With the Yankees, Clemens won two World Series titles off the bat, sending Sox fans into a state of déjà vu from the Babe trade, despite most fans not having been alive back then. His postseason play was on the level that Boston had wanted so badly in '86. In 2001 his record was 20–3. Before retiring, he recorded his 300th career win and 4,000th career strikeout. Clemens was indeed the Greatest Pitcher of All Time. "It kind of always hurt when he won that World Series, but he wasn't going to do that for the Red Sox. He had given up on the Red Sox. They had a pretty good system in place, and he chose to go to New York, where they don't really treat the superstar like a superstar," Moran said. "He had no respect for the organization. I think Clemens forced his way out of Boston, and so really, why would you want someone who at that point did not want to be with the Red Sox?"

But to Shaughnessy, the pitcher's demise in the eyes of the Sox fans was both unfortunate and unfair. "Clemens got the crap kicked out of him," he said. "People just didn't appreciate it. He won 192 games here and got no love in return for that."

The Caveman
There was a time when Red Sox fans unconditionally loved outfielder Johnny Damon along with his long, Jesus-looking hair

and untamed beard. With 20 homers and a .304 batting average, he played an invaluable and pivotal role in extinguishing the 86-year curse and bringing the 2004 World Series championship to Boston. In Game 7 of the 2004 ALCS, Damon hit two home runs, the first of which was a grand slam, to help lead the Red Sox to the 10–3 victory against the Yankees that sealed the historic, unbelievable comeback. In that moment, neither Damon nor Red Sox fans ever imagined what would happen 14 months later.

Damon wasn't around for all 86 years of drought, but he was playing for the Red Sox in 2003. He went 0–5 at the plate on October 7, 2003 in Game 7 of the ALCS against the Yankees. Then, with the game tied at five in the bottom of the 11th inning, Aaron Boone hit the infamous walk-off home run, crushing the dreams of Red Sox Nation once again. Red Sox fans can list off a lot of reasons for hating the Yankees, but that one moment would serve as the kerosene that would keep the fire burning for another couple of decades. And Damon seemed to understand that when approaching free agency in May of 2005. Following a World Series win, he expressed his intent to remain in Boston, no matter how many zeros the big-spending Yankees threw at him.

Seven months later he was in pinstripes.

Hassett is like most Sox fans in that he swears he'll never forget Aaron Boone's walk-off homer. Calling it his most painful Red Sox memory, he remembers exactly what he was doing when it happened (about to sign his bar tab). He once viewed Damon, the caveman, the lovable idiot, as Red Sox Nation personified. "He seemed to be the embodiment of the difference between us and them. He epitomized what the Yankees fans hated about us and what we loved about the Sox," Hassett said. "It's more symbolic, really, than anything from a competitive standpoint. Baseball-wise, I was really okay with it. He had a poor arm and he would've gotten more than he was worth at that point. But he hits that grand slam in Game 7 of the ALCS at Yankee Stadium. He plays the role of the typical dirt dog, the hair. He looks like Jesus basically. He's just a scrubby-looking guy, and that was us!"

But as much as Damon's ultimate decision was business, it was politics. The face, which Red Sox owner John Henry once called the face of the franchise, became clean-shaven before the sun rose the next morning, keeping in line with the clean-cut standards of the Yankees and for a price of $12 million more than the Sox were offering. And as quickly as Damon chose pinstripes, Red Sox Nation turned their backs on a traitor. Jesus became Judas. "It was really like something you only see in wrestling. If he had gone anywhere else, it would've been okay, but he went to the Yankees. And overnight, he was this clean-cut New York pretty boy. It was the baseball equivalent of 'turning heel' in wrestling," Hassett said. "And that is what did it for me. It was so easy for him to change that it felt like everything he seemed to embody before was fake."

Damon had joined the ranks of Boggs and Clemens of Brutus and Benedict Arnold. The betrayals just kept coming. "It's like we kept getting beat up by our neighbor over and over again, only for members of our family to join the other side," Hassett said. "It's the Montagues and the Capulets."

Shaughnessy said the Damon backlash serves as the best example of how unreasonable Sox fans can be, getting extremely emotional over what's simply a business transaction. "When they leave, there seems to be a growing, in my opinion, an immature issue regarding players leaving and playing for the Yankees, which is best explained by Johnny Damon," he said. "I thought that was really bad. I find that extremely immature. Damon did a great service here, and there was no comparison with what Boston offered and the offer that he left for. It wasn't the difference of a few dollars. It was significantly different, and the Yankees showed far more faith in his future, and they turned out to be right."

Moran also takes the position that Damon and other players shouldn't have their decisions held against them. "It's a big business. Who would ever deny or want to deny any player from going out and getting what's best for his family?" he said.

But try getting Red Sox Nation to see it that way. The booing was relentless whenever Damon set foot back in Fenway Park. McDonald said that he's never heard a player get booed louder than Damon. All that Damon had done for the Red Sox wasn't necessarily forgotten, but it was null and void. He had three good years with the Yankees, one in which he won a World Series but another where he sat and watched as the Sox won one without him. Damon then spent three seasons with three different teams before being demoted to wandering free-agent status in August of 2012. In 2011 the Red Sox actually claimed Damon off of waivers from the Detroit Tigers to help them make a run at the playoffs, but even if Red Sox Nation was prepared to forgive and forget, which is debatable, Damon wasn't. "They eventually forgave Buckner, but that was different," said Hassett, who seems unlikely to ever have a change of heart about Damon. "He chose to be a villain."

El Tiante

There was one exception, one Red Sox player who made it to New York and back without being disowned by Boston. In fact, he was welcomed back with open arms. After a memorable and legendary career with the Red Sox from 1971–1978, pitcher Luis Tiant went to the dark side for two seasons. He currently resides in New England and has been working as a consultant to the Sox for the last two decades. He also has a Cuban sandwich shop at Fenway Park called El Tiante. Tiant beat the system.

The Sox had taken a bit of a gamble on Tiant. The righty from Cuba is fondly remembered for his Fu Manchu mustache and a cigar in the corner of his mouth. His odd pitching deliveries would contort his body into all kinds of positions. Sometimes he even faced away from the batter as he wound up. He had a stellar breakthrough six years with Cleveland, but after a pair of injury-plagued seasons with the Indians and then the Minnesota Twins, it was uncertain whether or not Tiant had already peaked. Turns out he was far from being done with baseball.

His first year with the Red Sox was slow, as Tiant posted just a 1–7 record with a 4.85 ERA. But he easily won over the hearts of the Fenway Faithful the following season with a 15–6 record and a league-leading ERA of 1.91. He only got better from there and posted three 20-win seasons. His most notable games occurred against The Big Red Machine of the Cincinnati Reds in the 1975 World Series, still one of the greatest World Series to date and a time of insanity for the city of Boston. In Game 1 Tiant went out and pitched a 6–0 complete-game victory while also hitting a single and scoring the Sox's first run. In Game 4 he threw an incredible 163 pitches in another complete-game victory, again scoring what turned out to be the game-winning run. And then in Game 6, one of the most memorable World Series games in history, Tiant's no-decision ended with Carlton Fisk's dramatic and controversial walk-off homer in the 12th inning to force a Game 7.

Leccese can't think of a single player more endeared to the fans in Boston than Tiant, who he described as having the charisma of David Ortiz times two. "In 50 years of going to Red Sox games and going a lot, I don't think there's ever been a player that was as loved in Boston as much as Luis Tiant. I don't even think Yastrzemski was. Yaz was respected, but I don't think he was loved like Luis Tiant. Jim Rice was respected but not loved like Luis Tiant," Leccese said. "If you had been in the ballpark in the '70s, where not only was every seat taken but every step in the aisles was taken—before the fire department stopped it—if Tiant was pitching, almost 40,000 people would be chanting 'Loo-ie! Loo-ie!' There wasn't a player in my lifetime who was more beloved by the fans in Boston."

By the time Tiant left for the Yankees, or the "Junkees" as he famously pronounced them in his thick, Cuban accent, Tiant was at the end of his career. And when he returned, he never received the customary booing that is reserved for Red Sox players that do the unthinkable and unspeakable. During a game in the late 1980s, Leccese remembers spotting Tiant, who was coaching for the Savannah College of Art and Design. "I was at a game, and I looked up six to seven rows behind me in the stands, and he was there with a bunch of kids," he said. "He looked nervous. I'm not sure if he'd been back at Fenway. People started to notice him, and pretty soon there was a long line stretching down the aisle for Luis' autograph. When he came back, people were just so happy to have him back."

El Tiante was inducted into the Boston Red Sox Hall of Fame in 1997 and has retreated to Southborough, Massachusetts. "He loved baseball, he loved playing in Boston, he loved the Red Sox, he hated the 'Junkees' and he was a hell of a pitcher," Leccese said.

To Red Sox fans, signing with the Yankees is like signing on the devil's dotted line, but it's not the only kind of breakup that they've endured. Leccese has seen Red Sox breakups go one of two ways. "When players leave the Red Sox, there's really two kinds," Leccese said. "There's the ones where we blame the player, who decided to walk away from Boston and there's the ones, where we blame the front office, where they were traded or weren't given reasonable contracts." This determines how Red Sox fans will respond to a player during a breakup and whether they slash the tires of the player or manager.

A close comparison to the Babe trade is the trade of Sparky Lyle—who had 69 saves in five seasons in Boston—to the Yankees in 1972. Arguably the second-worst trade the Red Sox ever made, it was another personnel decision that was one-sided. Boston got virtually nothing for him. The Sox received Danny Cater, who hit just .262 in his three seasons in Boston, and a player to be named later. That turned out to be Mario Guerrero, who only lasted two years with the team. Lyle, on the other hand, went on to have a phenomenal career, becoming the first relief pitcher to win the Cy Young Award. He also won two World Series rings with the Yankees. "Every time he got a save," Moran said, "it hurt."

Then after the 1980 season, Sox general manager Haywood Sullivan traded Fred Lynn and "the Rooster" (Rick Burleson). Worse still, he lost catcher Carlton Fisk, the future Hall of Famer who hit the most dramatic home run in team history during the 1975 World Series, to free agency when he accidentally mailed Fisk a new contract a day after the deadline. Fisk then signed with the White Sox. It was as if the greatest band of the 1970s had broken up. "When Fred Lynn and Carlton Fisk were let go, I think that was like a punch in the stomach to a lot of fans, because it really hadn't happened too much before. No one had really experienced two great guys like that leaving at the same time," said Moran, noting that free agency was still fairly new and that he'd never felt more betrayed by the Red Sox. "Fisk, he was a hometown guy. He hit that home run to beat the Reds. Losing Fisk, that was a big blow to the team. I think they lost the trust of their fans. At the time it was apparent they were just shooting for money and did not make wise decisions. They were not a great organization."

Because the three players had come up through the Red Sox farm system and are still loved and talked about by Red Sox Nation today, the dismantling of the team fell solely on the shoulders of Sullivan. The Rooster, who was loved by the fans for his Dustin Pedroia-like work ethic, even returned in the early 1990s as a coach for the Red Sox. They were the kind of Sox players who are cherished long after their time and were invited back to 100th anniversary celebrations at Fenway Park. They are the ones that got away. "No one ever blamed those players," Leccese said. "There's nothing more exciting to a Red Sox fan than to have a player come out of their minor league system. You feel like you know them because you saw them when they were kids. Maybe you were at their first game; it creates a bond."

And in 2012 Red Sox Nation lost another fan favorite when hated manager Bobby Valentine had first/third baseman Kevin Youkilis traded to the White Sox. Youk's batting stance was untraditional at best, but at times he was the best hitter the Red Sox had in their lineup, stepping up in the absence of Manny Ramirez or during the slumps of David Ortiz. He was unbelievably dependable at first base, going a record-setting 238 games without an error. And he was welcomed to the plate every game (even on the road) with a booming "Yooooooouk!" that sounded like fans were booing. He was such a part of Boston that he even married the sister of legendary Patriots quarterback Tom Brady. "Youk has always been a fan favorite," McDonald said. "He was a guy that should have played in the NFL—the way he goes out and plays the game of baseball, always playing hurt, and it didn't matter, and he always tried to play through it, and fans knew that."

The trade was bittersweet for Sox fans. Youk and Valentine had an issue earlier in the season, when Valentine publicly questioned his physical and emotional commitment to the team. The relationship between manager and player was obviously strained, and fans believed that Valentine was responsible for driving off their beloved baldy. But at the same time, all good things must come to an end. With the promising young talent of Will Middlebrooks, another Boston-groomed player ready to step in for the older, injury-plagued third baseman, it was simply time. Following a tip of his hat, Red Sox fans erupted into their "Yoooooouk!" cry one last time as "the Greek God of Walks" stepped up to his last at-bat with the Sox and fittingly hit a triple. "He always said how much he loved playing in Boston right up to the end, and the fans didn't blame Youkilis," Leccese said. "He didn't have control over being traded. So when he came back for his first game, he was cheered."

And that he was. He returned to Fenway the next month in a ChiSox uniform, receiving yet another booming standing ovation as he went 3–for–4 with two doubles and a run against his old friends, giving the Fenway Faithful a second chance to get closure from his departure. "The ovation he received was one of the loudest I've ever heard for a returning player," McDonald said. "He always knew that he was well respected in this town, but I don't think he could truly appreciate that until he left and came back and got that ovation."

Moran agreed wholeheartedly. "I think people just really wish him well, wherever he goes," said Moran, who at the time of that statement, might not have even considered the possibility that where Youk would be going next was none other than New York, and not to Citi Field either. In December, Youkilis did the unimaginable and signed a one-year, $12 million-contract with the Yankees, begging the question of whether or not the "Yoooooouk!" cheers at Fenway would transition into boos. The verdict won't be out officially until a pinstriped Youkilis first steps up to the plate in Fenway, but judging by past history, it's likely he'll escape the crucifixion of the likes of Clemens, Damon, and Boggs, and fall into the unique category of Tiant, jumping ship in the dwindling years of his career but closing out forever as a Red Sox.

In the cases of blaming the front office, Red Sox fans can be just as harsh as they are on the players. In 2012 new manager Bobby Valentine was brought in to revive a team that had suffered a historic September collapse, going 7–20 and blowing a nine-game lead for the wild-card. But there was nearly a second Boston Massacre, as Valentine endured an entire year of loud and angry disapproval from Red Sox Nation. The fans tirelessly begged for his firing until it finally happened, following the horrible season in which the Sox lost 93 games and finished last in the AL East while Baltimore—yes, the Baltimore Orioles—made the postseason. "It was quite a culture shock for these players with Bobby Valentine. He's a totally different kind of manager than Tito, and you can forget the fact that he went a span of 10 years without managing in the big leagues," McDonald said. "That's a big difference. In those 10 years, the players change, the X's and O's are the same, but the players are different. The majority of these guys have had Tito for eight years, and it was a big culture shock for the players and for Bobby."

Valentine didn't have the best timing either. After a golden decade that featured two World Series championships and a seven-year span of making the playoffs every season, Valentine came in to pick up the pieces, following the huge September collapse and two straight seasons in which the Sox missed the postseason. "I don't think it was a hatred for him. Fans were just upset," McDonald said. "How could this team go from two World Series in four years to just falling apart? This team just hasn't been winning, and I think—even if it was Francona and they failed to make the postseason again—I think it would have been just the same."

Among the Red Sox's history of subpar management, Sullivan will always be remembered as the guy that let go of Boston's beloved Tiant and Fisk, while Sox owner Frazee will forever be the man who sold the Babe and the Red Sox' winning ways down the Charles River. But when manager Terry Francona and GM Theo Epstein left soon after the 2011 collapse, leaving the team in shambles, the fans didn't blame them. It was these men that had brought Red Sox fans to the promised land, and they would never be anything short of gods. "Theo Epstein and Tito Francona brought this team two World Championships, which this city hadn't had since 1918, and that's how we'll always see them," Leccese said. "Theo Epstein and Terry Francona should never have to buy a beer in this town, because they brought us two championships when we had been starving for 86 years."

Nomaaah!

Not all players leave with such appreciation or unanimous well wishes from the fans as Fisk or Youkilis. The ones that stop hustling, exaggerate injuries, attract negative media attention, or make selfish demands are the ones who, in the words of Moran, "are put in the rearview mirror." It's these kinds of players that Red Sox fans ultimately decide to cut ties with before stepping on the gas. It's for the best.

Shortstop Nomar Garciaparra was one of those players. One would have a tough time finding a Red Sox fan who denies that Garciaparra, a two-time AL batting champion and five-time All-Star, was one of the better players in Sox history. "Nomaaah," as fans would cheer when he walked up to the plate, was unquestionably loved. He was Mr. Boston.

But the relationship started to split at the seams before the 2004 season. Under the new management of Epstein, Garciaparra was included in talks to be part of a trade for Alex Rodriguez, who at the time was with the Rangers. The trade fell through, and Garciaparra returned for 2004, but he spent the first 57 games of the season on the disabled list with an Achilles tendon injury. Garciaparra was also approaching free agency at the end of the year, and Red Sox management believed he would be on his way out because of resentment over the A-Rod talks. Moreover, he said he would need considerable time off for the rest of the season because of his injury. It appeared that Garciaparra, who was supposed to spend his entire career with the Red Sox, was unhappy and had one foot out the door.

Before McDonald covered the Red Sox, he said that Garciaparra was his favorite player. He was the first player he talked to when he crossed the line from fan to reporter, stepping into the clubhouse for the first time in 2002. But meeting his hero was not what he had hoped. "I had such high expectations. I respect the way he played the game. He played the game hard, played the game right, but I was just disappointed by what I saw," McDonald said. "I didn't see the person I saw at Fenway all those years or watching on TV. To the time they traded him, I never saw that same type of person off the field that I did on the field."

When it came down to it, the Red Sox needed to improve their defense if they wanted to make a run in the final months of the season. Garciaparra was traded to the Chicago Cubs in a four-team deal at the trade deadline. "I love Nomar. I saw him as a hit machine, which he was, getting more than 200 hits in a year. I loved watching him play," Moran said. "But he was too inconsistent and he was injury prone. I think people know it. They know that getting rid of Nomar was not a bad decision despite his greatness."

And whether fans agreed with the deal or not, everything changed less than two months later. The Red Sox won the World Series for which Garciaparra had strived so hard. Red Sox Nation, though, realized that the trade may have been for the best. "It reached a point that he didn't want to play for this team anymore, and he made it clear, so they traded him. We won the World Series after. If he had stayed in this town, they would have built statues for that guy," Leccese said. "But he wanted out. Nobody wants to cheer for someone when they come back and say, 'I don't want to stay in your city.'" After the trade, Red Sox fans began to trust in Epstein, like they did in esteemed Patriots coach Bill Belichick.

If Nomar had stayed, there might never have been a 2004 World Series win to begin with. "I truly believe, and a lot of people feel the same way, that if that trade doesn't happen in 2004, that team doesn't win the World Series," said McDonald, who noticed the difference immediately after Nomar's departure. "He was miserable and when he left the dynamic of the clubhouse changed. The dynamic changed when he was traded, and I truly believe that if Tito doesn't make that trade, we don't win the World Series."

The Problem Children

Sports fans have an endearing habit of turning a blind eye when their heroes mess up, as long as they're still performing. As far as fans are concerned, if the *W*s are still coming in, what athletes do off the field or on their personal time is none of their business. When the San Francisco Giants won the World Series in 2010, a year after star pitcher Tim Lincecum was caught in possession of marijuana, the city erupted into cheers of "Let Tim smoke!" (See also: Bryant, Kobe; Vick, Michael; and Roethlisberger, Ben.) The biggest problem? Whether or not court dates interfere with gameday. But sometimes it gets old. Sometimes the ego outgrows the city; such was the case with slugger Manny Ramirez. "He had been so good for so long, and I just loved watching him hit," Leccese said. "He was an eccentric character, but it got to the point where he simply refused to play for the team anymore. The team had no choice but to trade him, and I think people just put him out of their minds."

For a while, Manny being Manny—which McDonald insists was real, not an act—was kind of cute. The power-hitting outfielder with a carefree attitude was certainly a character but a loveable one at that, especially when he was hitting home runs. And gifted players like Ramirez are allowed to be a little crazy. There were incidents like when he climbed into the scoreboard during pitching changes or talked on the phone during games. There was the time he high-fived a fan in the middle of the play, thankfully still getting the ball to Pedroia in time, and the time he spoke to media during spring training for the sole purpose of auctioning off his neighbor's grill. And, of course, there were the many hairdos of Manny, from his long dreadlocks, to the Chia Pet cut, to the style that can only be described as Al Sharpton bedhead. "Manny is in a category of his own," McDonald said.

Moran looks back fondly on the Manny years. "I was watching batting practice one day, when the ball came up to the wall, and you could not even try to catch it. It was still accelerating. That's how hard he hit," he said. "People forget that one of the reasons we won those two World Series was because of Manny. You need a guy that's the backbone of the team. I loved the stuff that he did. When he caught the ball on the wall and high-fived the fan, it was funny. It's funny how fast the talent just fades."

But there was also the constant toying with Red Sox fans over wanting to be traded before changing his mind at the last minute. There was the toddler-like tantrum, boycotting spring training to get what he wanted, though he never won, the sitting out for questionable injuries, and the recurrent lack of hustle to get on base. "I was usually of the opinion that the good outweighed the bad with him. He was one of the greatest, if not the greatest, hitters of his generation—such a force in the middle of the lineup," Hassett said. "But sometimes it was just like, 'What the fuck Manny? Run it out through first base, make an effort out in the field, stop hanging out with the scoreboard guys behind the Monster between innings.' We're not asking for much, I don't think. You would just scratch your head sometimes with that guy."

The first big incident was in 2003, when Ramirez missed a game during a Yankees series because he was too ill to play but was then spotted at a bar with Yankees player and friend Enrique Wilson. It surfaced that same year that Ramirez tested positive for performance-enhancing drugs. The Red Sox, who must have had an idea of what was to come, put Ramirez on waivers, but nobody would claim him and his monster contract.

Still more importantly was what Manny did on the field. In 2004 he led the league in home runs, slugging percentage, and OPS (on-base percentage plus slugging), proving to be the key player on the team that won the World Series for the first time in 86 years. The World Series MVP was a hero. He was untouchable, and nothing could taint him. So it seemed.

Yet there was just something about Ramirez that was a little too familiar, something about him that hit a little too close to the likes of Clemens. He was hot and cold in both his play and mentality. In 2006 Ramirez spent half of the season hot at the plate—at one point going on a 28-game hitting streak—and then the other half sidelined by an injury, which many questioned. His 2007 championship season was not up to snuff with 2004's. He, however, stepped it up for postseason play, hitting four home runs (including a walk-off, three-run homer in Game 2 of the ALDS) and 16 RBIs while batting .348.

The 2008 season started off with Ramirez hitting his 500th home run, but his last season with the Red Sox would not be remembered so much for his play. He got in a heated, mid-game dugout altercation with his own teammate, Youkilis. This was the same game that memorably sent Coco Crisp flying to the mound at Rays pitcher James Shields and subsequently cleared the dugouts for an all-out brawl between the two teams. Ramirez had yet another altercation that season when he pushed the elderly Red Sox traveling secretary Jack McCormick to the ground. Just days before he was traded, the final Manny-being-Manny moment in Boston occurred. After being penciled into the lineup against the Yankees, Ramirez decided he would not be playing—just minutes before the game.

After that his days were numbered. It was way past three strikes, and Manny was out. On July 31, 2008, Ramirez was traded to the Los Angeles Dodgers in a three-way deal that also included the Pittsburgh Pirates. "Manny played great here and he hit great here. He was a very good demonstration of fans loving a guy, no matter what he did. He quit on them every now and then, and it didn't matter. He was such a good hitter. There was nothing he could do to disappoint them," said Shaughnessy, who fell off the Manny bandwagon long before most of Red Sox Nation. "Nobody wanted to hear it, because he was too good of a hitter. He shot himself out of town, and that made people mad. They finally turned on him and saw him for what he was personally."

The prize for the Sox out of the deal was outfielder Jason Bay, who made an immediate impact upon his arrival in Boston. Since then Manny has received two suspensions for testing positive for performance-enhancing drugs. After the second one, he chose to retire rather than serve his suspension. He bounced around from the Dodgers to the Chicago White Sox to the Rays for short, disappointing stints on each. He returned to baseball with the A's organization in 2012 but was released after serving his 100-game suspension. Red Sox fans can agree: they said farewell to Manny when the time was right.

In 2012 the Red Sox made history. On August 24 in the blockbuster deal of the year, if not many years, the Red Sox purged itself of the beer-drinking, fried chicken-eating Josh Beckett; the injured, over-the-hill Carl Crawford; the power-hitting but expensive Adrian Gonzalez; and utility player Nick Punto in a nine-player exchange with the Dodgers.

There was a time when Josh Beckett was the Red Sox's ace and when Carl Crawford and Adrian Gonzalez were pegged to be the Red Sox revivers. But following the September demise and the Beckett-led beer and chicken clubhouse scandal, the honeymoon was over. He and some of his bullpen mates also were in the country music video for a song called "Hell Yeah, I Like Beer." The finishing touch on his grounds for dismissal? His abysmal 2012 marks of a 5–11 record and 5.23 ERA prior to the trade. The guy, who went 20–7 from the mound in 2007 and led the Red Sox to a World Series championship, was no more. "With Beckett it got to the point where fans were asking, 'Well, what have you done for me lately?'" Leccese said. "After the whole collapse [of 2011], it's a tough market to play in because it gets so much coverage from so many media outlets, and people pay so much attention to it, and you always have to be saying the right thing. Those guys didn't always do it."

Crawford turned out to be a disappointment, like many players that the Sox have acquired in the past from within the AL East division. (See also, pitcher Torrez, Mike.) Acquired from the Yankees, Torrez allowed a three-run homer to Yankees shortstop Bucky Dent in the 1978 divisional tie-breaker game, which prevented the Sox from reaching the playoffs. Crawford, who the Red Sox signed away from the Rays in 2010, was a hitting and stealing machine until he got to Boston. Red Sox Nation waited and waited for his bat to heat up but to no avail. Crawford was a dud. He started 2012 on the DL, came back for one month, and then underwent season-ending Tommy John surgery. He lasted less than two years of his seven-year, $142 million contract.

And though Gonzalez did well for the Red Sox and was the biggest loss of the three, he did not live up to his massive contract and previous years' production. In 2012 he also was one of the leaders in a Red Sox mutiny against Bobby Valentine, sending a text to management, calling for a meeting about the failing manager. Following the trade he gave a big middle finger to Bobby V and the Red Sox front office in the form of a three-run homer in his first Dodgers at-bat.

But Gonzalez only hit two more home runs that season and batted under .300, Beckett won only two of seven starts, and Crawford remained on the DL. After taking on more than $270 million to its payroll over the next six years, the Dodgers didn't make the playoffs. The Red Sox, on the other hand, cleared their three highest-salaried players and some bad juju. McDonald, privy to what was going on behind closed doors, believed it was absolutely the right move. "Josh Beckett was miserable in Boston. He needed to move on," he said. "It was the right time for the Red Sox to move him. Adrian Gonzalez never turned into the kind of player for the Red Sox that he should have been. He did well, but he was brought in to put up numbers and win games, and that never really happened. Crawford is a great guy. His work ethic is unbelievable, but unfortunately it didn't work out in Boston. He's one of those guys who can't play in a market like Boston."

Fans generally agreed that it was time for a Red Sox face-lift, but now what? How was the trade going to fix the very broken team? "When you unload all those salaries, you've got to have something to show for it," Moran said, "and they don't have anything to show for it yet." Time will tell.

The Tragic Figures

And then there's Tony C. He didn't leave for an archrival. He didn't get traded unfairly or leave on a bad note. He left the Red Sox due to a rare and terrible fate that Red Sox Nation will never forget.

"It was a really tragic thing that Boston had to go through twice," Doyle said. "It's the most tragic thing that ever happened to the Red Sox."

Tony Conigliaro was the start of Leccese's love affair with the Red Sox. "I come from an Italian-American family from the Summerville and Burlington area, and when I was a young boy, the Red Sox brought up a young star, Tony Conigliaro, who was an Italian-American from the Boston suburbs. He was like me. He was 13 or 14 years older than me, but he was an Italian-American kid from the Boston suburbs, a big star, and he was my first baseball hero," Leccese said. "Every day I would clip stories out of the newspapers of him and paste them in a scrapbook. That was like the beginning of a real attachment. I had all these older men in the family—my dad and my uncles—and they all said the same thing. 'You're a hopeful little boy, thinking that the Red Sox are going to

Red Sox teammates surround Tony Conigliaro during a 1967 game against the California Angels. After the star outfielder was beaned and nearly died, his career would never be the same.

win the World Series.' They all said, 'They're a bunch of bums. They always were bums.'"

Conigliaro was no bum. He was just 17 years old when the Red Sox signed him in 1962, and he was brought up to the majors by 1964. The following year, he led the league in home runs with 32 and was the youngest home run champion in AL history. An All-Star selection in 1967, he reached the 100-career-home-run mark, the second youngest in MLB history to do so. It was clear that Conigliaro, who was both a chick magnet and a pitch magnet—he was known to crowd the plate with his batting stance and broke several bones from getting beaned by pitches—was going to do great things for the city of Boston. He was a hometown hero.

But it didn't end well for Conigliaro and it ended quickly. On August 18 of that same 1967 Impossible Dream season, Conigliaro took a pitch from California Angels pitcher Jack Hamilton that shattered his cheekbone. He was taken out of Fenway on a stretcher as his adoring fans watched, horrified. A doctor later told him that if the ball had struck him one inch higher, it could have killed him. Conigliaro admitted later that he had thought he was going to die. Although he lived, he endured severe damage to his left retina, and his career appeared to be over. Both Conigliaro and Boston were devastated.

"It was like everybody in New England was Tony C's dad. When he went down, it was a huge emotional letdown and yet at the same time, it served as the catalyst to drive that team to overachieve," Doyle said. After Conigliaro's injury the Red Sox went to the World Series for the first time in 21 years. It was also the team's first winning season in nine years. The Red Sox had breathed life back into New England, but there was still a gaping hole in the lineup where Conigliaro used to be. "People thought of him as one for the ages," Doyle said. "If he had stayed healthy, people had thought he was going to be like Ted Williams. If Tony hadn't gone down, Yaz probably wouldn't have won the Triple Crown, because Tony probably would have had more home runs than he did."

A year and a half later, Conigliaro made a remarkable return to the Red Sox in 1969, hitting 20 home runs and being named

Comeback Player of the Year. In 1970 he hit a career-high 36 home runs. "When he came back, it was almost like people were afraid to watch. They were almost afraid to see him fail," Doyle said. "When he had a great year, it was an incredible story."

Yet his eyesight began to deteriorate from the beaning, and it was clear that he would never be the same player he was before that fateful day. He was traded to the Angels, the very team that almost cost him his life, for one year in 1971. He hit just four home runs and batted .222 and retired at the end of the season. Like Leccese, Moran also had a strong connection to Conigliaro, who grew up in Moran's hometown. "When Conigliaro ended up playing for the Angels, no one wants to see a hometown guy play for another team, but people were more relieved and happy for him that he was back in baseball. It would have been an issue, but he was so badly injured, and everyone was happy he was alive," Moran said. "That whole story is really tragic, going through the tunnel, and he basically died, really a tragic story the whole thing. He was so good so quick, and then it was all gone because of one pitch."

A few years after retirement, the tenacious Tony attempted yet another comeback in 1975, returning home once again to the Red Sox. But he didn't even make it through the whole season, retiring for good and narrowly missing the Sox winning the AL pennant and reaching the World Series again. The lasting effects of one pitch ruined what could have been a Hall of Fame career. But Conigiliaro, born in Revere, Massachusetts, is still revered by Red Sox Nation.

Even for the most emotional Red Sox fans, time heals all wounds. They forgive and forget—and all the clichés—even the worst offenders. "It happens time and time again," Moran said. "Guys go, and when they come back they get cheered. Even Bill Buckner got cheered. When he came back, he got a big ovation. He always gave 100 percent, so why not give him a big ovation?"

Yes, Red Sox Nation even forgave Bill Buckner, most remembered as the goat of the 1986 World Series for allowing a ball to go through his legs, which led to the winning run in the 10th inning that kept the Mets alive on the night Boston could have closed it out. The Mets then went on to win it all. It didn't matter that Buckner, an incredible hitter, had played a huge part in the Red Sox reaching the World Series. It didn't matter that Clemens had left the game with a blister when the Sox were leading; or that closer Calvin Schiraldi blew the Red Sox's 5–3 lead with two outs and two strikes; or that Bob Stanley threw a wild pitch to allow the tying run. All of the blame flooded through Buckner's open legs; one error did him in. "If you were watching that series, you realize that Bill Buckner's error was one thing that contributed to their loss in that game and the series," Doyle said. "Buckner came to symbolize the failure and he owned a piece of it, but so did the whole team, particularly three or four other guys who had made worse mistakes. Yeah, he made an error, but it was in the 10th inning after they blew a two-run lead, and it wasn't even the end of the World Series. They lost another game after that. He should have been so insulated from this, but it was just 68 years of frustration being focused on one moment unfairly."

Then came the heckling, booing, and death threats that all but ran Buckner out of town before he was released mid-season in 1987. In his 1993 *Sports Illustrated* article, Leigh Montville wrote, "A convicted felon, the perpetrator of the most heinous crime can return from a stay in any prison and attempt to remake his life. This happens every day. Bill Buckner cannot be rehabilitated. No amount of good works or public penance can repair the damage he has done. He let a bouncing baseball slip through his legs." And that's exactly how Buckner must have felt. "If Tony C is the saddest thing to happen to the Red Sox, Bill Buckner's character defamation might be the most tragic thing that happened to the Red Sox," Doyle said. "People that understand baseball know it wasn't true, but it really did destroy his life. He felt terrible about himself for decades."

Every Red Sox fan that watched that moment still painfully remembers it like it was yesterday. Each remembers where they were and what they were doing. Some were likely just about to pop a bottle of champagne. Buckner, though, returned in 1990 to retire with the Red Sox and he received a standing ovation from the fans, who definitely hadn't forgotten but seemed to have forgiven. And in 2008, after the Red Sox had finally gotten those World Series wins, Buckner returned to Fenway once again to throw the ceremonial first pitch on Opening Day. He received a standing ovation that lasted for four minutes. The elephant in the room—Game 6 of the 1986 World Series—appeared to have shrunk. "Afterward, he met with the media and he was crying because of the reception he got from the fans," McDonald said. "He couldn't hold back the tears. He was really choked up about it. No matter what happens, when these guys come back, they're not forgiven, but it's like, 'Okay, you've always been part of the Red Sox family, and we take you back.'"

In similar fashion, Garciaparra returned on March 10, 2010 to sign a one-day contract with the Red Sox, so he could retire in Boston, where he felt he always belonged. That May the Red Sox celebrated Nomar Garciaparra Night in honor of his contribution to the team. In 2012 he, Buckner, Fisk, and many other ghosts of Red Sox past came back to Boston for Fenway's 100th anniversary celebration. All were welcomed back with cheers of appreciation. All grudges seemed to have been dropped.

Without the 2004 and 2007 World Series wins, however, McDonald said fans might not be so welcoming to their former heroes. "If the Red Sox still hadn't won, if The Curse was continuing on, I think that is a different dynamic," he said. "Because they won the World Series, it's a lot easier for fans to forget the past and move on."

And so for the players with whom the wound is still fresh, the damage too great, or the cut too deep, they are not without hope. "The fans are pretty generous here for the most part. If Manny came back now, sure, there would be memories of the home runs and good times," Shaughnessy said. "For the most part, when guys come back it's pretty good."

Leccese agrees, stating that even Damon will eventually shed his scarlet letter. "In five years when his playing career is over, and he comes back for some ceremony or something at Fenway Park, Damon will get a huge standing ovation," he said. "It will have receded into the past, and like any other breakup, after a lot of time goes by, you tend to remember the good times."

———•——

Born in Peabody, Massachusetts, Jess Lander, a writer and dating columnist for the *Napa Valley (California) Register*, is known to preach the gospel of Boston sports to anyone who's listening, and especially to those who aren't.

Acknowledgments

J on and Allie would like to thank Adam Motin, Jeff Fedotin, Noah Amstadter, and everyone at Triumph Books for their support and guidance on the project. We're looking forward to keeping this wonderful relationship going. Thanks to Jess Lander for her professionalism, thorough reporting skills, and for knocking her essays way out of the park. Thanks to Matthew Mayo for his enthusiasm, support of the project, and contributions. The authors would especially like to thank Fred Lynn for taking the time to contribute a foreword, Karl Ravech for an impressive introduction, and Bill Lee for being Bill Lee. Thanks to the following for their assistance in helping us shape this book and make it what it is: Tim Wakefield, Adam Pachter, Hank Garfield, Ben Cafardo, Bronson Arroyo, Sean Casey, Angie Frissore, Mateo Vosganian, Saul Wisnia, Mike Zhe, Bill Grogan, Dick Flavin, David Pesky, Pat O'Connor, Ken Walsh, Rob Cordrry, Rob Kissner, Nicole Chabot, Brett Rapkin, Brian Kiley, Glen Miller, Carol J. Merletti, Leah Tobin, and all of those who contributed. The authors would also like to thank Rich Tarantino for his love and support but not for sitting this one out. We missed the Sweater Pimp on this one.

Jon Chattman thanks...

I would personally like to thank the Boston Red Sox for picking 2012 to be their worst year in half a century. There is no greater gift for an author than to seek fans' positive comments during a season that's so historically negative. Moving on, I would like to thank my wife, Alison, for her patience with all of the hats I wear. I am also so amazed how natural you are as a mom. You have accomplished so much in your life, but Noah is your crowning achievement. I am in awe of your patience, dedication, and love for our son. Speaking of which, anything I do in my life from here on out—I do for my sweet boy, Noah. Whenever you pick up this book or anything I write, produce, or create—just know I do it for you. You are the greatest creation I've ever been involved with. You inspire me every day, and I love you so very much, my sweet little monkey!

Thanks to my parents, Gary and Patti—"Grandpa" and "Nannie" —for being such loving and giving people. Thanks to my dad for getting me interested in baseball in the first place and letting me win one-on-one games at P.S. 21. Thanks to my mom for her strong support over the years and for giving me the courage, when I was seven years old, to see *Gremlins* again after walking out, crying the first time. I think that decision helped shape me to be the man I am today. Thanks to my sister, Alissa, for her friendship and excessive liking of my posts on Facebook. On an unrelated note, I miss the days of shopping with you, buying overpriced movie posters at French Kisses in the city, and eating "tuna terrific" sandwiches at Mr. Greenjeans. I miss that place. Also, thanks to you and Jake for raising Ryan in a non-Yankees household. Speaking of which, I'll catch you on the flip side, Ryan. Thanks also to my mother-in-law, Barbara, for taking such good care of Noah.

I'd like to thank Allie Tarantino for being my copilot on this project and for being a wonderful, loyal close friend ever since the days of pork-chop sideburns and league "candy-throwing" T-shirts. I consider you, and all the Tarantinos, family. We have come a long way from being cocounselors at Elmwood and singing Toto's "Africa" at Finn McCools in White Plains. That place, by the way, probably closed down because they never let us on the mic. On another note, I'll trade you for your Dick Pole or Mark Zuckerberg card next time you see Bischop, forgive you for popping all of those dodgeballs, and blowing the big *Seabiscut* reveal in the last book. Thanks again to Jess Lander for adding so much to our book with her well-researched essays and to Mateo for introducing us. Your band is awesome. Thanks to Fred Lynn for coming through in the clutch.

Thanks to John Miele. From carrying apple-picking poles to colonoscopy car rides to wrestling fact-checks, I can't tell you how much I value you as a friend to me and my family. Thanks to Rich Tarantino for his friendship, attempts at a Pale Bros. reunion, St. Louis misadventures, and all those "Cheek to Cheek" moments. I missed you on this book, buddy. Thanks Alyson Tina, Keith Troy, and Cyrus Tarantino for being such loyal friends of mine for, respectively, 20 and four years. I'd also like to thank the following people just because they're all kinds of awesome: Carole and Jimmy Snuka, Robin Joseph, Andrew Plotkin, Larry Harbison, James Mullally, Nates Smith and Correira, Deb Ryan, every Tarantino, and Kuklis—but not Kevin Youklis (e tu Youk?).

Thanks to Bon Iver for his amazing second album, which has been the soundtrack to the first year of my son's life. And, finally, thanks to Yogi Berra for providing me with countless ideas for fake Yogisms that he'll never know about (and Allie T. wishes he never heard). This book, as mentioned earlier, is dedicated to my parents, wife, and son, but also to the memory of Rosalie Kaufman—a native New Englander who changed so many lives as our "Baba Dear."

Allie Tarantino thanks…

Thanks to my magical match and beautiful wife, Shira. Your positivity is a guiding light; you are an inspiring wife, mother, and artist. Thank you for your patience, input, and wisdom. Cyrus and Juniper love their "Princess Mommy." Cyrus, "I just love you" and the summer of 2012 we spent at Elmwood. It was made even more memorable when we stood on the warning track of Fenway Park.

Every time you see my book and get excited is a thrill. Someday you will write a book, and I can't wait to read it. You are an amazing artist! Juniper, our little "Cutie, Cutie," you got to visit Fenway Park and see Stephen Strasburg outduel Johan Santana before you turned one! Say hello to a life of baseball. Your smile brightens everyone's day. Mom and Dad, thank you for all your support and belief in me since I was little. Thank you for always surrounding me with books. It has turned out to be the best gift ever. To my Bash Brothers: Rich, Erica, and Jaxon...Rit, good call at Buffalo Wild Wings and glad we finally got to meet Jose Conseco or was it Ozzie?)...Looking forward to writing another book with you since you took the time off to roam Parts Unknown, Rhode Island, in search of elusive masked wrestlers. To my sister, Angela; Mike, and their boys, Michael, Matthew, and Nicholas D'Ambrosio. Thanks for putting up with my anti-Yankees tirades on Sundays; it's not too late for all of us to jump on the Washington Nationals bandwagon. Angela, it is a blast working with you and going on adventures with our kids.

Jon, from Pesky Zink to Johnny Pesky. Who knew what started with Raw boosters would someday turn into two books and counting? You can put your arm around me while you tirelessly put together shows, interview bands, scour the country for good music, and persevere for this and all the projects you balance at once. You are an amazing new dad and thanks to Alison and Noah for sharing you for the duration of the summer. Thanks to Ray and Aaron Goodman, my father-in-law and brother-in-law, who know how to tell a good story and make me laugh. Thank you to Triumph Books for the opportunity to author my second book.

The original APBA gang: Brian Rosa, Brian Mancusi, Joey Bonanno. My Ward School leaders past (Ken Regan, John Fogliano) and present (Franco Miele, Kimberly Peluso) and Mike Sgobbo and our seven-time champion, Ward Liberty. Wally the Green Monster, Liquid Carousel, @redsoxtriumph. Nate, Val, Autumn, and Tristan Smith. Randi Steiner, Mike and Eli Fetterer. Fred Bader for helping me get this far. Deb Ryan, Mike Izzo, Max Steiner, and Carlos Garcia for making our Stamford signing a success. Jeff, Bobbi,

Gregg, Hillari, Dani, Mike, and the rest of my EWD family, past and present, including: Jamie Rich, P.J. Murray, Big Dan Malone, the real Andy Greenspan, Dave Barkin, Andy and Brett Dymek, Cheryl Hajjar, Dave Nodiff, Paul and Steve Warham, and Adam Zimmer. Carol and Artie DeAlleaume. Mary Ellen, Greg, and Christian Locker. Dawn, Chris, Gabrielle, and Gavin Ferrante. Carolyn and Andrew O'Leary. Albert and Lynn Tarantino. Thanks to Leslie Feist for suggesting her "Cicadas and Gulls" as Juniper's first song ever. Thanks to Matthew Mayo for his quick responses, insightful words, and encouragement. Getting your essays inspired me at the start of this process. Adam Pachter and Hank Greenfield, thanks for answering my questions about *Fenway Fiction*. I really appreciate the time you took to be a part of this book. Thanks to Mike Zhe, who provided me info and direction on the Portsmouth Clippers. Thanks to Ken Walsh for directing me to Elmwood and continuing to be an inspiring force in New England. Thanks to Pat O'Connor for a wonderful conversation about his incredible Little Fenway. Best of luck with Little Field of Dreams.

Thanks to Bill Lee and his wife, Diana, for being so generous of their time in Boston at our book signing. Spaceman, thanks for being such a willing and interesting interview subject. I couldn't agree more with your Denis Diderot quote. In loving memory of fellow teacher and, more importantly, my mother-in-law, Cheryl Goodman. I know you are proud of how amazing Shira is as a mom. She learned from one of the best! For my grandparents, Connie and Victor "Vete" Ritacco and Mary and Albert "Terry" Tarantino. Grandma Mary loved baseball, and I loved hearing her tell me stories about Babe Ruth and Mel Ott.

Bibliography

Books

Cafardo, Nick. *Boston Red Sox: Yesterday and Today*. Illinois, West Side Publishing, 2009.

Chadwick, Bruce and David M. Spindel. *The Boston Red Sox: Memories and Mementoes of New England's Team*. New York: Abbeville Press, 1992.

Lee, Bill and Richard Lally. *Have Glove, Will Travel: Adventures of a Baseball Vagabond*. New York: Crown Publishers, 2005.

Mayo, Matthew. *Bootleggers, Lobstermen & Lumberjacks: Fifty of the Grittiest Moments in the History of Hardscrabble New England*. Connecticut: Globe Pequot Press, 2011.

Montville, Leigh. *Ted Williams*. New York: Doubleday, 2004.

Nowlin, Bill. *Red Sox Threads: Odds & Ends From Red Sox History*. Massachusetts: Rounder Books, 2008.

Pachter, Adam (editor). *Final Fenway Fiction*. Louisiana: Cornerstone Book Publishers, 2012.

Purdy, Dennis. *The Team by Team Encyclopedia of Major League Baseball*. New York: Workman Press, 2006.

Remy, Jerry with Corey Sandler. *Red Sox Heroes: The RemDawg's All-Time Favorite Red Sox, Great Moments, and Top Teams*. Connecticut: Lyons Press, 2009.

Shaughnessy, Dan. *At Fenway: Dispatches from Red Sox Nation.* New York: Three Rivers Press, 1996.

Newspapers/Magazines/Publications
The Boston Globe
USA Today Special Edition: Fenway at 100
Red Sox Magazine
Sports Illustrated Presents: Fenway 100th
New England Baseball Journal
Boston Red Sox Media Guide

Web
Baseball Almanac (www.baseball-almanac.com)
Baseball Biography Project (http://bioproj.sabr.org)
Baseball Reference (www.baseball-reference.com)
MLB (www.mlb.com)
Retrosheet (www.retrosheet.org)
Seacoastonline (www.seacoastonline.com)
SABR (www.sabr.org)
Little League World Series (www.littleleagueworldseries.com)

About the Authors

J on Chattman is an accomplished author whose credits include *I Love the Red Sox/I Hate the Yankees* (with Allie and Rich Tarantino) and the wrestling autobiography *Superfly: The Jimmy Snuka Story* for Triumph Books. His other books include: *A Battle Royal in the Sky* with Rich Tarantino for Pitch Publishing, *Sweet Stache* (also with Rich Tarantino) for Adams Media, and *Rock On!* with Ellen Rosner Feig.

In a career that spans over 15 years, Chattman has also written for a variety of newspapers, websites, and magazines—specializing in pop culture, music, and film. He started his career as a beat reporter for a local newspaper, went on to become managing editor for a small chain of papers, and for the past eight years has focused on blogging and online writing. Throughout his career, Chattman has written for various outlets including The Huffington Post, *New York Post*, and Spinner.com.

For over seven years, Chattman has owned and operated thecheappop.com, a pop culture humor site that specializes in down-to-earth celebrity interviews and music and entertainment reviews. In 2011 he launched A-Sides Music, a site featuring his sessions with established and up-and-coming musicians and its live entertainment off-shoot A-Sides Live!

Chattman is currently working on two other book projects, plans music and comedy events in and around New York City and Westchester County, and was selected as one of the "Rising Stars—Westchester's Forty Under Forty" in 2011 by the Business Council of Westchester. He lives in Westchester County, New York, with his wife, Alison, and their son, Noah.

Allie Tarantino is the co-author of *I Love the Red Sox, I Hate the Yankees* and *How the Red Sox Explain New England* from Triumph Books. By day he is a school teacher who shares his love for writing, reading, and baseball with his students at William B. Ward School in New Rochelle, New York. He lives with his wife, Shira, and children, Cyrus and Juniper, right in the middle of the Red Sox-Yankee rivalry in Connecticut. Details from his visits to two dozen major league stadiums can be found on his blog www.alliebaseballtour.com. His many ballpark trips include a visit to Olympic Stadium to see the Milwaukee Brewers play the Montreal Expos. He hopes to one day return baseball to Montreal, so his website www.lastexpostanding.com can become obsolete. Allie maintains a third baseball blog, www.ihateyanks, devoted to his hatred for the New York Yankees, which most likely started when he was snubbed by Lou Piniella at Yankee Stadium for an autograph. However, the moment was saved when Hall of Famer Jim Rice interjected and signed his scorecard. His love for baseball is directly attributed to his parents, Diane and Ralph. They frequently took the family to the ballpark, while his dad introduced him to Cadaco All-Star Baseball and APBA. Allie and his dad are frequent competitors these days on Whatifsports.com. Allie owns an extensive collection of Boston Red Sox and Milwaukee Brewers memorabilia, his favorite American and National League teams respectively. His baseball card collection includes rookie cards of Robin Yount, Kirby Puckett, Mike Greenwell, and a signed Little League card by an eight-year old Mark Zuckerberg. Although proud of every wiffle home run he hit off his brother Rich, his greatest sports achievement was collecting seven hits including one home run in the first softball doubleheader attended by his son, Cyrus. As for coaching, Allie is a successful elementary school girls' basketball coach who has won seven New Rochelle City championships with cocoach Mike Sgobbo. Allie has been employed at Elmwood Country Day Camp for 25 years where he has served as Athletic Director and has a basketball court—Allie's Arena—named in his honor. He spent three years as an assistant coach and statistician for the New Rochelle High School varsity baseball team. As a member of SABR, Allie looks forward to bringing his growing family on annual trips to Fenway Park and Citizens Bank Ballpark.